DEAR MOM AND DAD . . .

Mom, do you remember when I was fourteen and I told you a deep, dark secret of mine? Do you remember how upset you were, and how we both cried about it? I think you also remember all the talks we had, and how I wanted to be changed into a girl, like Christine Jorgensen . . .

What I'm trying to get the courage to tell you is that I'm a transsexual—one whose desire it is to become a physical member of the opposite sex—and have been all my life. Now I'm in the process of doing something about it . . .

I've decided—after countless days of just sitting and waiting for the right time to die, wondering each day when I got up if I'd have the guts to end it all before the day was over, and, at the same time, realizing that Danny was no more, and that now there was only Canary, the name I call myself—that I want to live.

CANARY

The Story of a
Transsexual

by
Canary Conn

CANARY

*A Bantam Book / published by arrangement with
author*

PRINTING HISTORY
Nash edition published 1974
Bantam edition / July 1977

---

*Bantam Books are published by Bantam Books, Inc. Its trade-
mark, consisting of the words "Bantam Books" and the por-
trayal of a bantam, is registered in the United States Patent
Office and in other countries. Marca Registrada. Bantam
Books, Inc., 666 Fifth Avenue, New York, New York 10019.*

PRINTED IN THE UNITED STATES OF AMERICA

*To Dick Irving Hyland,
whose wisdom and foresight
helped to make this book happen.
And to Sylvia Cross,
whose editorial guidance
and encouragement
made it a fait accompli.*

CONTENTS

LADIES AND GENTLEMEN —
CANARY CONN

"The assembly will be ready in about fifteen minutes." A young woman put her head inside the doorway. I smiled at her trying to overcome a fainting feeling by concentrating on her face as she walked toward me. "Dr. Lopez asked me to come back and check with you to see if you're all right," she said. Something about her was very calming.

"I'm feeling a little faint," I said, "but it's really much better than I'd expected." After all, I thought, it had been only nine days since my final operation and there was still a great deal of healing my body had to do. So much had been happening so quickly, that I knew the full impact of the past few days hadn't really hit me yet.

"I'm Barbara Jefferson," she said, extending a hand. "I'm a medical student here at Stanford."

"Hello. I'm Canary Conn." My hands were almost blue, and shaking uncontrollably. I tried to breathe evenly to stop the shaking. At first I suspected it was fear of the coming event; but now I was beginning to worry that there was something wrong and that my body was on the edge of a total collapse.

Dr. Lopez had made the journey as easy on me as he could. He always took the time to make sure I was comfortable. The wheelchair I sat in was just one of the many small details he had thought of. Except for a brief shopping expedition that morning in the shops on the first floor of the hotel, I hadn't had to deal with any of the problems of our journey from Tijuana to Palo Alto.

"Can I get you a blanket? You seem awfully cold." Before I could answer, the girl moved to a cabinet and opened one door after another until she found a thin, rough blanket about the size of a standard baby's blanket. When she helped me tuck it around myself, I felt a little warmer.

"You know, Miss Conn, I don't know much about transsexuals. They don't talk about . . . well, your kind of situation very often in school." She seemed a little nervous. "I don't know exactly what a transsexual is."

"Well, a transsexual is a person who is born one sex but who has a lifelong identity with the opposite sex. It's a problem of gender identity—genitals don't seem to match up with feelings inside."

"Are you the same thing as a transvestite?"

"No." It occurred to me suddenly that she might think I was simply a man dressed up as a woman, although that seemed really ludicrous to me. "You know, I now have female genitals. Dr. Lopez just did the second operation a few days ago."

"Is that why you're not feeling well?"

"It does take a while to recover from the surgery," I said. But it was worth every minute of it, I thought; it was worth the pain and the torment. For once in my life I felt *right* inside my body. A child's sense of himself as male or female is formed pretty early, and I had spent a lot of time feeling uncomfortable about the external appearance of my body.

"I'm really interested in what you're going to say in the lecture. It's really astonishing," she said, "to think that you . . . " Flushing, she broke off, then smiled at me tentatively. She looked down at her watch, then back at me. "Well, look, you've got just a couple of minutes. I'll give you some time to yourself."

"Okay," I said, thinking for a minute about the lecture, about all the things I wanted to say. Slowly, I stood up to make sure my dress was straight, and smoothed a hand absently over my hair. Barbara reached out and took the blanket from me. She folded it and placed it on a table.

"Hey, you know, that's a really far-out dress. Well—good luck with the lecture." I smiled at her, remembering how hard I had wished for my *first* dress.

THE CHRISTMAS DRESS

Rain had been pouring out of the sky ever since I had arrived at my grandparents' house. An icy wind shook the windows, frosting the glass. It was one of the coldest nights ever recorded in Jerome, Idaho. But it was also Christmas Eve 1955—a special time for a six year old with just one Christmas wish.

As my grandmother moved about the house, she hummed to herself. There would be a squeak followed by a rattle, every time she walked over the iron grating that covered a heating vent in the floor. Over and over again, I would lift my head from my play to count the sounds—one, two, three. Each time I made my wish, I closed my eyes, hoping this would insure Santa's attention. "Please, Santa," I whispered. "Please, I just want . . ."

"What are you doing on the floor with your hands over your eyes?" The voice echoed suddenly through the bedroom, startling me. When my eyes flew open, though, I was relieved—it was my grandmother, Gigi. Her eyes had a familiar smile as she put out a hand to help me up from the cold floor.

"You don't have your house shoes on, Danny boy. You'll catch your death of cold running around barefooted," she said. "Come along. We'll find you a good thick pair of Granddaddy's socks to wear."

If anyone else had interrupted me, I would have been upset. But Gigi issued her commands in such a friendly, polite manner that I obeyed without hesitation. Gigi was more than my grandmother, anyway. She was my friend. I often wondered why her hair was gray

4

while my mother's hair was black. She was a grand-mother. Were grandmothers supposed to have gray hair? Perhaps gray meant friendly. Whatever the reason for her gray hair, Gigi was my friend, and she left me alone a lot to think and to play. That was the most important thing to me.

Sometimes, she would spend hours on one side of the house because she knew I wanted to be left alone for a while. We both knew I was an odd child, but my differences brought respect from her. She rarely challenged my right to privacy.

I shivered a minute. The floor in the other room had been cold. Now, standing in my grandparents' room, I was chilled. Grandma was digging through the dresser drawers. Silently, I wished that she would hurry and find those wool socks.

"Here, yes. Here," she said, handing them to me, "these will do you just fine." With a little grunt, she straightened. There was a satisfied look on her face. As I took the socks from her, we both smiled.

I sat on the floor to pull the socks on, and she hurried from the room to get back to her tasks. Almost immediately those familiar sounds in the kitchen resumed. I wiggled my warming toes, and looked about the room. White lace and brown wood. It was beautiful! The bed was French Provincial style. The paintings were all reproductions of paintings by French artists. Even the smell in that room was French, for my grandmother liked French perfumes. That is why my grandfather began calling her Gigi in their courting days.

The doorbell rang. Granddad! Grandma might have liked French things, but she loved my Irish grandfather. His hair was pure white and cut into a flat top. He told me once that his hair had been like that since his early twenties.

"Hi, Granddad!" I greeted him. "Can I see your false teeth?" He grinned at me as he hugged me. As if he had been waiting for my request, he reached into his mouth and pulled out the upper bridge. I squealed with joy as we shared this ritual greeting.

"Danny boy," he asked, "have you let Santa know what you want for Christmas yet?"

"No, he hasn't," came a voice over my shoulder. I looked back. Gigi seemed to be pouting a little.

Of course I had let Santa know, but I hadn't told anyone else. Though my big sister had confided that she believed with all her heart that there was no such person as Santa Claus, I told her that this Christmas I would prove her wrong. I knew Santa was real. Besides, I had a very special wish.

In a little while we had dinner—roast beef and mashed potatoes. When he had finished, Granddad pushed back his chair and asked me if I would like to watch him stoke the furnace. He always made a ceremony of it for my benefit. First, Granddad would carry me down a long set of stairs to a dark, musty place. It frightened me a little. When we reached bottom, he'd reach above his head, give a couple of waves with his arm, and there would be light. Light made the place fascinating rather than scary.

There were dozens and dozens of hunting rifles. Moose heads were mounted on the walls. Other animal heads were lying on the tables. I once tried to count all the fishing poles, but there were so many I had to stop—I'd forget which ones I'd already counted. In the middle of the floor there was a huge hole where, my grandfather told me, a giant troll lived. I didn't really believe him, but if I pretended that I believed him, he would give me freedom to wander while he was working.

Granddad was very practiced at furnace stoking. He would take a shovelful of coal from the pile on one side of the room, and after a momentary hesitation, he would heave the coal across the room into the furnace. He never missed—not once. He usually repeated the process about ten times. When he was finished he would lay the shovel down, cross the room, and shut the furnace door. As it clanged, he would call out to me. While he was working, I would wander around, fingering the many objects which cluttered the basement. I kept one eye on him, though. Usually, by the time he had finished, I would have circled the entire basement. This time I had found something new. It was a doll.

"Danny! Come on now, it's time to go!"

It was a beautiful doll. Maybe if I carried it upstairs with me, my grandparents would let me have it. Yes, that's what I would do.

"Granddaddy, I'm over here!" I answered. I was very excited. This was something I had hoped for from Santa. I examined the doll closely—it was new. Perhaps Santa had come early and placed it here for me by mistake.

Granddad was standing near me. He had a puzzled look on his face. I asked him if the doll was for me. Did he think Santa had left it down there by mistake? He smiled but nodded his head no. It wasn't for me— Grandma had found it in the backyard next door. The little girl who used to live next door had left it when her family moved away. They hadn't left a forwarding address, so Grandma had put the doll there in the basement. It was to be saved for a needy little girl someday.

I hugged the doll very carefully before placing it back into the box of soft paper. There was a lump in my throat, but I wasn't going to cry. I didn't want Granddad to be upset with me. Besides, Santa hadn't come yet. I was sure I would get my wish.

Gigi had finished all the baking and cooking for our family feast the next day. Granddad was settled back in his easy chair, smoking one of his favorite pipes while he read a *National Geographic*. We were quiet for a while after dinner, but the air was thick with excitement and good smells.

When the time came for me to go to bed, my grandmother took me by the hand. We went into the small bedroom where I had been playing much of the afternoon. She helped me clear my bed of the dozens of toy soldiers I'd made with Granddad's pipe cleaners.

"Now," she said, "you be a good boy and go to sleep. Santa will be coming to visit us soon. Remember to say your prayers. Thank God for making you a healthy little boy."

"Yes, ma'am," I answered. She smiled as she left the room. For a minute I wanted to call her back to tell her about the doll I had found in the basement. Granddaddy had said they would give it to a needy little girl.

But I wasn't needy—I knew Santa would bring me what I'd wished for.

My excitement kept me up for hours in the cold night. I could hear my grandparents talking for a while, but gradually it became very quiet. I thought each little noise was Santa, but my curiosity couldn't outweigh my fear of being discovered, should I get out of bed. I slept for a while.

I woke to hear conversation in the front room. The words were blurred by the howling wind and rain, which had turned to sleet. It was Santa, I knew. I wanted to run into the front room and meet him, but my bed was warm, and I was too befuddled by sleep. Besides, I'd be scared if I really came face to face with Santa Claus. I had heard he would never return if he were confronted.

There was a creaking sound, then all the whispers were gone. I felt dizzy with excitement. I wondered what color the dress would be. I hadn't chosen a color, but yellow would be just right—it was my favorite color. I didn't care about the fit or the style, but the color was very important.

The excitement gave me courage. I slipped out from between the covers to the cold floor. It was dark, and I couldn't find the light switch. I would have to find the front room without lights. Somehow I found the door knob and carefully pulled the door. There was a shrieking sound! I froze. There was no further sound, so I left the door where it was and slipped through the narrow space. Another shrieking sound might have wakened someone. There seemed to be a little light in the dark house, but I found my way mostly with my feet, and as I neared the living room the warmth of the furnace warmed my cold feet. If I had found the light switch I could have put those wool socks on. I reached out with one arm. My hand brushed needles and there was a tinkling sound. That had to be the tree.

I knew that at the bottom of the tree was a cord with a switch for the lights, and that there were over a hundred lights on the tree. It had taken Grandma and me most of that day to decorate it. Now, more than at any other time, it seemed part of my Christmas. The lights were soft and varied. It was a beautiful tree.

I glanced around the room, wondering if I had surprised Santa Claus, but it was too late. Sighing, I knelt down to examine the names on the gifts under the tree. There were many with familiar names—my cousins, uncles, aunts, parents, and sisters—but I couldn't seem to locate mine. Here was Janet's; here was Dee's. . . . All the presents under the tree were for other people—there was nothing for me! I felt dizzy for a moment. Could it be? No. No, I wouldn't believe it. I looked down again, and suddenly, there was my present—"To Danny Boy from Santa."

That was my name, all right. Suddenly, everything was fine. It was my present, from Santa Claus himself. I picked it up and examined the package carefully. It didn't feel like a doll, not even in a box—it was the wrong size. It was the right size box for a dress, though.

I couldn't wait to find out. I began to twist and tug the ribbon on this special present. At last I would prove to everyone that I was a little girl, not a little boy. Certainly, if Santa gave me a dress, as I had asked, no one could dispute the fact. As I pulled the wrapping paper off, my eyes must have been shining. I yanked off the tissue paper and saw the glimmer of yellow.

It was a dress, a bright yellow dress. I hugged the dress to me. It had finally happened! I had proof now! Nothing else could matter. All the names the neighborhood children had called me were meaningless. I jumped at a sudden sound, stuffing the dress back into the box.

It must have been the wind. I wanted to go back to my bedroom. There, I was sure to be caught, but in the bedroom I could try the dress on. I grabbed the box and the dress. Leaving the warmth of the furnace didn't bother me now.

There was a mirror on the back of the bedroom door. Pulling the dress from the box, I grinned at my image. I was spilling over with happiness. I looked so pretty, just having the dress in front of me. And now I wouldn't have to hide myself while I wore it. This was *my* dress. Santa had given it to me. No one could ever take it away.

I hurried to take off my pajamas. The icy cold didn't matter. Kicking my pajamas away, I slipped the dress over my head—it fit! It even fit. I looked at myself in the mirror and started to cry. Why did I have to be a boy? It wasn't right. Nobody liked me for what I was. I was different; I was too pretty to be a boy. I knew I was a girl like my sisters.

The buttons in the back were a struggle, but it was a familiar task; I had been dressing in my sisters' clothes from the time I was three years old. Blinking back my tears, I reached to check the last button again.

"Danny? Boy, what are you doing with that dress on? That isn't for you." I gasped with shock. It was my grandmother. No one had seen me in girls' clothes before. I was only six years old, but I had a real fear of being discovered.

"Grandma." I was crying again. "This is *my* dress. Santa gave it to me. This *is* my dress. It's even my favorite color—yellow. See?"

"Danny?" There was confusion in her voice. "You're a little boy. Little boys don't wear dresses. Santa wouldn't give a dress to a little boy. You've made a mistake. You've opened the wrong present." It was hard to answer her through my tears. I wanted only to prove to her that Santa had given me the dress. Then she would believe me.

"Come here, Grandma," I said. "Look at the package." I took her hand and, sobbing, led her to the box on the bed. Releasing her hand, I searched for the tag.

"Here! Here it is," I exclaimed. She was surprised to see my name on the tag. There was no doubt I had opened the right present. She lifted her eyes from the tag slowly, looked at me, then looked away.

"Well," she began, "there's certainly no doubt that this present was addressed to you, but I think maybe Santa made a little mistake." She looked at me again. "Why don't we look under the tree for another gift? I'm sure we'll find the one meant for you."

I was crying again. I pleaded with her to understand that Santa had gotten me exactly what I had wished for. She seemed to shake her head a little. I could understand her confusion, but there was no confusion for me. My name was on the tag.

"What's going on here?" came a voice from the door. "Danny, what the hell are you doing in that dress? That's supposed to be your sister Dee's. . . ."

"John, hush up," my grandmother interrupted. "We have no idea who this dress is for. All we know is that the present was addressed to Danny. No matter what I tell him he refuses to believe Santa could have made a mistake and put his tag on someone else's present."

Granddaddy seemed quite put out. He spun around and left the room. In a minute, he returned. His face was red. One hand was clenched into a fist.

"Now, listen young man. This is going to stop, right now. You're a boy, not a girl. Even though this present had your name on it, it was meant for your sister. Now, get that damn dress off, right now. We'll go find your present. It's probably got your sister Dee Dee's tag on it."

It wasn't fair. I was humiliated. If the dress was for Dee Dee, why did the tag have my name on it? It didn't make sense. I was a girl, just like Dee Dee, even if they didn't think so. Santa had brought me just what I had wished for. I wasn't going to let them take it away from me.

Granddad disappeared again. My grandmother began to urge me to take off the dress.

"No! No!" I screamed. "I'm not going to take it off. Not ever!" I stared up at her. She wasn't my friend. She didn't understand. I hated this stranger who stood before me. I hated both these people who had made me feel so degraded.

"Now, look. Look." My grandfather was smiling as he reentered the room with a shiny gun set and a cowboy hat. "*This* is your present. I was right. Santa switched them somehow."

I couldn't accept the possibility of a mistake. I hadn't wished for a gun set; I had wished for a yellow dress. This was a yellow dress. I wasn't going to give it up. Where were my parents? I didn't want to be there anymore. No one seemed to understand. Granddaddy pulled Grandma out of the room. In just a couple of minutes they were back. Both of them were smiling.

"We've decided," Grandma began, "you can keep the dress on until your parents come tomorrow."

"Danny boy? Okay?" Granddaddy asked.

It wasn't okay. It was just a reprieve, and I knew it. The smug look on their faces reflected my certainty that my parents would leave me with no alternatives. But I wasn't going to give up easily. They couldn't shake my conviction that I was a girl.

I couldn't go back to sleep. I kept the dress on, but the magic was gone. Once my parents came, there would be only anger and humiliation. They wouldn't be able to see why I wanted the dress.

Eight o'clock Christmas morning I got out of bed and went to the window. The wind had quieted and the sleet had turned to snow. Snow covered everything in the yard. My decision was clear. I would take off the dress. I would swear to my grandparents never to mention the dress again—if they wouldn't tell my parents. That was it, plain and simple.

Hurrying, I removed the dress and pulled on a pair of Levi's and a sweat shirt. I could hear my grandfather yank open the basement door. He would be going to stoke the furnace for the day. I knew I had to move quickly.

"Granddaddy?" I was quiet. If Grandma was still asleep I didn't want to wake her yet.

"What is it?" he answered me gruffly.

"Uh, Granddaddy," I went on, "I just wanted to tell you I'm sorry. I won't ever wear the dress again if you promise not to tell Mommy and Daddy."

His face softened as I told him of my decision. I felt good about it. This would be the last time I'd ever do this, I was thinking. I was trying to reassure both of us of my masculinity. Granddaddy picked me up in his arms, telling me he was proud of me. He understood, he said; it was the principle of the thing that had made me put the dress on. I was glad we were friends again. The previous night was the first time he had ever been mad at me and I didn't like the feeling.

"What are you fellows so happy about?" Grandma asked, as she came into the kitchen. She was smiling. Granddaddy explained my decision. She nodded in agreement when he told her of my request not to tell my parents, then she took me from Granddaddy and hugged me.

"Let's look under the Christmas tree and see about the gun set and that cowboy hat your grandfather showed you last night," she said. "I hope it's still there." She put me down and I ran into the front room. The new present was lying in its box, near the tree. As I picked up the hat, there was a knock on the front door.

Granddaddy went for the door while Grandma disappeared. My sisters rushed through the door when he opened it. Behind them were my parents. I waved the hat at them and hurried to my bedroom.

There was Grandma, quickly putting the finishing touches on the dress box. She had crumpled up the paper I had so eagerly torn off. But the new paper that she was putting on was the same as that I'd torn off. I managed to swallow my surprise, but as I stood there watching, I suddenly realized that there was no Santa Claus—that my grandparents had purchased those gifts for me and my sisters. If there really was no Santa, as Dee Dee had been telling me, then it was just a cruel mistake that my wish for a dress had been fulfilled. Maybe feeling like a girl was just part of my imagination, like believing in Santa Claus had been.

But the feeling that I was a girl trapped in a boy's body was one I had already identified, and although I gave up my belief in Santa Claus that Christmas morning, I was to find my gender identity problem an increasingly difficult one to deal with.

"GIVE THE KID A BUTCH!"

Although I was not an only child, I can remember wishing at times I were. There were three of us: Dee Dee, the eldest, me, and Janet. Dee Dee was a rebel; she was the one to tease and tantalize my parents. Although Janet and I might have laughed at a scheme of hers that didn't work out, we were well aware that Dee Dee's rebellion sometimes made it easier on us.

Janet was my closest friend. She was the youngest, the angel. She just wanted to be included, but the impishness in Dee Dee would leave Janet out whenever possible. Janet and I were partners in any games I chose to play. I guess that's why we got along so well. Although Dee Dee was dependable, I trusted Janet— even when I dressed up as a girl. She never breathed a word to my parents and played right along. Janet was outgoing, in contrast to Dee Dee's shyness. They fought often and violently, though, and relied on me to resolve many of their arguments.

The one thing they have in common is looks. Both of them are dark-skinned, with dark brown hair. They look like my parents. It was a standing joke around our house, however, that I was the milkman's son. My skin has always been milk white, smoother and softer than my sisters' skin. My hair is blond, my eyes blue. In family pictures, I looked like a visiting neighbor.

My looks disappointed my father, although he never came right out and said it. My effeminate appearance was cause for a continual challenge from him to "stand up and be a man."

"What are you, some kind of sissy or something?"

14

he'd say. "If you can't do the work, maybe we can get your little sister to do it!"

As I grew up, I realized that most of this kind of talk is common among men. But in my early years, I was very much aware that I wasn't a boy, let alone a man. As far as I was concerned, what they said about my being a sissy was right. Sometimes the word hurt, though.

One crisp January morning in 1956, when I was six, comments about my "girlish" locks prompted a trip to town. As we rounded the town square, I heard snow-birds chirping. The trees were covered with icicles. It was cold, really cold. Tugging at my little parka didn't help. It must have been close to zero that morning. As I walked, my breath formed little clouds. If my father's hand hadn't been tugging so hard, I would have enjoyed them.

He seemed remote that morning. His collar was pulled up around his face, and from my vantage point, he seemed taller than his six feet. The dark shadow on his face intrigued me. Would I have a beard, too, when I grew up? Although his eyes squinted against the cold, I could see them, brown, and unconcerned. I slipped on the ice, watching him, but his big hand pulled me up-right again. I flew across the ice as though skating.

His quietness bothered me. I felt he was mad at me, or disappointed in some way. Lately, he had ig-nored my questions. It had occurred to me that my grandparents might have told my parents about the Christmas dress, but surely that wouldn't have changed his mood so drastically.

We passed the Jantzen Theater, and I brightened. Saturday and Sunday matinees were a chance for us kids to get outside the small town and into another world. Ten cents paid the entrance fee and bought an all-day sucker.

Then, the candy-striped pole was turning in front of me. Uneasiness crept over me. I didn't like the bar-ber shop. It was a male haven. Women were discussed in sarcastic tones. They certainly weren't wanted in this masculine place. My father pulled the door open.

The warm air was welcome against my chilled

face, but my uneasiness grew when I saw the gruff faces that greeted our entrance. Once acknowledged, the half-dozen men looked away from us and settled back to their *Sports Illustrated*s. Dad greeted two barbers, busy with customers. The third, Rex, was to be my barber. I was afraid of Rex.

He was tall, a redhead with freckles on his face and arms. His neck was thick. It reminded me of a football player's neck. Once, while I was there getting a haircut, I overheard him talking to another man about the war, and about how he, Rex, had been a marine. When he spoke, he growled, just like a big dog. For this reason, more than for any other, I feared him.

"Hi, Rex," my dad said, walking toward the empty chair in front of the barber. "My kid here is beginning to look like a sissy. Can you fix him up for me?"

The words stung. My dad didn't have to say that in front of all those men. Why had he? Now they all were staring at me. I felt like a cornered animal. Fear held my tears back. Even Rex was glaring at me. Was I his enemy?

"Well," he said, hesitantly, "what kind of haircut you want?"

"Ah, give him a butch," Dad said. I turned to beseech my father, but he wouldn't meet my eyes. One of my friends at school had a butch—it looked terrible!

"Well, I can give him a butch, but I can't make a man out of him," Rex said. "That's your job." He laughed, and the sound echoed throughout the shop. They were all laughing at me, even my father. I started to run out of the shop, but my father's hand caught mine. He held me so tightly that a spasm of pain shot through my arm.

"About how long you think it'll be?" he asked Rex casually.

Rex smiled. He told Dad it would be about an hour or so. Dad nodded his understanding, then addressed himself to me. He was going across town to attend to some business, but if I didn't want a licking, I would stay right there and get my hair cut, like a good boy.

My first impulse was to run when he let go of me.

I didn't care if I saw him, or anyone in that town, ever again. I didn't want a haircut, and I certainly didn't want a butch. I hated Rex. He was cruel, and he played on the cruelty of the other men in the barber shop. As I stared at Rex, my father slipped out the door. There was no time to protest. I was alone.

I thought Rex had motioned me into the chair, so I climbed up. The sooner it was over, I thought, the sooner I could leave.

"Get out of that chair!" Rex growled.

I started, and muttered my protest. "But, I thought you wanted me to sit down. I . . ."

"In *this* barber shop," Rex cut in, "the men go first. The girls wait their turn." I could hear the other men laughing. My chin started to tremble.

"I'm not a girl," I said, as I fought my way out of the barber's chair. It was hard to ignore the stares of those men. I took the first empty chair and blindly grabbed for a magazine. I put it up in front of my face, and took a deep breath. Although I knew I was a boy, I felt like a girl and deeply resented having to defend myself in that way.

"Sure you don't want a doll, kid?" The laughter became a roar. I began to cry, great silent tears. I felt alone, but somehow I knew this was something I would have to battle alone—for a long time.

I eventually managed to control my tears. Other than an occasional tremor, I felt rather poised. At first, peering carefully over the magazine, I sneaked looks at Rex, but his face was so distasteful to me, I chose to keep my head buried in the magazine until I had to move.

"Hey! Hey, you!" It was Rex's voice, but I ignored the taunt. I didn't want to cry anymore. "Hey, you, little girl, aren't you listening to me? It's your turn to get up here."

I couldn't ignore him. Carefully, I put the magazine back on the table. As I got up, I noticed the faces in the shop were new ones. I had been too busy with the struggle for self-control to notice the customers coming and going. Perhaps he would say nothing in front of these new people.

"Come on," he said. Impatience edged his voice. I hopped up onto the chair as he put the board across the arms. I sat on the board. It was the only way I could sit tall enough for him to work on me. A long barber's sheet whipped in front of me. His rough hands tucked it around my neck. There was a sweet smell, a little stronger than my father's shaving lotion. I looked down from my perch and studied the brown and black hair scattered on the floor. Why wasn't there any blond hair? I felt odd again.

I heard water running, and felt the splash as Rex rubbed it into my hair. His fingers dug into my head, and I felt he was trying to hurt me. But my hatred of him wouldn't let me show the hurt.

The clippers buzzed as he shaved my head. They seemed like a large mechanical bird, diving and sliding over my skull, as my hair fell in clumps. My back was to the mirror, but I could imagine the transformation.

"What's wrong, honey?" asked the ghastly, familiar voice behind me. "Does the little girl feel a little afraid of Uncle Rex? Why, don't you know Rex is going to make you look like a boy, for a change? He's cutting off every bit of that pretty hair of yours."

These comments brought surprised looks from the men along the wall.

"You like looking like a girl, huh girlie? You play with dolls?"

I didn't answer his crack. I played with dolls, but I wasn't going to feed him more ammunition to hurt me with. It was a trick I had already learned to recognize.

"Why don't you answer up?" Rex continued, mocking. "Your daddy once told me he caught you dressing up in your sisters' clothes. That right?"

The look in those eyes along the wall changed, narrowed. I couldn't run, and I wouldn't scream. It was true, but I felt so ashamed when he talked about it. It was a humiliating thing, suddenly. The warmth in my face was my only protection against the ridicule in their eyes. But there was one man in the corner who didn't seem to despise me. There was concern, a kind of worried look, on his face.

The clippers clicked off, and the chair spun

around. I was confronted with a bald-headed baby in the mirror. For a minute, I didn't recognize myself. Then, all I could think of was the pretty blond hair, gone, lying strewn across the floor. I would never be the same again. I cried, in trembling sobs that shook my whole body. I didn't care if they saw me cry. I didn't want to live anymore. I looked ugly. I hated myself.

"Snap out of it, you little sissy," Rex growled. In one last effort, he whacked me across the back of the head with a brush. I screamed then, with the pain.

"What the hell are you doing to that kid? He couldn't be more than six years old. What are you doing to him?" a new voice exclaimed. In the mirror I could see the man rise from his chair in the corner. He moved quickly to the back of the shop. Rex looked surprised. He raised his hand suddenly, then he dropped from sight.

I looked down. Surprise made me hiccup and blink back my tears. Rex was lying on his back. There was blood coming from the corner of his mouth, and his eyes seemed huge in his pale face.

A strong arm encircled me and lifted me out of the chair. I buried my face gratefully in a red-checked shoulder. He walked with long strides to the door, hesitated and grabbed our coats, then yanked the door open.

I didn't even have time to be cold. He marched briskly past two shops and swung through the door of the third. Gently he lowered me and we sat down.

"You all right, son?" he asked softly. I felt as though he understood the hurt I felt. I was trembling too hard to tell him anything. In answer, I swung one arm around his neck and squeezed tightly. I had found a friend. His hand rubbed the sore spot on my head, as he held me on his lap and whispered assurances over and over. I felt that everything would be all right. He couldn't make the last hour disappear, but he could battle that cruelty with his gentleness.

After a while, I climbed into the chair beside him at the table, and sipped at a cup of hot chocolate. Dad and I spotted each other at the same time. He had a kind of sad smile on his face. The stranger turned to me and, with a hand on my shoulder, asked if he could have a talk with my daddy. I nodded, and they stepped away.

I couldn't hear their words, but I watched their faces. After a few moments, they shook hands. With a waved good-bye, the stranger left the shop. That was the last I ever saw of him.

A LITTLE BOY
DISCOVERS HERSELF

The fields were green for as far as I could see. Corn stalks stood lazily crooked in the summer sun. The only sound as we bounced along the road was the motor of the old pickup. I started to say something to Uncle Ed, but stopped. I didn't want to spoil the clean, quiet feeling around me that I associated with the country, and especially with the farm. Up ahead, I could see the mailbox and the lane leading down to the farm, which was off to the right.

This summer I was to stay a week, rather than last summer's three days, and I had been looking forward to the visit ever since I had suspected I might get this return invitation. Last summer had been a time to play alone in the fields and around the farm, to throw rocks at the cows, to chase the chickens and watch their feathers fly, and one day, to discover a great secret.

Cousin John was waiting to greet me as we rounded the final curve toward the farm. He was jumping up and down and waving his arms. I waved at him, then looked beyond him to the small farmhouse. Built of rocks, boulders and cement, it was cool in the summer and warm in the winter—two requirements for a house in northern Idaho. The house was surrounded by tall oaks and maples, and was filled with good smells.

My Aunt Mary was crossing the yard in front of the house, waving her arms and yelling her greetings. She was a stocky woman, probably no taller than five feet, but, without a doubt, loud and outgoing enough to make up for her height. I enjoyed her type of pushiness; it always made me feel at home.

She was just the opposite of Uncle Ed, who had not spoken five words to me since we had left the town. I'd never known him to swear or to raise his voice to anyone, although he must have had occasion to in the course of a lifetime of farming.

There was kissing all around when I got out of the truck. I even kissed Johnny, who was seven, one year younger than I, and although he was a nearly intolerable brat, I permitted him to be my playmate. Although I was familiar with the routine on the farm, Aunt Mary quickly took me aside and explained what she expected of me, when the meals were served, and asked me whether I would like to sleep with Johnny or on the floor.

Sleeping with Johnny had one big disadvantage— he wet the bed. There is nothing to compare with the sensation of a cold Idaho night interrupted by a warm burst of urine—at first, a welcome bit of warmth, but gradually changing to a cold, uncomfortable dampness. I awoke each morning with a wretched odor resembling ammonia filling my nostrils, and wet pajamas. It was no fun getting out of bed. I decided that this year I would sleep on the floor, despite assurances that I was doubly safe because, not only had Johnny stopped wetting the bed, but it was summer.

We spent our first day doing chores. Johnny and I were expected to pile manure, clean the chicken coop, and more. It didn't take long to finish our list and receive permission to go play. Johnny led me to a field where there was a pond full of frogs. Imagine, if you can, what two young boys would be interested in doing with a pond full of frogs.

We did. We caught over 200 of them before sunset. It was such an absorbing task that we didn't notice Uncle Ed's discovery of the frogs in his water trough (our storage space). While he scolded us, the cows that had been following him got into the yard, and one of them approached the trough.

As Uncle Ed was winding up his lecture, I caught a glimpse of the cow, and nudged Johnny. We watched in disbelief as the cow swallowed a frog whole. The cow's eyes bulged in surprise, as though it had been given a sudden goose, and it reared—something I don't think I've seen a cow do since. Aunt Mary came running out of the farmhouse and joined in the laughter.

We chuckled about the cow during dinner, but Aunt Mary made sure we knew that catching frogs, and putting them in the water trough was something we weren't to do anymore. When the rest of the family adjourned to the living room to watch "Rawhide," I found a flashlight and slipped out the back door.

There weren't any lights for miles. It took my eyes a few minutes to adjust to the dark beyond the light of the farmhouse. I shone the flashlight bravely in several directions, reminding myself of the lay of the land. A few times I shook the flashlight to reassure myself that there were batteries inside. Being stuck out there would have been awfully scary. Slowly, I made my way across an empty pasture, behind the old oak tree to an abandoned storage shed.

As I fumbled with the rusty padlock, I listened for any sounds other than the crickets' chirping. I prayed that the lock had not been replaced, and that I would be able to remember how I had placed it on the door. After a minute, I freed it from its mooring and carefully opened the door. The squeaking noise seemed faint enough. I shone the flashlight eagerly around the dusty room and fought down the electric shock of excitement mixed with the undeniable feeling that I was becoming another person.

Although it was difficult in the dark, I located the pile of books and magazines I had piled on top of the clothing necessary to rejuvenate my female self. One hand steadied the flashlight while the other removed the musty objects. Maybe one day in the coming week I could leave the shack, perhaps walk in the fields for a while.

Aunt Mary was calling me. I pushed away the last magazine and uncovered my prize—dresses, purses, nylon stockings, underclothes, and more—everything a little girl could want to play dress-up. I chuckled to myself in anticipation, then covered them again as quickly as I could. I let myself out of the shack.

"Danny! Danny!" my aunt yelled again.

I ran through the fields to approach the farmhouse from the other side so that Aunt Mary would not be able to guess where I had been.

"Where you been, boy? Land sakes, I derneer called my head off for you!" she said.

"I was sitting in the pasture, Auntie, listening to the crickets." I tried to catch my breath.

She just smiled and explained that there were wolves in those parts, and they would think nothing of gobbling me up for a late-night snack. I wasn't to wander too far from the house at night. As she talked, I noticed a noise I'd heard every night I'd ever stayed on the farm. Before now, I'd dismissed it. But perhaps this had something to do with the wolves. It was a sort of gnawing sound.

That day, I'd fed the pigs and collected eggs from the chickens, so I knew it wasn't chicken or pig sounds. But it *was* an eating noise. As we reached the yard, I asked her about it. Aunt Mary smiled faintly and nearly ignored me, but I asked the question again.

"Well," she said slowly, "it's not a pretty sight."

She had whetted my appetite now, and she knew it. We turned and walked in the direction of the pigs' trough. About halfway there, she halted suddenly and lifted one arm, pointing to the pig pen. I gasped. Just beyond us, not more than ten yards away, stood a hundred ravaging, hungry rats.

I could just make out one of the big ones. His teeth extended some two or three inches below his mouth, and when he saw us standing there, he merely paused a moment before returning to his feast in the pigs' trough.

Little shivers ran up and down my back and I wanted to turn and run away from the sight, but I couldn't lose face in front of my aunt. After all, I had insisted on coming down to see what was making the noise. I guess she felt my eagerness to get back to the house, for she wheeled me around and began warning me again about straying from the house, and in particular, about staying away from the pigs' trough at night. I asked her how long the rats had been there. She just shook her head, saying that they were at the farmhouse before the family had moved in—and that was over twenty years before.

The next few days went pretty much as the first had, with the exception of my trips to the secret hiding place—those were made during the day. Each time, though, I was limited to only a few minutes in my imaginary world for, just as I had found some time to rush to the shed, take off my clothes and put on the female clothing, someone would call me and I'd have to hurry to reverse the process in order to respond without arousing suspicions.

It was about halfway into the vacation before I was left alone, or at least thought I was. I'd gone off right after lunch to the anthills on the north end of my uncle's farm. I had asked Johnny if he wanted to accompany me but he had refused. One of his favorite television shows was on.

The anthills seemed like miniature civilizations that grew and fell at an amazing rate. Sometimes I helped them destroy themselves. I got really interested in them that particular afternoon and must have stayed away from the house a couple of hours. By the time I'd returned, the three of them were gone, and there was a note on the table. Aunt Mary explained that she and Uncle Ed had some business in town and that Johnny had gone along for a doctor's appointment. I couldn't believe my eyes!

Without hesitation, I ran for the storage shed. I grabbed the door, not caring for niceties now that no one could see me, and sighed with relief as I entered. Pulling off my clothing I thought over which dress would be the best-fitting. None of them really fit, as the clothes were old and a bit misshapen. I'd taken a mirror from my aunt's room, but that day I wasn't concerned with how I looked in the mirror. I decided to forgo that, and just imagine how I would look if the clothes were really mine and a little more stylish.

I felt just like a little girl dressing in her mommy's clothes. After a few minutes of talking to my imaginary boyfriend, I decided to venture out of the shed. Excitement soared through my body as I felt for the first time what it was like to be a girl outside. It was beautiful.

I ran through the alfalfa field in my bare feet, not caring about the small pebbles bruising my feet. This was a new me, a me I hadn't really had time to understand. The clothes were just an expression of feelings that didn't seem to match those of other boys my age, but I loved the feelings, and I loved the girl who was me when I was alone. I didn't understand, but I didn't really have to. For about a half hour I explored the farm in my new self and in my dress, as well.

"Sissy!" the voice said. It had come out of the bushes. I turned quickly to greet my cousin. He was standing behind a bush with a devilish look on his face. I thought fast. First I asked him what he was doing home. He had talked his way out of the doctor's appointment at the last minute, because, after all, he was going to look around and find me.

"Want to play?" I asked him, grinning, acting as though I had some great secret to share, some nasty forbidden game. He went for it. When he asked why I was wearing girls' clothing, I told him about friends in my neighborhood back home who did it, and it was fun.

I led him back to the shed, and he chose some clothing—after he had swallowed his surprise at finding them. We played until we heard the pickup.

Still wearing our dresses, we ran to meet them. Aunt Mary and Uncle Ed were surprised but not really disturbed by our game of dress-up with the clothing I had found. For the next three days, as though it were a dream, we were allowed to dress up—and no one made fun of me. My aunt even took a picture of us.

Johnny got tired of the game after the first day, but he still enjoyed dressing up as a man. He played my husband. We had three quiet days. Then on my last day there, my uncle came in and asked if Aunt Mary could speak with me privately. We rounded the corner of the house slowly. I knew what was coming. Aunt Mary was humming in the kitchen, and her hands were covered with flour. She looked up at the squeak of the kitchen door and smiled at me.

"Now, listen here, Danny," she said, "you're a little boy and you're going to have to take that dress off. It's one thing around here, and I've let you do it for the past three days, but your parents are coming. I can't let them see you like that." She turned back to her bread-making. I watched her and tried to decide how to tell her of my feelings, how to explain, but . . .

"Ok," I said softly. "I'll go change right now." I walked back to the deserted shed and slowly made the transformation back to my male self.

The country had provided my freedom to dress as I wished, but I had nevertheless felt guilt as a result of culturally imposed dress standards and sex roles—even at the age of eight.

LEARNING TO HATE ISN'T HARD—
FOR A SISSY

Because it was the first day back to school, Dad drove my sister Dee and me that morning. After slipping the car into neutral, he turned around a little and reached over the seat. This was a manly gesture of luck, I knew, but as I shook his hand, I wondered why Dad felt the obvious need to reassure me. What exactly was this thing they called junior high school?

Dee left me shortly after we entered through the front of the antiquated main office building, hollering that she had to meet some friends of hers before the first session. That was a little inconsiderate, I thought, but in my anger, I lost some of my initial fear.

She had pointed to a little sign. It turned out to be the first in a series which led me to the auditorium. As I walked, I studied the students who surrounded me. There were definite class distinctions. Most of the students were very poor and showed it. They wore old clothes, torn tennis shoes, and patched shirts. I wondered if anyone would notice my somewhat baggy white pants. Mom had insisted I wear them.

The day was hot already. It must have reached over a hundred later on. Each time I filed into a classroom with the others, I remember the combination of heat and warm bodies made me feel faint. But junior high school meant I was growing up, and I relished the thought of it. Only the thought of P.E. (physical education) class disturbed me. I didn't like what I'd heard about it.

As I entered the auditorium, one of my friends

from elementary school waved at me. I returned the gesture but looked around as though searching for someone. Allen Kelly and I had been members of the same gang of neighborhood kids, but I didn't want to share my first day with him. He frightened me a little, because he really seemed to enjoy picking on other kids. We could laugh together when it came to teasing the girls, or talk when one of us was lonely, but he was the bully sort. Besides, I'd heard he spent time in a juvenile home for stealing something from a neighbor's house.

I wandered over to the left side of the auditorium, but still didn't see anyone I wanted to join. There was an empty seat near me so I took it, carefully keeping my eyes straight ahead. I felt self-conscious as usual.

Soon, the public address system began squealing with feedback. A loud voice, which immediately reminded me of Orson Welles with a Southern accent, told everyone to quiet down. I braved a look to each side of me, since everyone seemed to be twisting around looking for talkers. The voice boomed again, and looking at the stage, I connected it with a tiny bald man who turned out to be the principal.

Once again, I joined in the search for those violating the order for silence, looking bravely to either side of me.

His voice boomed through the loudspeakers again. "Shut up!" That did it. Other than an occasional cough and the sound of a nose being blown, the little man on stage had our attention.

"Now, children," he began, "hereafter, when I or any of the teachers in the junior high school tells you to be quiet, you will be quiet. If they have to tell you to shut up you'll get this." He held up a long board full of holes. I was later to learn what the paddle felt like, at the hands of one of those teachers.

"Now, you will listen for your name and your homeroom assignment as we read them. Before we do that, I'd like to tell you a little about the school in which many of you will be growing up during the next three years. The name of our junior high school is Mark Twain. This school has been here for over fifty years, and many of you here today have parents who once at-

tended this same school. As a matter of fact, I have met
two children so far whose parents were students of *mine*
many years ago." With this the bodies around me began
a search for those two as if they were going to stand and
identify themselves. The principal went on.

"For those of you who think junior high is a cinch,
you've got another think a-coming. It's all work—no
play. For those of you who work, there will be personal
rewards later on in life. But those of you who play, believe me, will have a very unhappy three years. I can
guarantee that!"

I felt threatened, and I didn't like that. It wasn't
right, I thought, to threaten us on our first day. Of
course, I'd work, but only as hard as I had to to get
passing grades. I never particularly liked school, and if I
couldn't play a little, well, it was going to be pretty aw-
ful. I listened half-heartedly to the droning voice. When
he had finished, a little, skinny, gray-haired woman
with wire-rimmed spectacles came to the microphone. It
turned out that she was the school counselor.

"These will be your homeroom assignments. Listen, closely, for I'll repeat them only once and then go
on to the next. Andres, Chapel #2; Anderson, Chapel
#2 . . ."

The first day was a good one. Other than the heat,
my only complaint concerned my math teacher, a lady
named Schmidt. During the first ten minutes of class
she paddled one boy for talking. It wasn't the board that
bothered me, it was the humiliation—having to stand in
front of the class afterward. Miss Schmidt had gray hair,
like my grandmother, but that was where the resem-
blance ended. She fit my picture of a real witch and
seemed even to speak with an evil snap, like the cracking of a whip—meant to sting. Her seventh grade math
class had one advantage, though. Most of the class was
female; that made me feel more secure.

Physical education classes, for the first few days,
were really minus any education, physical or otherwise.
We were told that our shower rooms were being worked
on, so we could use the time period for talking or working on other class assignments. This was the time in
which I first got to know some of my classmates.

There were, I decided, three types of boys. First, the Mister America's—those who could obviously be the Stars, no proof needed. These boys were either tall and well-built or shorter and mean-looking. They had an air about them that the Cattle looked up to. I called this second type Cattle because they did anything that the Stars or the coaches directed them to, and they never thought of doing anything that wasn't required. Cattle made up the vast majority of every P.E. class I ever attended. Even after I left school, I could still see this type of person in society, ambling along aimlessly. They did just what was expected, never exhibited any creativity, and never expressed any desire to excel in anything.

The Cattle were a step up from the third, and smallest group, though. The boys in this group were pigeon-toed, uncoordinated, smaller-than-average, skinny, effeminate, dumb, or otherwise unable to keep up with the majority of the class. They were immediately identifiable Victims. I called them Victims because these unfortunates (of which I was one) were constantly being subjected to humiliations and degradations at the hands of students and coaches alike.

"All right boys, listen up," came the voice from one side of the auditorium filled with boys. My reprieve was up. "Today you get down to the dressing rooms, dress in those gym shorts you brought from home, and meet me right back here where we'll get started on your physical fitness tests."

As I walked to the dressing rooms, I felt my heart sink. So far I had avoided classification as a Victim, but that was about to end. I'd taken special care to wear long-sleeved shirts, and pants and shoes with a definite toughness about them to avoid comments on my effeminate appearance. A couple of the tougher-looking guys in the class had talked to me as if I were one of them, asking me about the number of fights I had been in.

At one point I described a fight in which I had single-handedly taken on four fifth graders—I was only in the fourth grade—and had done a real job on them. What I was actually describing was a fight in which a sixth grade football type had beaten up four

fifth graders because they wouldn't chip in to give him
his lunch money—different from the way I told it, but
the story suited my purposes. I was playing the punk
role to the hilt, but my masquerade was soon to end.

The locker room was small and crowded. This was
the first time many of us had worn gym shorts, and
those who could afford new shoes were pulling on
squeaky new tennis shoes. I was horrified at the idea of
undressing in front of so many people.

As I fumbled with the combination of my locker, I
cringed with embarrassment at the screams and laughter
of my classmates. I kept my attention on my locker,
afraid that by looking around me I would embarrass
someone else. Many of the boys acted as though undressing in a crowd was nothing new, but there were
others who seemed as uneasy as I was about exposing
themselves to others.

"Alright, you punks, quiet down in here. Shut up!
You hear me?" It was the coach, a man nobody wanted
to tangle with. Suddenly the only noises in the room
were grunts, as each of us dressed. I was stalling, hoping someone would come in and tell me I didn't have to
do it. Slowly, I unbuttoned my shirt, exposing soft white
skin and a skinny torso. Everyone around me was
nearly dressed. The stink of perspiration was stronger
there than in the halls and classrooms. I waited for a
minute, expecting howls of laughter and pointed remarks, but no one seemed to notice. I sat on the bench
and took off my shoes, slowly revealing the pale skin of
my feet. For a moment I hated my feminine-looking
body. As I reached to unfasten my pants I noticed the
coach, returning to our midst from his office.

"How many sissies we got left?" he mocked, gazing around at the few boys left. "Listen, girls, if in one
minute you don't have your clothes off and your gym
suits on, and if you're not out of here, there's going to
be five licks for each of you. Now, get the hell out of
here!"

My inhibitions were forgotten. I finished unzipping
my pants, pulled them off quickly, and yanked on my
gym shorts just as the coach came back into the locker
room, holding a paddle.

"What's your name, honey?" he asked, looking right at me. I thought there had to be some mistake, because although Dad might call me honey, a man like Coach Tex would never do that, or so I thought. I looked around me at the few boys left. As I faced him again, he screamed.

"You, that's right little lady. You think I can make a man out of you?" Fear struck hard at me. These words had come from anyone who had ever hated me, all through my life. I didn't want to be singled out as a sissy, even in front of just a small number of classmates. The word would spread. Once the tag was on me, I was a Victim, and I'd be accorded the treatment of a Victim.

"Yes, sir," I said, afraid to raise my voice to him.

"What's that, little lady? I can't hear you," he shouted.

"Yes, sir!" louder this time, despairingly.

"Listen here, sissy, when I tell you to get your clothes on and get the hell out of here I mean it. And when I ask you a question you're going to answer me like a man. Do you understand me?"

"Yes, sir!" I yelled. My voice cracked and went into a girlish scream. The boys who hadn't left yet broke into a laugh. This amused the coach and he faced his audience.

"All right, everybody out."

I started out, too, but his huge hand caught me by the shoulder squeezing hard. As he whirled me around to face him, I saw the fire in his eyes. I could see now that his face was pocked and scarred, and one eye opened wider than the other. His hair was cut in a razor-type flat top that revealed a red spot in his scalp as he bent to talk to me.

"Listen, punk, I don't like you and that's because you're a sissy. If I had my way, you and all your friends would be over in the girl's P.E. class where you belong, but the law doesn't allow that. So you listen, and you listen good."

I was listening, but there was a new emotion in me. I won't let this creep humiliate me, I was telling myself, over and over again. My anger was new, and it

strengthened me. When his speech had ended, he let me
go. My shoulder burned where he'd grabbed me, but as
soon as he released me, I ran from the room. He was
screaming that he hadn't told me I could go, but I didn't
care.

As I entered the gym, stares met me. A few were
sympathetic, but many of the boys sneered, as if to isolate themselves from me, so that it was clear which side
of the fence they were on.

We were busy for the next few weeks proving our
physical prowess in what the coach called the ball-buster
examinations. I was always at the bottom of the list,
although I tried to give my best in each test. Other than
making a snide remark when I came to the front of the
line for a test, the coach seemed to have forgotten our
encounter.

I'd become one of the quickest to dress for class,
but there was a new problem—showers. For the first
two or three weeks I managed to skip them without notice. One day, though, one of the Stars noticed my hurried dressing. As he crossed the locker room, I knew
there was going to be trouble.

"You ain't takin' a shower, huh?" he drawled.

"Why . . . no," I answered, trying to plead ignorance with my voice.

"The coach asked me to watch for him to see who
wasn't takin' no showers," he said. "If I's you I'd jest
get in there and take mine. Otherwise, you gonna be
reported."

I resented his orders, but I didn't want the coach
on me again. Undressing, I hurried off to the showers
stark naked.

"Hey! That looks like a girl. Get that sissy out of
here!" I ran down the long, wet, tiled hall.

In the showers I was confronted with a dozen late
showerers—all of them naked, but hairy. They all
seemed to have pubic hair—everyone but me. "Hey,"
one boy yelled, "look at that. He hasn't got one." I
wanted to run, but grabbed a bar of soap and started
lathering myself instead. It surprised me that most of
the boys were larger and hairier than I was. I hadn't

realized I was so small, but then I'd never had the chance to compare before.

One of the larger boys walked past me and knocked the soap from my hand. As I bent to retrieve it, another boy stepped over and kicked it from my reach. Shrugging, I stepped under the stream of water and rinsed off.

When I left the shower room, there were more comments, but I'd grabbed a towel and draped it around my hips to forestall any more comments about the size and condition of my pubic area. I hurried to dress so I wouldn't be late for my next class. As I bent to pull my socks on, I felt a thump on the back of my head. Turning, I felt an anger build in me. It was the Star who had told me to take a shower.

"What did you do that for?" I asked, my head buzzing.

" 'Cause I wanted to," he said, trying to make his voice high and squeaky. "The coach wants to see you, right now." He shoved me in the direction of the coach's office. By this time I had the attention of the whole class, and their encouragement to fight back, but I was no match for that hulking bully. I walked toward the coach's office, not even having had the chance to put my shoes on.

"Why don't you fight, pussycat?" someone yelled.

"Come on, chickenshit. What's wrong, you yellow or somethin'?" another yelled.

I was yellow, but I wasn't dumb. There was no use in my becoming a punching bag for some bully's fists. Why should I be hurt so someone else could enjoy it? I could still hear the heckles in the coach's office.

"You know what you're here for?" he grumbled as I shut the door. I nodded.

"You say 'yes, sir' or 'no, sir' when I ask you questions. Is that clear?"

"Yes, sir," I answered, trying to make my voice sound masculine.

"What's your name, boy?" he asked, sounding bored.

"Uh, Danny. Danny O'Connor."

He appeared to be writing some kind of report.

Although I could see he'd put my name on the upper left-hand corner, I could make out nothing else. I glanced around his office. There were plaques and pictures on the wall, some of them of boys who had starred in athletics. I wondered what it would be like to be one of them instead of myself. The coach looked up for a minute, and I detected a smirk on his face.

"You're going to take this note home to your father, if, of course, you have one, and have him sign it," he said. "Now, you know what I told you about getting along in this class. I thought I made it clear I didn't want any sissies." I was mad. I didn't want any more of this verbal abuse.

"I'm not a sissy!" I screamed. "I hate you and I don't care what you do to me; I'll never come here again." I took the note from him and ripped it in two.

His face flushed red as he stood up and reached for the paddle leaning against the wall. My anger kept me firmly planted. It wasn't fair, I told myself; not taking a shower doesn't deserve this kind of treatment. He reached across the desk and pulled me over it.

I felt every blow, but I didn't cry. When he had finished, he pushed me away so that I stood up and faced him. His face was contorted with anger.

"Now you say you're sorry, or I'll give it to you again." I stood there, silently watching him.

By the time he had finished with the second batch of blows, I could feel only a numb burning in my rear end. It hurt, but I wasn't going to apologize. Not to him, or to anyone. He screamed at me to apologize to him. I still kept my silence, and watched him. His rage seemed to change to something else, for he reached around me suddenly and opened the door.

"Get the hell out."

As I tried to walk, the pain struck me. I couldn't move. He booted me in the rear and I flew out the door, breaking into tears. I felt a wet spot on my pants and realized that I had urinated. Shame washed over me, but I ignored it, just as I ignored the people who watched as. I walked by them. The bully was standing near the door, as though waiting for a chance to continue his abuse. Without a second thought, I walked

straight toward him and instinctively kicked him as hard
as I could. I didn't wait to see where my kick had
landed or what damage it had done, but I listened to his
screams of pain with satisfaction.

The bell rang for the next class.

As I ascended the stairs, I noticed a crowd of students around me. They all seemed to draw away from
me and stare. My face was red and teary, but they were
staring at my feet. A girl I knew from one of my morning classes was staring down and biting her lips, as
though confused by what she saw. The floor was cool
on my shoeless feet. Embarrassment stopped my tears,
but I wasn't going to go back to that locker room. My
next class was math, I realized; that terrible old Schmidt
woman would be sure that I was humiliated further. I
stopped, leaning against a window sill, and sobbed.

When I had taken a breath to calm myself, I noticed a tall, younger-looking man with a cap like the
ones coaches wore approaching me.

"What's wrong, son?" he asked quietly. I started to
answer him, but decided against it. He would surely
side with Coach Tex. He bent down on one knee and
took my arm so that I faced him. I watched his face as
he looked down and noticed that I wasn't wearing
shoes. The crowd of students around us was quiet, but
they pointed and stared. The coach stood up, looked
around us, and sighed. He pulled me to his side, and we
began to walk through the crowd of onlookers.

"All right you kids, go on to your classes or I'll
take you all to the office," he bellowed. I didn't look up
to see if they obeyed him, but I heard the scurrying feet.
We walked in the direction of the administration office,
but he twirled me around and ushered me through an
old, scratched-up door with the name Coach McCauley
on it in fresh-looking gold letters.

He lifted me to the top of a huge old oak desk and
as he sat me down, I felt a burning, wet feeling on my
bottom.

"Well, now, son, what's the problem? Where are
your shoes?" I noted the obvious concern in his eyes.

"I left them in the locker room," I squeaked. It
was difficult to speak after all those tears.

"Okay," he said, "why don't you tell me what's made you so unhappy so we can get to the bottom of this and help you?" I nodded, and started telling him the story, keeping it as brief and as honest as I could. My relief at his sympathy was so great that I felt no need to take up any more of his time than was necessary. A coach was too important, I thought, to waste his time on long, involved stories. He had been pacing as I talked. When I finished, he turned to me.

"Now, don't worry about going back down there to retrieve your shoes. I'll send one of the kids from my sixth period class for them. I'm not going to say you were right for not wanting to take a shower, because you have to realize the rule wasn't made up just to embarrass you. It was made so everyone would stay clean. You know, some of the kids—in fact, most of them—don't take a bath or shower anywhere else."

"I do!" I interjected. "I take a bath every morning before I come to school." He nodded his head in acknowledgment.

"Okay," he continued, "but you must understand you were wrong in disobeying the rules. Now, as for Coach Tex beating you, I have no proof of that, so . . ."

Although modesty made it difficult for me, I decided to get back at Coach Tex by proving what I'd said was true. I stood up, and unbuttoned my pants. My rear still stung, and I knew that it would be very red. I could feel the cool air on my bottom and I faced it to him.

"Oh my God," he said. "I can't believe this. He had no right to do this to you." I looked down in surprise, then blinked in further surprise—my underwear was bloody. I started to faint. The coach grabbed me and carefully lifted me onto the desk.

"Now, just lie here quietly and I'll be right back with some help. Okay?" There was a hint of fear in his voice. The pain came back, and the humiliation I had felt a few minutes earlier at the hands of Coach Tex washed over me again.

Coach McCauley came back with the school nurse. I recognized her because she had visited my second period science class to lecture on the productive uses of bacteria in industry. Whenever I saw her in the halls, I pictured a walking bacteria culture, for she looked the type; but just then I was hurting too much to even laugh at my own joke.

Later that day, when I arrived home, my parents were in an uproar. Dad had come to pick me up, but he hadn't said anything. I didn't know that the principal had called Mom right after he learned of the unjust beating I'd received. For a while I didn't know whose side anyone was on.

Dad kept screaming that I was wrong, but Mom challenged him every time with her conviction that I hadn't deserved that kind of beating, no matter what I'd done. I sat in the middle of the argument and kept my views to myself. Finally, they decided to take the school administration's offer. In return for not bringing charges against the school and the coach, the school would place me in another P.E. class and would see that I was never under the supervision of that coach again. After that, I even made a deal with my new coach, Coach McCauley, that I could skip showers if I cleaned up after my classmates.

For the first month or so of the school year, things had been relatively calm on the bus that took us to and from school. Although we got loud and played tricks on each other, it took a while before some of the meaner pranksters got tired of their simple games and sought out unsuspecting prey. Coming home on the bus one night, these bored individuals looked for a victim, and picked me.

"Hey, blondie locks, why don't you come on back here with us boys? We got a seat for you."

"I don't want to." I was annoyed at the name the voice had picked for me, but I didn't want to go to the back of the bus and challenge them. Today, though, I was sitting next to Dee Dee, and the name hurt a little more because she was there.

"Don't pay any attention to those creeps," she said. "They just want to pick on you the way they picked on little Billy Joe Davis last week." One day, when I'd been home sick, those same bullies had strung Billy Joe up by his feet from the roof of a nearby bar. If

I hadn't been home, I'm sure they'd have chosen me as a better candidate for their fun.

"Why didn't the bus driver stop them; didn't he see them?" I asked Dee, even though I had asked her this question every time the incident had come up.

"He saw them all right," Dee admitted. "I was going to tell him what was happening, but he seemed to have already noticed and he was just sitting there, as if he were enjoying it."

"Come on, little blondie locks, what's the matter?" the voice called again. "She's not afraid, is she?" There was a burst of laughter from the back of the bus, and everyone around us turned to look at me. I could sense Dee coloring with embarrassment. I knew Mom and Dad would hear about this later. As we walked from the bus stop, she spoke.

"Why didn't you just go back there and shut them all up," she asked, trying to keep her voice low. "You know none of them are anything but bullies and Dad said people like that are always chicken themselves. They pick on people so everybody is afraid of them and won't challenge them. Danny, don't you understand that if you let these things go they'll only get worse? Either you get it over with soon, or they'll do something to you like they did to Billy Joe."

How could she understand that I just didn't want to fight? I would defend myself if they came after me, but I didn't want to fight anyone. As we neared the house, I saw Janet climbing into a treehouse we'd built just a few days before. I ran to join her, waving at Dee, who was still grumbling.

A strange car pulled into the driveway a little later that afternoon, and our parents got out. I ran over to the car, trying to talk to Dad first, hoping that Dee had decided not to say anything about the incident on the bus.

"Where'd you get this one, Dad?"

"This is a loaner from the brake place," Dad said. "The car broke down this afternoon. Not bad, eh?" Dee and Janet came running up to greet them. I went back to the treehouse, and sat inside, waiting.

"Danny! Damn it!" I heard the roar, and scrambled out of the treehouse. He was standing at the back door, shaking a fist at me. "What the hell you mean you didn't go back there and take care of those lugs?" he yelled. "A son of mine, yellow? What's been happening to you lately? It wasn't more than a month ago you had trouble with guys in your gym class; now you're getting pushed around by a whole new bunch. What the hell's happening?"

How was I supposed to know? It wasn't a whole new bunch, but I knew he'd get mad if I brought that up. The boy I'd kicked never bothered me again, but some of the boys who'd been watching kept picking on me.

"Well, answer me!" Dad shouted.

"Wha—What? I didn't hear you Dad." He shook his head.

"I said, what's wrong with you? How come you don't stand up for your rights? You're my son. My son is not a coward. You know what to do with people like those s.o.b.'s who pick on you. What's wrong with you, you turning yellow? I thought I told you a thousand times that when your sister is with you I'm relying on you to protect her. How can I let you alone with her if you won't even protect yourself?"

There was no answer I could make to him. I'd lost his respect.

"Now, Dad, don't be too hard on Danny," Mom broke in. "It's not his fault that every bully in school picks on him. After all, it's not as though he goes out looking for the trouble."

Dad turned to Mom and they began talking quietly. They went inside and as they shut the screen door, it squeaked loudly. I thought about what I was going to have to do.

I decided I had to fight those bullies. I had to gain respect from my family, from the school. I couldn't let fear hold me back anymore.

I felt weak as I boarded the bus the following afternoon. This was it, I knew it; in a little while I'd be dueling with those bullies, like a New Orleans gentleman, dueling for my honor.

Dee wasn't on the bus. I hoped she wouldn't make

it. It would be much easier to make up a story about single-handedly wiping out the back of the bus. But, what if I lost? After all, what made me think I could take on six or seven guys anyway?

"Hi there, blondie locks, baby. How's my little girl doing today?" a boy said, as he came toward me from the back of the bus. It was the one they called Haight; Ronald, I think his first name was. He was the ringleader of the gang I was about to face. Although he was only two or three inches taller than I was, he was twice my size. As he approached me, I felt fear tighten my stomach.

I wanted to make friends with him. Why did we have to fight? What a silly business this fighting stuff was, anyway. As he brushed by me, he slammed an elbow into the side of my head. My head was still aching as Dee climbed aboard the bus.

"What are you holding your head for?" she asked. "Somebody hit you or something?"

"No," I answered, quickly taking my hand down. "I've just got a little headache or something."

"Well, I see that one they call Haight is back there," she went on. "Has he said anything to you? I mean, did he try to pick a fight yet?" I could sense a tinge of hope in her voice. Did she have any idea at all that I might be genuinely afraid of these bullies? That I was no match for them? That I had no interest in proving my masculinity?

"Here come some more of them," my sister said, leaning over to alert me. "See that tall one? That's Jerry Finnigan. He's the one who got kicked off the football team for fighting the coach last year. Those other two used to be in a gang called the Scorpions. My girl friend Angie—you know, the one I told you had gotten pregnant last year—well, she told me that she used to go with one of those two. I don't remember which one, just now." I looked out the window for a minute, then back at my sister. I didn't really care.

The bus driver was revving up the engine. There were only two more people standing outside waiting to enter the bus. There was a clank, and I knew that the front door had closed. There was no way out now. As the bus pulled out, there were cheers from the back of the bus.

"Hey, blondie locks, you're next," said a voice. "You're next!" echoed another. "Yeah, we even brought the rope today," said a third. I turned to my sister for comfort.

"I didn't see any rope, did you?" I tried to smile.

"What difference does it make?" she answered coolly. "You know what you're going to have to do if they start anything. What's the difference?" The bus rounded the first of a series of turns that would put us on the main highway. I carefully watched each person get off the bus, and waited.

As if it were planned, about halfway home, one of the bigger guys Dee had pointed out to me came from behind and grabbed my arm. He was trying to pull me up and over the back of the seat. My sister was screaming. Everyone in the front of the bus turned around and watched, open-mouthed.

"Come on, blondie locks. We gotta surprise for you in the back. We want to share a little secret with you." He jerked at me angrily for resisting him, and began to shout. "Come on, you punk. You're coming back with me. Come on! You little son-of-a-bitch, we're going to teach you a lesson. We don't like sissies riding our bus. . . ."

Something snapped in my arm. I jerked it away from him and Dee dug her nails into the guy, sending him away cursing.

"How's your arm?" she asked, turning back. I checked my arm carefully, trying to mask my embarrassment that she had protected me. Nothing was broken. I tried to reassure her.

"Hey, queer," one of the voices called. I recognized it—Ronald Haight. "You think you're going to get away, don't you. Well, you're wrong. You, and that ugly sister of yours—we're going to get both of you." I wondered briefly why the bus driver didn't stop the bus. I watched all the faces staring at us. Then Dee Dee screamed. One of the creeps from the back had thrown a book at her. It hit her in the head and she began to cry. That was what I needed. I climbed over her.

"I'll kill you!" I screamed. "I'll kill you!"

They thought it was funny, at first, and I could see they were laughing. But as I ran to the back of the bus, the smiles on their faces disappeared. I guess they realized it wasn't a game anymore.

Haight was the first to get up from his seat and face me. As he rose, I raised my right hand in a fist and smashed it straight into his throat with all the strength I could muster. It so surprised him that he fell back, clutching his throat as though I had strangled him. Seeing him in retreat encouraged my desire to make him pay for the hurt done to my sister. I pounded on him.

"Stop him! Stop him!" he cried out, hoping to gain the aid of his friends. "Stop him! Please!"

My rage cooled a little. I looked down at Haight, his face full of tears and blood, and felt nauseated at what I had done. It wasn't right. I straightened up and looked around. One of the two my sister had recognized had pulled a knife, saying, "Hey, man, don't try that shit on me. . . ."

Again, the anger rose and I felt my face flush. Did he think I would run from him because of a knife? In the seat next to me was a pile of Haight's books. I grabbed the top one and threw it straight into the face of the knife holder. It happened so fast, they were all too astounded to move. The guy with the knife dropped it. Then I made my move.

I began to swing my arms madly and connected time and time again. Each time I found my mark, I pounded, or scratched, or slapped.

There was blood on the front of my shirt, and some of it was mine, but it didn't matter. I was getting the better of him. And the others? They had run to tell the bus driver! The only one left was the one Dee had said was kicked off the football team. And he was holding his hands in front of his face, pleading with me not to hurt him. This time I laughed out loud.

"Now who's the chicken?" I screamed, feeling chills come over my body. "Now who's yellow?" I screamed again, looking around for another to challenge me. I was relieved when no one stood, for I realized suddenly how badly I was hurt. My nose gushed blood and my right eye was swollen half-shut. I turned to walk back to my sister. Ronald Haight was babbling.

"You're going to pay for this," he said, through his blood-filled mouth. "You're going to pay; I'll see to that." I continued walking, right toward him. He began to cry, just like a little child. He was fifteen—two years older than I was—and twice my size, and I had made him cry. Me, little blondie locks. Suddenly, the pain didn't seem as bad. I looked to the front of the bus. The driver was standing in the aisle, talking to my sister.

"They deserved it," she was saying. "They threw a book at me and had been picking on Danny for several days." She nodded. "They deserved it."

"Well, these boys say your brother started it," the bus driver answered. "They say . . . well, I'm afraid I'm going to have to report this to the principal." He was a coward, a big man who could have stopped it all right from the beginning, just by threat.

"Shut up!" I screamed at him. "Shut up and leave us alone!" His eyes opened wide, and he seemed to crumble.

"N—now wait a minute. You can't talk to *me* like that," he said shakily. I felt strong and confident.

"Who said I started it?" I asked. He pointed at one of the boys who had been sitting in the back of the bus.

"You say I started this?" I grabbed his shirt collar. "You the one who said I started this whole mess?" The boy had slicked-back, hood-style hair and greasy, smelly clothing. He and his friend wore motorcycle jackets— leather ones with silver stars on the shoulders.

"Uh, no, no, not me, man—I didn't see nothing! Ah, well, that is, I know you didn't start the fight—not you, that's for sure, man." I grabbed his friend.

"You say something bad about me?" I asked. "You got anything bad to say about me or my sister?" As I asked him this, I glanced over at my sister who watched me in awe.

"Uh, no, man—I didn't see anything, man. I'm just riding the bus, that's all. I didn't see anything—I don't know anything about it." I held onto him with one hand and turned to the bus driver, who started to protest.

"Now, listen, if you think I'm going to let you run this bus . . ."

"Shut up!"

"Now, wait a minute here; you can't talk to me like that," he said. "I don't have to put up with that kind of talk from anyone."

"You shut up or I'll get Billy Joe Davis, the kid you let them string up the other day, and we'll all make a trip to the principal's office where you can tell your story."

He was becoming sickly looking. He had permitted a weak-looking, effeminate thirteen-year-old to push him into a corner.

"You have no witnesses to that," he whined.

"Oh yes, he does," chorused a dozen voices in the bus.

"And we'll tell the principal everything!" Dee chimed in.

The bus driver turned away without a word and took his seat. He started the bus, and pulled out onto the highway. Dee looked at me with pride and concern in her eyes. She wiped my face with some tissues people around us had donated. They seemed eager to help me, as though thankful for what I'd done. Was this what it was like to be a man? To be able to overcome your enemies? To conquer those who do you harm?

I remembered that day in the locker room. Even that s.o.b., Coach Tex, would have been afraid of me, now. Shaking my head, I looked to the back of the bus, thinking about what had happened. With surprise, I noticed that all of the hoods had gone. Ron Haight was back there alone, holding a handkerchief to his nose.

Okay, I could justify what I'd done, but for some reason I felt sorry for him. He'd asked for it, maybe, but I could identify with the way he must have felt—defeated, humiliated, and alone.

I got up slowly, testing the ache in my arm. As I walked to the back of the bus, Dee called that it was almost our stop. He saw me coming and looked away, staring out the window with a fierce concentration. When I was even with him, I extended my hand. He seemed to pull away, not looking at me.

Then, slowly, he looked towards me and noted my hand. His face relaxed a little and he extended his hand. He pulled the handkerchief down, and I noted that he wasn't as badly hurt as I'd thought.

"Friends?" I asked.

"Friends," he grumbled.

As I left the bus I realized how much easier it would have been on me to stand up to him from the beginning. Until challenged, a bully uses aggressive behavior to mask his insecurities and fears. But when his bluff is called, the mask is ripped away, and the bluster turns to apology. To this day I remember the triumph of calling a bully's bluff.

THE SEARCH
FOR A CONFIDANTE

It was a hot, clear, beautiful day. Just summer, too—June 21st. We were done with school for a while, the three of us, and we were going to Wisconsin for two weeks. My father's brother had sent round-trip tickets for Dee Dee, Janet, and me. It was our first bus trip, and the first time we had ever visited my uncle's family.

All of us were glowing with excitement as Mom and Dad kissed us good-bye. We mounted the bus steps and settled in eagerly. Our excitement made the forty-eight-hour bus trip speed by. We were still grinning when we stepped off the bus to greet my aunt, my uncle, and my five cousins.

She was a rounded woman, with a smile that never stopped. The cousins seemed a little apprehensive, but they welcomed us warmly. The eldest two, both girls, took to me almost immediately. They wanted to accompany me wherever I went, and to introduce me to all their girl friends.

My uncle was a former army colonel. He had played football while in college. He was the kind of man who always seemed to intimidate me. However, that day must have been a special occasion. He complimented me on how much I'd grown and how manly I seemed. Both he and my cousins seemed to tell me exactly what I needed to hear. They helped to soothe some of the fears I had been living with the past few years.

Although I seemed to have an undeniable attraction for girls, my uncle's unquestioning acceptance of my masculinity surprised me. I found that my uncle, unlike my father, showed me a different kind of approval that went beyond respect and understanding.

He woke me early one morning and asked my help with a project. He had ordered a number of fifteen-year-old trees and needed help digging the holes to plant them in. He surprised me, but I was determined to prove my manliness.

I worked until my hands were raw and my back was sore. I was obviously exhausted, and my uncle's admiration was clear. My own satisfaction astonished me.

Every time he said: "Good man!" or "Danny, you're quite a man," I would stare at him, trying to detect sarcasm or ridicule, but there was none of it in his face or his words. He confused me. He confused me, but he pleased me. I began to put on exhibitions for my cousins. I wanted to show them how many push-ups I could do. One time I did twenty-five—that surprised even me!

I felt as if I were becoming a man, and it seemed to be happening to me just as it had happened to others all around me. I wanted that. I wanted to be normal. But, even as my security in this new self grew, the old feelings recurred.

One time I watched my sisters and cousins as they lined up in front of the house for a quick picture. They were dressed in Sunday dresses, ready for Mass. Their soft-looking clothes brought something out in me. The girl in me seemed to be getting stronger. Gradually I began to feel I would have little choice—she would come out and live.

One evening my cousins went shopping with my aunt, and, as my sisters had been out all day with my uncle, I was left alone in the house. It was as though I had planned it. When I had insisted on staying home alone, I puzzled even myself, but when they walked out the door, something clicked. Almost immediately, I began looking around the house for girls' clothes that would fit me. At first, I was content just to take them out of the drawer or the closet to look at them. But the urge became stronger.

I've heard many times that children faced with gender problems sometimes get sexual gratification from wearing the clothes of the opposite sex. It wasn't that way for me. It wasn't for sexual feelings that I wanted to wear those clothes. I rarely thought of my genitals as more than another appendage of my body. I knew their function, but that had nothing to do with my feelings. I wanted to put on the clothes to feel somehow right in myself.

That evening I dressed for only a short time. I had a feeling they wouldn't be gone long. When they pulled up to the front of the house, I ran out to greet them. It was hard not to show my guilt; just a few minutes before, I had been wearing my cousin's clothes.

I got at least a dozen chances to dress again. Although my aunt and uncle quite often insisted that I accompany them, there were many times they accepted my wish to remain at home.

It wasn't until we boarded the bus to return to San Antonio that the irony struck me. The guilt was almost unbearable. I wanted to talk to someone. I needed to explain to someone why I would work all day with my uncle to impress him with my masculinity, and then plot for moments alone to express my femininity.

Janet and Dee Dee were asleep.

I hadn't had much chance to talk to them during the past two weeks. Now, when I had both the chance and the overwhelming desire to talk with them, they were asleep. I wanted to wake them, but as I thought about it, I lost the courage. As I started to feel heavier, sleepier, I put the thought out of my mind. I slept.

In the long month since our return from Wisconsin, I couldn't shake the guilty feeling that had begun on the bus, coming home. I could feel the need for someone to share my problem with becoming stronger. This person would have to be trustworthy—someone who would keep the secret as long as I requested them to. I had no close friends living nearby. There was virtually no one but my family to confide in.

One sunny day in July, I asked my father if I could accompany him to work that day. He was a wholesaler of various kinds of merchandise and spent most of his day riding around, making deliveries. I thought, if I could find some way during the day, I would tell him of the overpowering urges I was feeling.

My father had come to accept that his son was a little different from other boys. Although he didn't like the idea, I think he realized that there was nothing he could do to change it. I'd tried many times to prove myself different from his opinion of me, but nothing could shake his disillusionment. I wanted him to accept my need to become female, but I couldn't find a way to explain my feelings.

We sat in silence in an old '56 Plymouth, traveling along the San Antonio Expressway. It was very crowded at that time of morning. I stole glances at him from time to time, but Dad hadn't even looked my way since I had asked if I could come along. I thought I knew what was bothering him, but I couldn't find the courage to confront him.

The night before, I had succumbed to an urge to become my female self. On many other such occasions, I would sleep the entire night in a nightgown, waking early to remove the garment before someone could come in and find me. No one knew about these actions until last night.

Yesterday I had made a very unorthodox move. I purchased two nightgowns, several pairs of panties and a dress from money I took out of my savings. During many sleepless nights, it had become more and more apparent to me that I was, or was becoming, a girl. No matter how I fought these feelings, they always returned. Usually, when I wanted to dress as a female, I borrowed something from one of my sisters, but I wanted some clothing of my own that I could use for experiments on myself.

So, when I retired, I hurried to my bedroom, closed the door, and, under cover of darkness, slipped into one of the nightgowns. It was soft. I felt normal. I decided I would definitely tell someone my secret before the end of the week. The night was hot, so I slipped out of bed to open the door in hopes of starting a light breeze. Instead of sleeping under the covers, I stretched out on top of them. If I awoke early, there was no need to fear discovery.

Sometime in the middle of the night, I awoke when my light went on. I struggled to make out the person who was standing at the foot of my bed, but I was blinded by the sudden light. Then, just as suddenly as the light had gone on, it blinked off. By then, I was fully awake—and very afraid. Who was it? I asked myself, over and over. My fear grew as the night passed into morning. I fantasized that I would come out of my room in the morning to face a firing squad. Or the police. Or my father.

I was filled with a deep humiliation. What would my father think of his son? Surely, he would accept no excuses for my behavior. Slowly I gathered the courage to find a way to discover who had come in and to explain honestly that I believed I was a girl.

When I heard my father in the kitchen, cooking breakfast, I decided to test him. Pulling off the night-gown wistfully, I dressed in male clothes. There proved to be no need for a test. As I walked into the kitchen, he looked away. He refused to look at me, despite my attempts at small talk, until I asked if I could go with him to work. He looked at me just long enough to nod his head in approval.

We spent most of the day in silence, but I began to feel comfortable with him again. I couldn't help but feel that he was beginning to warm to me. He seemed to have chosen not to believe what he had seen. For my part, I was relieved. I loved him, despite the feeling that I couldn't confide to him my deepest fears and hopes, and I didn't want to face his humiliation or his ridicule.

There had been many other times when I had accompanied him on his deliveries, for he was often glad to have company on a long journey. But that day, as we rounded the last corner before the house, I felt a special need to improve my standing with him. I wanted to do something "masculine"—something he liked. Fishing! He would enjoy a weekend of that. Although I detested anything of that sort, I wouldn't really mind the sacrifice.

"Dad?" I began, "how's chances of you and me

going up to the Dam and fishing this weekend, maybe Sunday?"

Dad looked at me in obvious surprise. He pulled to a stop in the driveway before he answered.

"Did I hear you right?" he asked. "You want to go fishing? What's wrong with you? You sick or something?" Well, I thought, maybe he was right. I might have been sick, but I wanted to be normal. I didn't want to hurt those I loved. I took a deep breath.

"I just think it's time we guys spent a little of our lives together."

He smiled as though to reassure me I didn't have to worry. I knew then he would never breathe a word about what he had seen. He agreed Sunday was going to be our day.

Now I was glad I hadn't brought up last night myself. I knew it would only mean problems. It had taken a long, scary day to eliminate one possible confidant, but it had been worth it.

For the next few weeks I tried desperately to prove myself, again and again, to my father. It seemed to be working. But I still needed someone to trust with my secret. I decided to test my big sister, Dee Dee.

Mid-August. It was a muggy Texas evening. I had been dropping hints all day about my birthday. Each year it seemed money was short when my birthday rolled around. This year I wanted to warn them early so they'd have plenty of time to save. Dee Dee was sewing—Mom and Dad had purchased her an old sewing machine. She had spent days just learning to thread it.

I was handy with mechanical things, or thought I was, so I had tried to help her. She seemed to be more aggravated than pleased by my attempts at aid, but I couldn't be angry with her—I respected her too much. She would be getting her driver's license soon, and that spelled independence.

Dee Dee was pretty and very popular. My parents used to say that if she charged people money for her time, she'd be a millionaire. Although it was going to be difficult to tell someone, I was hoping I would be able to tell Dee Dee my secret. I had picked that night. She looked up as I walked through the doorway of the bedroom she shared with Janet.

"Yes, I know. Someone's birthday is coming up. And we'd better start preparing for it!" We both laughed. Dee Dee had a way of making me feel important. I loved her for it.

I'd brought an article into the room with me. It was an uncommon bit of news for our part of the world. A man had escaped from a mental institution and had murdered a man in Dallas by cutting off his penis with a welding torch. Only after a massive statewide police search was he found. And it was near our home that he'd been apprehended. He was being held in the county jail awaiting trial. The most interesting thing about the case, for me, was that the individual was a female impersonator. The San Antonio paper had pictures of him on the front page. One picture showed him as a woman, but I felt worried too. I wasn't like him. I didn't want to hurt anyone, even though I, too, dressed as a female. Did this tendency in me mean I'd end up the way that man had?

The article seemed good ammunition for a test of Dee Dee's feelings. When I had all her attention, I pulled the article out of my shirt pocket. She seemed very surprised, since I rarely read the newspaper. What would cause me to clip something from the paper?

"What's that?" she asked.

I quickly unfolded the article and showed it to her. She gazed for a moment at the pictures, once she had finished reading the article, then turned to me and shook her head as if in disgust. I tried to act awed by the article.

"It's terrible, isn't it. The other day one of my boyfriends, Jim . . . you know him?" she started. I nodded. "Well," she continued, "he was telling me about a park here in San Antonio where queers hang around. He said they wait until dark, then attack people— mostly little children from what Jim's heard. I remember seeing the place on one of our Sunday rides. I think it's called Travis Park."

I'd heard the name of that park mentioned many

times at school when kids made fun of the queers. Someone had even remarked, once, that I lived there. It was all I could do not to slug him. But Dee Dee had called the man in the article a queer, immediately. I wondered if dressing in women's clothing made me queer.

Maybe that was it. Maybe I was a queer and just hadn't accepted it. But I'd never felt like a queer. I'd never called myself a queer. I always assumed I was a *girl*. What did Dee Dee think about queers? I asked her.

At first she looked upward. Then she brought her brown eyes level with mine. After a moment, she spoke. "Well," she began, "I don't know that much about them. I'm certainly not an expert in this kind of thing. But . . ." She hesitated, leveling her gaze at me again. ". . . I think they're probably evil people. Jim once said that his brother Joe, who's in the navy in California, was approached by a queer. The queer wanted to go to bed with Joe."

"What did he do?" I asked. This interested me.

"I don't remember, exactly," she answered, "but I think he hit the queer or something. Anyway, Jim says in California being a queer is legal. They just have to carry some kind of card saying they're that way. Then the police will let them go." I was astonished.

"What does a queer do to another man?" I asked.

"I don't know." She shook her head. "I asked Jim the same question, but he refused to answer me. I guess they just hold each other." She looked up. "Wait. Here's Dad. Let's ask him." Dad was leaning around the doorway to say hello. I didn't really want to mention it to him so soon after the incident in the middle of the night, but it was too late.

"Ask me what," Dad said. He had a puzzled look on his face.

Dee Dee started telling him about the article and about our discussion of queers. Dad's expression changed to a very serious look. He told us about an experience he had had during the war.

He and a buddy of his who was stationed on the same ship had been out drinking. They picked up a couple of girls at a bar. All night, they bought the girls drinks and toured the town. The one thing that mystified my father was that neither one of the girls would let the men touch either their faces or their breasts—Dad and his buddy had compared notes when the girls had gone to the restroom. Dad finally got the idea that maybe those two weren't women after all. They didn't want the men to touch their faces because of the beards, or the breasts because they wore falsies.

My sister began to laugh. I joined her somewhat nervously.

Dad continued. He and his buddy decided to take the girls outside before they mentioned their suspicions. Once outside, Dad copped a feel—he touched the girl's face. He laughed as he described it.

"That queer had a heavier beard than mine, and he was running around in women's clothing trying to make out like a female." Without thinking I put my hand to my face. There were no whiskers growing yet. My face was as smooth as my sister's. I sighed quietly. I didn't want a beard at all.

Dad went on to tell us that he and his friend had beaten up the queers and resolved never to be taken in again.

I felt very uneasy. I wondered if that would ever happen to me. Was I a queer just for dressing in women's clothes?

"What," I asked, "do queers do to each other to have sex, Dad?" I was really curious.

"Well, one man takes another and has sex in that man's rear end."

"In the rear end?" I could imagine the pain of such a thing.

"Yes. And some even put the other man's thing in their mouths to have sex."

Dee Dee's face wrinkled up. She looked as though she were feeling sick.

"Okay," Dad said. "That's all in this lesson about queers. You two start getting ready for bed. It's almost time."

That episode had ruled Dee Dee out. She was

completely repulsed even by the word "queer." I had similar feelings, but I was glad of more information. That left Janet, who was ten, and my mother.

Now, Janet was my best friend. No matter what I told her I knew she wouldn't tell anyone. But she really admired me and I didn't want to tell her there was a possibility that her big brother was queer. She had seen me dressed as a girl before, but that had been at least two, maybe three years ago. I guess she thought of that as just a game we'd played. She probably thought I'd grown out of it.

By the time school started again, I had decided to tell my mother, and this evening was the time I had picked.

Dee Dee and Mom were in the next room, talking. I heard their voices, but my mind was concerned with the way I would tell her. I planned one opening, then discarded it. Each way seemed to fall short of the truth. I tossed ideas around. When I heard Dee Dee say good night and leave the room, I jumped up.

I walked into the kitchen and grabbed a glass of milk. Mom warned me to save some for breakfast. I nodded, but there was no worry in my mind. The milk was just a prop. I asked her if I could talk to her about something very important. She asked me immediately what was wrong. There was worry in her voice. I struggled for words—none came.

She asked again what the problem was. I couldn't answer her. Mutely I motioned for her to follow me. I left the glass on the table and went to my room. She walked silently behind me.

I sat on the bed. She started to turn on the light, but I asked her not to. Long hurried strides brought her to the bed. She sat beside me. I began to cry. She clasped her hands in her lap and urged me to tell her what was wrong. I took a long, shuddering breath.

"I . . . I think I'm queer. I don't know exactly what's wrong with me but as long as I can remember I've had a feeling inside that I was a girl."

In the darkness, I could barely make out her face. What I could see frightened me. She seemed to be in some kind of shock. Her eyes were huge, and they stared straight ahead. I went on.

"You see, I just don't understand, but I've always had this feeling. I've always thought that something was wrong. When I've had the chance, I've dressed like a girl, secretly, ever since I can remember. I wanted to tell you before but . . . "

"What?" Her voice was sharp, high-pitched. "I've never seen you dressed like a girl. Never. What are you talking about?"

I fumbled for words. If she didn't believe there was anything wrong, how could I tell her? Why should I jeopardize her opinion of me? Why should she question my masculinity? I wavered.

No—I was going to tell it all; I needed to let it out. It wasn't a game anymore. I couldn't turn back.

I rose from the bed and went to the dresser where I hid my collection of women's clothing. I tossed away the old shirts on top and gathered up the collection.

"What are these clothes doing in your room?" She was hurt, puzzled.

I took another deep breath. Carefully I explained how I had obtained the clothes. I told her how I chose times to wear them. The words came easily. It didn't really matter what she thought. I had let the secret out. Relief loosened my tongue.

My mother listened intently, as though she were a priest in a confessional. She didn't interrupt me. When she had heard the story through, she consoled me. It was all right now. We would talk some more about it tomorrow. She rose and kissed me good night. I was alone.

But I was not afraid. She had promised not to mention anything I had told her. I pulled on a night-gown and climbed into bed. Then, in the quiet night, I heard sobbing.

After a while, I felt nauseated. The sobbing hadn't stopped. I knew it was Mom. I had to let her know I wasn't really as sick as she thought. I had to let her know I loved her. Even if it turned out that I was a queer and not a girl, I would try to stop dressing in women's clothing. I didn't want to hurt her.

The floor creaked as I walked to her room. At the doorway I hesitated. I thought for a minute that I should take the nightgown off, but I wanted her to see that I wasn't something evil. I was the same person. I was still her child. That would never change.

Dad was snoring loudly on one side of the bed. If he awoke, there would be hell to pay. Mom was sobbing into the pillow. I was so upset by the sound of her sobbing that I nearly turned and ran. But she seemed to have heard me. Turning, she lifted her arms.

I started crying too, but climbed into bed with her. We held each other and tried to calm our sobbing. I was relieved to know that she loved me no matter how I dressed, but it hurt me to know I had made her cry. I held her until she stopped crying. When she fell asleep, I slipped away. The quiet early morning was peaceful. Slowly I made my way back to my own bed. I wanted only to sleep.

The next few months were trying for both of us. We considered my problem from all angles. Mom kept expressing her fear that I would harm my mental health if I wore feminine clothing. I had the opposite opinion. We searched for information on the concept of men who wore women's clothing. Even conservative San Antonio had some available to us.

About six months after I had told my mother, we noticed an article in *Redbook* magazine, written by the mother of a person who had changed sexes. We snapped it up. Parallels were inevitable. Mom was really upset by the article. The case history was almost identical to mine, but she kept denying it.

I became really afraid; she was threatening me with commitment to a mental institution. At first I wondered if I were really sick. Then, I began to wonder just how sick I was. Finally, I began to wonder about my chances of ever getting well.

One thing the article had mentioned helped me. A

transsexual was someone who had the anatomy of one sex but had a total identification with the other. That was me. I knew it. Now I had a name for myself. And it wasn't "queer."

FOOTBALL

"Run! Get out there and run, you little sonava-bitches, run!!!

"Alright, line up. That's it, ladies, you got it. That's right. Now we're going to see what yo-all children are made of. Give me fifty side-straddle hops. Ready? One, two, three, sound off!!!

"Come on, girls, move it, move it! There's no room for happy endings out here today, gentlemen.

"O'Connor, what do you think this is out here, a fairy tale? Where you been? Out in some dream world? Who the hell you think you are—Cinderella? Well, listen here, punk, this here is a football field, you got it? Yeah, and I'm your wicked stepmother, so you'd better move your ass."

The coach was a former drill sergeant in the marines, and as tough as they come. I don't know how I'd gotten through spring training, but I'd made it. There I was, a freshman in high school, on the football team. And I was going whole hog to prove once and for all time, to myself and anybody concerned, that I was a man.

"Alright, people, I don't plan to be here all night, so if you don't get your chores done today, I'll just have to leave you here so you can try it till you get it right. On your stomachs ladies. Get your asses on your stomachs! Thirty push-ups—now! Sound off! Up-down, up-down, up-down. Come on Hunter, get your fat ass moving. Judson, Peters, Balinsky—up! Up! Up!" I never really knew what was going to spill out of his mouth next, except that it would be foul and degrading.

This was another attempt at sports. I wasn't new at the game. I'd gone out in the fall of the eighth-grade

61

year for the junior varsity team at Mark Twain, but
after five weeks of hard work I'd been eliminated. The
same thing happened a few months later when I decided
to go out for the basketball team. I'd lost the chances of
playing on either team, but I hadn't wasted the time. I
was stronger now, and weighed almost one hundred and
thirty pounds. I was at a new school; we had moved to
a better part of town. The old school held a lot of bad
memories, so I really didn't mind. The new place
seemed to do me wonders.

Nimitz School, named after the admiral, was the
newest school in the city, and the front entrance was
flanked by naval cannons. It was huge and twice as
noisy as Mark Twain, and I was determined that those
around me would respect me. They did admire me, and
perhaps I surprised them a little. I looked effeminate,
but I had a super-masculine, "macho" attitude. I had
developed a command of four letter words and a hard
guy look, as well as a swagger. I wore leather boots,
Levi's, and made a point of being seen smoking cigarettes with some of the hoods at a small grocery store
across from the campus.

At home, I was in trouble. My urge to become female had grown stronger. I couldn't fight the battle anymore by simply going into my room and closing the
door. Mom knew now, and that made a big difference.
Any time anything of hers or my sisters' was missing,
she accused me. She often got very upset with me and I
feared that she would lose her temper and reveal my
secret to Dad. Football was insurance, of a kind.

After only one hour of our first day of practice
tryouts we'd done side-straddle hops, push-ups, knee
bends, frog jumps, five different kinds of sprinter's leg-
stretching exercises, two different kinds of painful leg
lifts, and sit-ups, sit-ups, sit-ups.

"Okay, sixty seconds rest!" called that familiar
voice. The rest meant that twenty of the people there
would be eliminated. If I concentrated on staying on my
feet and reacting, maybe I could avoid that.

The coach seemed like a nice, easy-going guy
when I talked to him in the gym, signing up for the
team. He even smiled when I told him I was going to be

his football star that year. Coach Swanson was a tall man who once had played football for the University of Texas. As the day wore on, he got tougher. I pictured him in spit-shined stormtrooper's boots, brandishing a whip, just like the man on the cover of one of the books I'd seen in the grocery store.

Slowly I moved my head first to the left, then to the right. It was nearly impossible—those muscles were sore.

"Now, ladies, we've only been playing so far, and even though it's a little hot today . . ."

"A little hot!" I thought. I had checked the thermometer in the locker room when I'd left there and it had said 110. It sure wasn't getting any cooler.

"Okay, before we go on men, I want you all to know that if you decide you can't take it you can drag your tails back to the dressing rooms. I don't want any man here to think that he has to do anything he doesn't think he's capable of."

At that last comment he had glanced directly at me. So, he didn't think I could take it, huh? He thought I was one of those who would walk back to the locker room with his tail between his legs? Well, he was dead wrong. I'd no intention of giving up now. Sure, I was tired. As a matter of fact, I couldn't remember a time in my entire life when I'd been more tired, but I had something to prove. I had to make the team. No one on that field knew how much it meant to me.

"Does anybody want to quit?" the coach's voice boomed.

"No, sir!!" we answered.

"Papa can't hear you, children," he responded, with a note of laughter in his voice.

"Yes, sir!!!" we screamed even louder. I could feel my throat strain and rasp.

He had us run—not just ordinary jogging, but a thing called wind sprints. Each time the whistle would blow we were off again, running to nowhere.

"If you guys don't hurry up, you're going to have to run them all over," he'd call, and, as if it were some kind of joke, he'd laugh and repeat himself.

I could feel my leg muscles from thigh to ankle

cramp, but I just kept on running. I couldn't give up, for I knew this was my only chance—I had to stick it out. I lost track of the number of hundred-yard dashes, and fifty-yard dashes, and other dashes and sprints we did.

"Come on, ladies, one more time. Keep it going," he'd say. "Keep running. This ain't no picnic, you know. This is a football field. I'm going to make men out of you yet."

I kept looking at the sky, because it seemed to ease the pain. First I felt like fainting, then vomiting, then it seemed as though death would be simpler. But I kept going—right foot, left foot, right foot, left foot. Then, I felt myself stumble, falling face down.

"Come on, get up, O'Connor," the coach called. "You're the champion; get up, son. You can't quit now. Get up." What the hell did he mean, I was the champion? I struggled to pull myself up and, as suddenly as I had fallen, I was back on my feet—and asking myself why. Why was I doing this to myself?

Then I noticed there was something peculiar going on. I was all alone. I was running on the field all alone, and I couldn't stop—I couldn't give up. I turned, after finishing another lap, and saw what was left of the first day's football tryouts. Two of the boys who had been following me had both collapsed on the ground not more than five yards from each other and were both vomiting. I glanced to my right and began another lap. There on the side was the rest of the team, hanging over the fence for support. There were only seven or eight of them, and they were all vomiting or crying.

"Okay, O'Connor, you can stop," the coach called out. I heard him, but I couldn't stop, I just couldn't. A blurry orange color in front of me wavered, then planted itself firmly. I ran directly into the coach.

"Hold it, son, hold it. You're the champ, you don't have to run any longer." I woke up in the coaches' office to the odor of smelling salts and the sound of a kind voice.

Coach Swanson was standing over in the corner of the room with a piece of paper in his hand, shaking his head.

"I just can't believe it," he was saying. "Out of more than fifty kids I end up with less than a dozen. I just never thought that those clowns would ever have the guts to walk off the field on the first day of practice." The man who'd been holding the smelling salts for me, Coach Allen, answered "Swannie."

"Look, coach, it's not as bad as all that. Just go to Smith's office tomorrow with an announcement."

"How do you mean?"

"Well, just ask Smith to announce that you want all the boys who went out for football today, whether they completed practice or not, to report during their noon hour to the coaches' office."

"Oh, yes, okay, I get it," the coach said with sudden enthusiasm. "I tell them I've decided to give everyone a second chance—something about having been given a second chance once myself in high school. That's it. Wow! What an idea!" All of a sudden, he noticed me. "O'Connor, what are you doing there, still on the table? If you haven't anything more to do, I can arrange for you to run a couple more laps!"

"No, sir," I answered, "I was just leaving."

I didn't want to leave. I was just beginning to understand the inner workings of the coaches' office. It was really funny. The last person standing at practice was me. A pseudo-male had out-endured all the heroes and superstars. I could sense the coach's disappointment in me, and in the others.

As I walked into the shower room, the last of the guys who'd been at practice walked out. Passing me, he patted me on the shoulder, congratulated me on my endurance, and called me the champ. It was odd to be the winner of anything. I thought that I was just meant to lose. At least, I *had*—and for a long time. As I pulled my shorts off, I remembered the first day I'd taken a shower in the seventh grade, in junior high school. I'd overcome my fear of that, now. I took a long shower in the deserted stalls.

Dad had told me to call him when I was finished, and he would pick me up, but for some reason, I felt invigorated and decided to walk home. It had been quite a day. I made my way slowly down Dresden Lane,

the street on which I lived. This feeling was something
to cherish. I'd actually proven to myself that, if I really
put my mind to it, I could do anything. To stay on my
feet was such a simple accomplishment, really, but as I
walked, I savored the picture of Dad's face when I
would tell him I thought I'd made the team.

How was it, though, that I was always thrown into
the position of having to appease the image that I
wanted my father to have of me? I'd had very little indication in the last few years that I was becoming any
more of a male than I had ever been. The changes in
me had come from facing up to people and situations I
normally would have feared, but, on the whole, I
couldn't see any signs that I was anything like the boys
around me.

It was cooling from the infernal heat of that afternoon, and my strained muscles were beginning to move
without pain. My fresh sense of well-being was inspir-
ing. I began to think that perhaps, at last, I would be
able to resolve my never-ending guilt feelings about
who and what I was—through sports and athletics.
Maybe I could go for the top. I'd surprised myself today, and perhaps I would be able to surprise myself in
other things. Maybe long-distance running. Maybe even
the Olympics.

"Danny boy, how's the football star?" my mother
joked as I entered the front door of the new three-
bedroom house we were renting. It wasn't home yet.

"How'd it go, son?" Dad spoke up, with an anxious look on his face. "Did you make the team? You're
almost an hour late. I thought you were going to call me
so I could pick you up." Suddenly I was nervous.

My earlier convictions seemed to fade. What if I
were wrong and the coach decided I was too frail to
play on the team, just as the coaches had last year?
What if, after all the suffering I had endured today, I
was eliminated before I even had the chance to prove
myself?

"I can't say for sure, Dad, but of the fifty guys
who started out today, I was the only man left standing." That made me feel important, using the word

man, I mean, in front of my father. There was a little sparkle in his eye every time I did it.

"Well, how about a big, juicy steak and fried potatoes for my football player?" he said, with a nod toward Mom, who was folding laundry in the front room. She nodded.

Food had never tasted better. With very little encouragement, I accepted a second steak. This football stuff was really neat. I was becoming a real celebrity. The *coup de grâce* came after dinner, though. Dad walked to the refrigerator and pulled out a bottle of icy Lone Star beer, the beer favored by most every Texas he-man I'd ever seen.

"Here you go, mister," he said, smiling as he popped the top off with an opener lying on the counter. "Here, have a beer on your old Dad."

The first two weeks were tough. I made the team, but, other than a few minor scrimmages, I hadn't had a chance to prove myself. It did seem though, each time I went up against a team member in blocking drills, that I somehow always ended up on my ass with some lug lying on top of me, his sweat dripping on my face through my helmet and the coach yelling for me to get up.

I was the one member of the team who would have been picked unanimously by both the entire squad and the coaching staff as the most likely not to succeed as a blocker. My assigned position, however, was offensive right guard. I was furious. My dreams were of star quarterback or end, the receiver of touchdown passes and of fame.

"O'Connor," the coach's voice boomed, "counting your change again?" I straightened. "If you expect to stay on this team, you're going to have to learn to block. Got that? Block! Block! Block! Put the brad to the number, son! Kill the man! That's the only secret of this game. The man in front of you is your enemy. That clown is a motherfucker. Kill him, you got that? Kill him!"

It was hard to concentrate on blocking when everyone smelled so terrible. We were issued uniforms

once a week, and we'd been wearing these through six
full days of practicing. Sweat had matted and hardened
into the jersey. Some of the guys had brought Right
Guard the first couple of days to try to squelch some of
the sickening b.o., but we all soon give it up as a lost
cause.

Hot. I bent to one knee and quickly pulled my helmet off to wipe my sweaty hair from my eyes. On the
bleachers at the far end of the field were a group of
spectators. One of them, who I could barely make out,
was Louise Ballard, a sweet girl who'd taken a liking to
me. She was beautiful, and reminded me of Elizabeth
Taylor, except Louise's face was thinner. I was flattered
by her interest in me, but it was becoming easier to accept the fact that girls found me attractive.

As I rose and put my helmet back on, I saw her
wave. The coach was glaring at me, so I quickly returned the gesture and headed for the group to do
wicked stepmother's latest grueling exercise.

"All right, ladies," he growled, "you've had a couple of days to bone up on the running plays you were
given, so let's try them out. Come on, you clowns, line
up. Let's go!"

A couple of hours later we'd gone through every
practice play the coach had given us. He sent us to the
water fountains with instructions to take a quick break.
As I pulled off my helmet, I remembered Louise. I'd
forgotten her, but the bone-tired ache made it easy to
understand why. After sucking up as much water as I
could hold, I raised my head in the direction of the
bleachers—they were empty.

"All right, horses, one more drink and we'll start
charging you. Back to reality! Come on, move it!"
Back to running plays. I actually enjoyed them. We
learned the quarterback sneak, and how to get run over
by missing the lineman you were supposed to block.
And then, there was the infamous, semi-illegal wedge
play, the coach's secret weapon. If any of us breathed a
word of this play we could expect to be instantly booted
right out of the smelly locker room.

When I played on defense, one block and tackle
maneuver gave me a chance to show off in front of the

entire team. The one thing I could do very well was fall
down. In this play I picked two of the biggest guys on
the team to play against. They were to simulate an inside run through the middle, one man carrying the ball,
one man blocking. My chance to show off came from
the position I was playing. I was a defensive guard, and
I was supposed to tackle the ball carrier. They made
their move.

The ball carrier weaved back and forth to try to
slip by me. The guy trying to block me was eager. As I
approached him, I spun, ending face to face with the
guy carrying the ball. It wasn't supposed to go like that.
I was supposed to tackle him hard and rough, but it was
too late for that. If I didn't do something in that instant,
he would be around me. All I could think of was to put
my arms around him in a bear-hug fashion and fall
down.

As we practiced each day, I wheezed less and performed more. At home I received encouragement for
my growth as a man and, Louise, more hooked on me
than ever, commented more on my tawny look than on
my blue eyes. Other than a few plays in the scrimmage
game with Whittier High School, I hadn't had much
chance to show the coach what I could do. I eventually
got down to the line, the first game, the first *real* game.

I was too nervous to sleep. At 5:30 A.M. I
watched the sun inching over the horizon. We'd been
battered, drilled and beaten into shape, but all of us had
butterflies about this game. Although I didn't have to
report until 7:30, I knew there was no more sleep for
me that day. Besides, I wanted to make sure I had
enough time to put myself into the proper mental attitude—winning. This was something Coach Swanson
had instilled in us.

"Remember, men," he had said, many times, "you
think victory, you get victory. You lose, and you have
hell to pay."

After a while I could hear Dad moving around in
the kitchen. Smells of bacon, eggs, and hashbrowns began to fill the air. It was the family's favorite meal, as
well as the thing my father cooked best. But that morning, the smells and the routine events were special. I

savored the meal slowly, and watched my father eat with his usual gusto. As I rose from the table, Dad spoke.

"What time does the game start now, son?" As if he didn't know. He'd asked me the same question at least a thousand times in the last two weeks.

"Oh, is there a game today? I didn't know that." I chuckled. Dad held his belly and laughed, then slapped me on the shoulder, saying he was really proud of me. For some reason, that old guilty feeling crept back over me and I left the room trying to understand. First I wanted to put the guilty feelings out of my mind— ignore them—then I began to analyze them, putting labels on my reasons for being in football. It was a front, for sure, though no one knew it other than myself. Dad was proud of me for the first time in my life. He was actually proud of his son, who had been a walking mockery of what his father had wanted and had wished for for so long.

The female person in me began coming back. I tried to stop it, but the urge was strong. This super-male image I was creating before my father wasn't me. I sat on the bed in my room, struggling to sort it all out. This always seemed to happen on the edge of something important. Glancing at the clock, I made a decision. It was ten to seven. I would jog to school, so that I could be alone for a while. Dad wanted to drive me there, I knew, but I couldn't do it. As I reached the front door and turned to say good-bye, Dad stuck his hand out.

I thought I was going to cry.

"Good luck, son," he said, "I know this day means a great deal to you. Believe me, whether you win or lose I'll be proud of you just being on the ball field." I shook his hand, but it wasn't enough, so I hugged him as I said good-bye.

Mom rushed out from the back of the house and gave me a quick hug and kiss good-bye. She had pulled her bathrobe on quickly. There was still a sleepy look around her eyes and her hair was tousled. This was becoming a real send-off. As I left the front porch, both of them hollered, "Yeah, Nimitz!" and I blushed and ran a little faster.

The quiet streets were still cool. I rounded a corner and decided to cut through the park, rather than head around it. The quiet reminded me of Idaho and my summers there with my uncle, my cousin, and Dad. I missed those days of clear streams and snow-capped mountains.

"Listen, you guys," a tall, thick-looking boy was saying as I came into the locker room, "the coach is going to speak to us. Shut up, you guys, back there, the coach is speaking." Mike Jordan was star quarterback, a leader by his very nature, and I resented him.

"Now, listen, gentlemen," Coach Swanson began. He licked his lips. "You all know that I've been talking to you a long time about this game. I've worked your asses to the bone because I want to be sure of victory. I want this team to go all the way to state finals this year and it's important that each and every one of you remembers that fact every minute out there on the field today. This is no street rumble, gentlemen. It's not a scrimmage. It's the real thing, the real McCoy, and I know you're not going to disappoint me."

String positions, I thought. Get to the point, coach. As if reading my mind, he spoke up.

"Now, I'm not going to pressure you into thinking that the team out there is a bunch of pushovers, but just the same, I don't waste my time on losers. Just remember that."

He looked different this morning. His face, usually so placid and sarcastic, was flushed and seemed hot. His speech was slower, more deliberate, and missing one very obvious element—degrading remarks. No "s.o.b.'s" or "ladies" or "clowns." Just "gentlemen" and "team."

"Now to the part you've been waiting for—your string assignments. I know you all want to know where you stand, but I'm going to hold back until after the end of this first game. Each man has one last chance to better himself in this game. Got that?"

"Yes, sir," we answered. He dismissed us to suit up and go play. The jerseys were clean and smelled fantastic, for a change. As I pulled on my cleat-soles shoes I realized what the difference in today was. No one was joking. It was the quietest I could remember. The coach reentered to inform us we had just three minutes to get our asses upstairs. Climbing up those stairs was like moving in a fantasy world. I could hear the echo of hundreds of little cleats against the cement. I glanced at my uniform, pulled the helmet on and left.

We walked straight out of that place, through the open space in the bleachers, into the crowd of roaring, laughing, stomping people. We jogged to the right side of the field over to the team managers. I'd been a team manager before, and tried to compare the anxiety with this.

"Hey, Danny," someone called, over and over. At first, I ignored the voice, uncertain as to who would page me that way. In curiosity, I finally cocked my head—it was Louise. I couldn't figure out how she knew me until I realized that my jersey had a number on it. We hadn't had numbers on the practice jerseys. I was suddenly proud. Dad, Mom, my sisters, and Louise were going to be proud of me.

As we all sat down on the bench, I could feel the wind touch my naked calves. It was almost cold, and I thought about winter.

"Jordan, Canby," the coach hollered. "Out on the field for the coin toss." I watched the two captains scurry to meet the referees and two members of the opposing team. We watched in anticipation as the coin was flipped. The coach grumbled in protest. All right, it would be defensive.

The team fought off repeated attacks by our opponents. It was a hard fight and we weren't winning. I kept asking myself why I was still sitting on the bench. What would the spectators think? At the end of the first quarter I got to my feet and began pacing back and forth behind the bleachers. With one minute left to the sounding of the gun ending the first half, I directed my frustration—carefully.

"Coach, uh, Coach?" I asked, trying to be as casual as possible.

"Yeah, O'Connor, what is it?"

"How's chances of me going in for this last play?" I asked, trying to seem cool.

He walked away from me. The gun sounded. We convened in the locker room.

"You're failing me, men!" the coach screamed. "You're failing me and I'm not too happy with you." He singled out those who had been messing up and concluded with a rather lengthy condemnation of the entire team for allowing it to happen. My face heated in shame although I hadn't even touched the field.

"Gentlemen, the score right now is nothing to twelve. In five minutes, you're going to go back on that field and win this ball game. Add one thing to your run—touch the red flags for luck. We're going to need all we can get."

How ridiculous, I thought. What luck? If he'd just let me into the game I'd show them all.

The last half of the third quarter saw the first touchdown for the team when we returned the kickoff all the way from our twenty. In the last minute of the third quarter we managed to tie the ball game up.

After that we scored again, and by the end of the last quarter we had twenty points. I was trying to think of good excuses for my father and the others. I was done with fooling myself. I wasn't big enough, or coordinated enough, or strong enough to go against guys my age in any kind of body-contact sport. There was a vital ingredient missing in me, too—aggression. I couldn't bring myself to attack the man across from me. My physical strength, or lack thereof, didn't seem to bother my teammates. My passiveness did.

On our way back to the locker room I tried to ignore the fact that my uniform was the only one without mud or grass stains on it, but I was horribly embarrassed. I didn't say anything because I didn't want to stand out. Everyone else on the team was jumping and screaming. I undressed as quickly as possible, decided to forgo the shower as unnecessary, and dressed in my street clothes.

How could I tell them their Danny was a failure? Dad tried to act as though the coach had made some mistake, but it kept on happening. He couldn't ignore the failure of his fourteen-year-old son.

Soon, Louise started to ignore me. I decided that if

she didn't like me for myself rather than for my accomplishments, we weren't really going to be friends.

It took the coach six weeks to figure out how to kick me off the team. The rest of the year was very quiet for me, and I decided that all I could do was take it easy and try to forget the erosion of my carefully built masculinity.

TURNING POINT

Every school year seemed to start the same way. In southern Texas, fall was the time of year for hot, bright sun and still air. Classrooms were well over a hundred degrees, empty. In a crowded one, the combination of bodies and heat made them uncomfortable. This morning the halls were full of confused, aggravated, and worried students who were finding their way to first period classrooms. Today we were allowed to be late, but tomorrow was the end of such privileges.

"First period, English literature, Cornbluit, 212" was my litany, murmured in counterpoint to the loud voices of other students as they passed me. It helped me to think and to walk in a somewhat straight line.

I had just passed the main office on my way to the stairs, when I ran into Bill Braun. He was headed for Spanish, a course he had failed miserably last year, and it was in the room right opposite 212. Punching his arm as a friendly hello, I began to trade news with him as we walked down the hall together.

"Well, here we are, old buddy," I said, as we neared the end of the hall. "I'm not really ready for school this year at all, but I expect I'll get used to it in time."

"For sure," Bill answered, smiling. "See you in an hour."

Someone called my name and I whirled around. It was Pete, my best friend. Although we'd known each other since junior high school, it wasn't until our freshman year, when he inspired me to play the guitar (or attempt to, anyway) that we became close. Three of us formed a neighborhood rock group, and spent most of our free time practicing and playing. Some considered us "pros" because we had had a few paying gigs, but I'd argue with the term. In two and a half years I learned a lot, but the prime lesson was how much I still needed to learn.

During the past summer we hadn't seen much of each other, since we both had jobs in grocery stores, but the gap in our relationship was small. Apart from our common musical interests, we were both interested in journalism. In our sophomore year we wandered into a journalism class, offering our services as willing and experienced photo lab technicians in exchange for the use of the school's wet lab and printing room. We never told anyone that we actually knew very little about working in a photo lab, but somehow our adventurousness made up for our lack of knowledge and we learned fast.

"Hey, Pete," I said, "what's been happening with you? Still involved with the annual?"

"Yeah, they roped me into taking most of the pictures for the annual *again* this year," he answered, shrugging his shoulders as though he didn't really enjoy it. "How about you, 'Sports Publicity Editor'?" He said my title as though it were in capitals, with quotation marks around it, and I smiled. Just then, the three-minute-warning bell rang. Pete waved and rushed off.

Funny, I thought. Until he'd mentioned it, I'd almost forgotten about the title. I'd been called into school a week early to help prepare the first issue of the school newspaper, but it didn't seem to mean anything special. Pete and I had top experience in the journalism department, but I thought of it more as goofing off than as really "working" at something.

I turned my attention to the small crowd of prospective classmates who'd gathered outside the door of room 212. The consensus was that this new instructor—Mrs. Cornbluit—was a temperamental, demanding one. One girl was so concerned about it, she told us she was going right down to the counselor's office on her lunch hour and try to swing a transfer. It seemed like no one had anything good to say about this teacher. Junior English had been taught by a strict, dull, somewhat close-minded woman, who tended to change the subject when things got interesting.

My lack of interest hadn't been entirely her fault, though. Besides school, I had worked a part-time job at the grocery store and had spent a good deal of time practicing the guitar, so that it seemed I never got any sleep. At any rate, Miss Watson had left a bad taste in my mouth when it came to English; in her class I'd earned a "D" as a yearly average, which was the worst grade I'd ever received.

"What are you students doing standing out here?" a blond, somewhat chubby woman said. "If any of you are in my class . . ."

"What class is that?" Bill asked, breaking in.

"You see the number above the door, don't you?" she bellowed. "It says 212, doesn't it? I assume none of you would be stupid enough to stand in front of a classroom that wasn't yours, this late into first period. My name is Mrs. Cornbluit, and any of you here that are to be in my first period class better get moving before the tardy bell rings, or you'll find yourselves on the way to the office!"

With that, she turned and reentered her classroom, and we followed. The room was full of strangers.

"Wow! This looks like a real 'winner' class," I nudged Bill.

"Yeah, for sure. I wonder where she parks her broom?"

"C-O-R-N-B-L-U-I-T" she was saying, her voice booming rhythmically. "Write it down. Remember it. It's 'Cornbloot.' Mrs. 'Cornbloot.' Get it straight now, and you won't lose points for calling me 'Corn-blew-it.'" There was a chuckle from the class, then a mild hum of conversation.

All in all, she wasn't as bad as we had originally been led to believe. She even cracked a couple of jokes, and she did indicate that the class would have many discussion periods during the course of the year. That whet my appetite a little. When the bell sounded, announcing the end of the class, I realized that this teacher was going to be something different. I didn't realize exactly how, though—not yet.

"Hi, Danny. What's the news from Cornbluit?" Bill asked. He was standing right outside the door as I left the classroom. "Is it just like I told you or is it just like I told you?"

We grinned at each other. It was just like he told me, although some important differences were to come up.

"Look at the board," the woman hollered as she entered the classroom, breaking into the conversations. "Look at the board; there's your assignment. Now get busy reading. It says thirty minutes and that's just what you have before your first class discussion."

For the past three weeks I had been busy adapting to the new schedule and the requirements of this final year in high school. By my reckoning, I could pass with a lot of careful listening and a minimum of homework. This class, however, was going to be my worst. Today was sunny and the sky was clear. Already it was becoming hot. It was almost nine o'clock, and I was very aware of the young, cool morning and of the potentially smoldering day. Reading the assignment became very difficult.

"Time's up!" Cornbluit chirped, as though she considered the assignment a race. "Did you all find the poems interesting?"

Interesting? I couldn't get much meaning from any of them except "I Wandered Lonely as a Cloud," by Wordsworth. I bent my head into the book, trying to fit the authors with the proper titles for the oral examination we were bound to have.

"I said the time was up, Mr. O'Connor. That means you should close your book. And since you seem to be so interested in what you've been reading, suppose you answer the first question."

Me? There were thirty other kids in the classroom and probably every one of them was more qualified to speak out. Not only did the subject at hand confuse me, but I was terrified of speaking in front of a class. Speech classes hadn't made a bit of difference.

"What was the title of the first selection?"

"Uh . . ." I was stalling for time to remember which selection was first.

"You do remember the first selection, don't you, Mr. O'Connor?"

Well, when all else fails, talk about what you know. "I Wandered Lonely as a Cloud."

"Yes. Well, very good so far," she said, cracking a slightly surprised smile. "Well, now don't leave us hanging. Who was the author? Who was the poem written by?"

I felt a little more courageous. I knew that one. "Uh, Wordsworth, William Wordsworth."

"What was the basic theme of the poem?" she prompted.

Well, she had asked, so I'd tell her what I thought. When I had finished with my reply, she questioned another student. I was allowed to gather my composure while others gave their answers to her probes. My interpretation of "I Wandered" had been a little unusual, and Mrs. Cornbluit had nodded in interest as I spoke. I could feel a new kind of self-respect growing.

While I was collecting my books to leave the class, she came over to my desk, and stood there until I looked up at her.

"You know, Dan, that was the first time I'd ever heard such an interpretation of that Wordsworth poem. I wonder if you'd like to write us a short story, using that interpretation, and read it to the class for extra credit."

I stared at her in surprise. "Uh, well . . ." I looked down, wondering how I could avoid committing myself to something I'd have to spend time on.

"Fine, fine," she said, as though we had an agreement.

"But . . ."

"Now, it's all settled. Dan, I've been looking at your grade average and the extra credit would do you a world of good."

"Sure. Well, I'd be glad to," I said, falling into a deep hole that was going to take a lot of work to get out of. Just the thought of it made me weak. And yet, the theme of loneliness had struck a chord in me and the assignment was not altogether an unwelcomed one.

The rest of that day I tried to figure out a way I could avoid giving the report. I could buy a *Cliff's Notes* on "I Wandered." *Cliff's Notes* is a series of books that summarize just about every major literary work in existence.

But *Cliff's Notes* wouldn't have my interpretation of the poem, and Cornbluit would be sure to detect foul play.

There were legitimate excuses I could make about other claims on my time. My job at the grocery store demanded a lot of weird, changeable hours, and I didn't want to cause any more trouble with my job than I already had. My hair was long and I refused to pin it back or cut it for work, because long hair made me feel much better about myself.

As I headed for home I tried to make a decision. There had to be a way out of it. If I couldn't think of one soon, I had a lot of writing to do.

When I arrived home after work that evening, to a darkened house, I realized that my open literature book on my desk was a hint I'd left for myself to get straight to work. In the quiet, with everyone else in my family asleep, my first impulse was to shut the book and forget it. I could come up with some kind of excuse to put it off, but then I remembered Cornbluit's words of praise for my interpretation.

Somehow those words kept me going late into the night, and the sense of achievement I felt boosted my confidence when it came to getting up in front of that class to read the report. Although I expected ribbing from my classmates, I wanted the extra credit she would give me, anyway. It amazed me when the class got into a lively discussion at the end of my report; we argued right up to the final bell.

After that, the class seemed almost entertaining, which surprised me immensely, and Mrs. Cornbluit seemed to change too. As I made my way down the hall of the second floor to number 212 one morning, I could see her unlocking the door.

"Well, good morning Dan," she said, with a strong

New Haven accent. "How's the writing going? Written any new songs?"

That's why I was there early that morning, but most mornings I would have come here early just to talk, even if I hadn't had anything to show her. I'd learned a great deal about this woman since the first day. She was intelligent—not just intellectual, but really wise—something I'd rarely found in a high school teacher. She encouraged me, too, especially in creative endeavors.

It was as though she had some kind of unusual sensitivity to how I felt inside. When she found out about my interest in music, she encouraged me to write a song, and then to sing it for her. Although I'd tried out for the school choir three years in succession and had failed each year, she convinced me that my voice had a unique, pleasing sound.

"Well, I knew you could sing, Dan," she had said one morning when I had finished demonstrating a song I'd written. "I'll give you extra credit if you perform this song in front of the class." This woman's confidence in me drove me on, despite my fears. I presented the song to the class that day, and did very well. One performance led to another, then another, and I fast became the talk of the school. No, it wasn't hard to see why I enjoyed coming early to class, for like an old proverb of my grandmother's: "Left alone I might falter, but give me someone who believes in me and I'll conquer the world."

Many times I'd considered telling her of my problem, but I wondered if it would make any difference to her.

Cornbluit wasn't afraid to discuss anything with me, and I liked that. Even though I'd never mentioned my personal problems to her, she provided support just by letting me know she was there if ever I needed her. When we hugged each other good-bye that year at graduation, both of us sensed that it would be the last time we'd see one another.

"Good luck, Dan," she had said. "I know that if you can just keep your confidence up, you'll set the world on fire."

Those words echoed in my mind—"keep your confidence up"—and it wasn't long before a new friend helped me discover that I did have within me the power to set the world on fire.

MEETING JOHANNA

"Play it again, Danny. It's really beautiful." She smiled at me, this beautiful blue-eyed blond girl who loved me. Johanna was a kind person, intent on learning as much about me as she could, and interested in my music. She fascinated me. I plucked a string and smiled back at her. "What's the name of it?"

" 'Can You Imagine,' " I told her. She reached over and hugged me.

"Well, it's the best birthday present I ever had. Thank you, very much," she said. I'd written the song some days before and it was all that I could do to keep the secret until today. Song-writing was something that came easier since I'd met Johanna, and there was a different kind of satisfaction in doing it. When I sat down with my guitar, the songs just came. When I sang the songs, my voice somehow performed as I wished it to. There was a coffee house near my home, and I'd even performed there a couple of times, to very good, approving audiences.

Johanna and I had first met on a journalism convention trip I had taken with my journalism class. She had come from another school district in San Antonio, but we had ridden up in the same bus. As we got acquainted, I had no thoughts of involving myself with a girl, but our friendship had rapidly become a very close one.

My parents thought she was definitely the one for me. Johanna had a glamorous manner that impressed all of my family, including me. We could talk for hours without tiring of each other, and we could be warm and cuddly with each other. But our relationship was a source of confusion for me as well as satisfaction.

I was holding her now, comfortably in my arms, and thinking about her, about how pleased she'd been with her birthday present and with me. The past couple of years I'd been dating almost constantly. Lovely young women who wanted to become part of my life seemed to find me. I'd had a lot of good times, but Johanna, in the past couple of months, had affected me differently. This time, with this girl, this feeling was love, as close as I could ascertain.

"Johanna," I said, getting to my feet and putting her down gently, "what do you say about us going on a picnic? You can cook chicken, and I'll spring for it out of the money I've saved from my last job."

"But Danny, you know you don't have enough money to waste it on picnic stuff. Why don't we just go for a ride this Sunday. I'll make sandwiches, nothing fancy, okay?" Okay, so I was close to bust and I didn't have a job right then, but she had hurt my feelings. I didn't want to eat stuff from her parents' house.

In my way of thinking, the guy in the relationship was supposed to be the one with the money. I'd been working almost constantly for three years, and blowing my money constantly—on booze, guitar equipment and Saturday nights with friends and dates.

It didn't bother me until something like this came up. But it was something that I didn't want to fight about, either. Johanna was more important to me than my confused ideas about manhood, my manhood.

Sunday was one of those freak days which crop up every now and then in southern Texas in mid-February. The sun was as bright and as hot as it would be in August, but the grass in her front yard was bright green, not summer-dry. Already, my shirt stuck to the back of the car seat, even though it was only 10:00 A.M.

The porch was cluttered with cats—six of them belonging to Johanna's family, and two who were probably just visitors. They meowed, and swirled about my feet. Reaching down, I petted one, then another, then the rest, laughing. As I straightened up, the door opened slightly.

"Hi, Danny," said a voice connected to a nose sticking out from the screen door. "Johanna said she'll be out in jess a minute."

From the sound of the voice and the height of the nose, I determined that it was Lannie, Johanna's little sister. She appeared at all the worst moments, announcing herself with a tiny giggle, full of smiles and unintelligible conversation.

"Okay, Lannie," I said, and turned to walk back to the car to put the top down. My first car was a convertible, and although I'd had the car since August of the previous year, I'd been working so much I hadn't really used it very often just for enjoyment. When I had the top down I jumped into the car to present my cool "sportsman" appearance.

My image was important to me, but before I had met Johanna I wasn't too concerned about the way I looked to females. The show was for the boys, and I cared about what they thought of me, and how successfully I could show a super-masculine image. Sometimes I could do it quite well, but I was always guilty about those times, because I felt so strongly that it was all a game, and that I was just acting.

Johanna confused my feelings about how I wanted to act. I'd been playing a pseudo-Robert Mitchum with a touch of Tony Curtis when we met, and she dug it. But the act was for the guys; I knew if I wanted to keep her around, I'd better get on the ball and find a *real* me.

With a squeak, the screen door opened. Lannie was valiantly holding the door open for her sister, who didn't really need the help. Johanna was wearing a yellow shorts set, and had her hair held back with a yellow head band. She was carrying a huge picnic basket. Her blond hair, straight down her back, glistened in the sunlight, each strand catching a glimmer and sending it back. She was beautiful, but part of her beauty was that she had something else, too, something I hadn't figured out yet.

I swung out of my side of the car and let her slide across the seat. It was something I felt a really cool guy did for his girl, and I liked it.

"Ready for Brackenridge Park, Johanna?" I

asked, as I got back into the car and started the engine.

"Look," she said, pointing to the basket. "You haven't even looked at the picnic basket." I laughed.

"I was just waiting for you to get uptight about it." Reaching over, I flipped up the lid. "That's not enough. I can eat ten times that much. Poor Johanna. Oh, well, I guess she can use a day of dieting."

"Well, well, what do you mean by that, Danny O'Connor?" She jumped up in the seat, her hands tucked on her hips, and stuck her tongue straight out at me.

"I mean I love you, you little fart," I said laughing. "I guess if you're nice to me and, well, if you rub my back, I'll share the feast with you."

She reached up and tugged my ear as if to let me know she couldn't be teased any longer, then she grabbed my arm and put it around her shoulders.

"I love you, too, Mr. Fart." We drove slowly down the steep road through Olmos Park, which was adjacent to Brackenridge, passing Alamo Stadium.

"Our next game is Friday. You going to come?" Johanna asked, taking my arm from around her and putting her hand in mine. It was hard for me to answer her. A year ago, I'd gone to a game with a bunch of my friends. Before that time, I'd always gone with my Dad, but he had something else to do that night. When we went down under the bleachers at half time for hot dogs, I knew there was going to be trouble. Some intuition had held me back, but the guys had fussed about my reluctance to go, and I shrugged off the uneasy feeling.

But I had been right. Before I had even reached the bottom of the ramp, someone had called out names, trying to entice me into a fight. Although I was an old hand at ignoring such things and avoiding confrontation, a couple of guys rushed me suddenly and gathered a group. I can still remember the faces of those creeps circled around me, calling me names, slapping me from one to the other, and finally pounding their fists into me as though I were a punching bag. When the cops pulled the gang off me, the first one leaned over and asked me if I was alive.

"I'll have to think about it, Johanna."

The day was a beautiful one. We found a spot to deposit the basket, and went for a hike. It seemed to be the traditional first picnic for young lovers, but there was one difference. I could feel today that Johanna was ready for sex. It wasn't a feeling I could pinpoint, but it was familiar.

Before I'd met Johanna, I'd been dating a girl named Sally who, although we didn't consider ourselves steadies or anything, had indicated clearly that she was willing to have sex with me. Sally was an inch or so shorter than I, with dark brown eyes that reminded me of my sister. Her brown hair hung to her waist, a tiny waist, and the rest of her was in good proportion to that waist.

Almost every guy I knew wanted her, except me. When she suggested we go to her house when her parents were away and her little brother was at their relatives' house, I made it plain I didn't want to get her into trouble. That was a good answer. It had satisfied her and dozens of others. It had even made me popular in the eyes of overprotective parents, who encouraged their daughters to date me because of my virtuous reputation.

The guys at school thought I was a "real cutter" and I let them think that. It helped my macho image, so I didn't argue. Someday I'd try sex, but it wasn't something I was ready for, not yet.

When the sun started moving below the horizon we headed for home. As Johanna climbed into the front seat she chattered about her school's games and how she planned to try out for cheerleader in the spring. Her enthusiasm bothered me sometimes, but I figured it was something I'd have to get used to. After all, I wasn't perfect either, by any means.

"What do you think?" she asked, "I mean, do you think I'd make a good cheerleader? After all, I'm in really good shape and Kristy Warner, our head cheerleader, is really sickly looking and she made it—and right to the top. But then, I probably should practice a little more. It never hurts to get a little more exercise. Dad says that when he was a swimming champ at Texas

University he used to exercise three hours a day, whether he swam or not. Can you imagine that?"

"What time you got?"

"Ten of seven. Hey, you know, I'm sure glad I asked Mom and Dad for this watch for Christmas. It really comes in handy in the dark. It glows, Danny, look, Look. . . ."

After I dropped Johanna off, I realized something. This cheerleader business bothered me. I couldn't help thinking that if she made it, I would be just another guy on the string. I loved her, I was suddenly very sure of that, but I wasn't sure at all if I could take the chances involved in sharing my confused, mixed-up life with anyone. I mean, could I actually take the part of a man in society? Was it fair, to myself or to anyone else, to even think such a thing? I knew that I wasn't a man, as I'd always known it, and the guilt I felt for thinking about involving Johanna was weighing on me. And I was becoming afraid. There was something I had decided to do and it was about time to do it.

The sun was just beginning to rise over the horizon as I hurried to dress. In snatches, I read the brochure again, and noted that it was open at eight o'clock sharp every morning, Monday through Friday. I grabbed my boots and began tugging them on.

"What's up, bub?" Dad asked, appearing at the doorway of my room. "How come you're up so early this morning? It's uh, only ten of seven."

"Well," I said, stalling long enough for an excuse, "I thought I'd go to school early today. I've got to finish that darn sports publicity brochure on the track team." Dad made a face and turned away. In a minute, I heard the water in the bathroom. I didn't tell him that the brochure was done over a month ago. He wouldn't really care, and I didn't want him to know what I was really up to—not yet.

When it was five minutes to eight, I climbed out of my car and walked across the empty parking lot. I walked into the building, slowly.

"U.S.M.C. Recruiting Office," I read. Hesitating for a moment, with my hand on the doorknob, I took a deep breath and thought about paratroopers I'd seen in movies who'd pause before they jumped out of an airplane for the first time. "Yep," I told myself, "I'm going to be a marine."

"Hold on there, son," a voice called from behind me. "I haven't opened up yet. You're going to see the recruiter, are ya?" He was a short, rounded-looking guy with a bald spot on the back of his head. I could see right off, by his uniform, that he was a marine, but it wasn't until he turned to let me in the door that I noticed the sergeant's stripes on his arm.

"My name's Sergeant Bradley," he said. Now his accent was more obvious. "Well, son . . . "

"Danny O'Connor," I said, sticking out my hand to meet his. "Glad to know you."

"So, you want to be a marine, huh?" He raised one eyebrow in question. "What's your reason, son; I mean, now how come a young feller like you thinks he wants to be a marine?" There was an emphasis I didn't like on the words "like you," but he probably tested everybody like that.

"Well, I . . . I want to be a man." At that moment I truly thought that the Marine Corps could perform some miracle, that this was my only way out. I could stop being a disappointment to my parents, and I wouldn't get the chance to disappoint Johanna, who was in love with me. It wasn't fair to think that I could have any kind of life with her the way I was. That's why I was there.

"What's the chances of me enlisting today?" I continued. "I mean, could I leave today? Could I be on my way to boot camp today?"

"Now, wait a minute there, son. Hold on. First I have to know how old you are."

"Eighteen. I was eighteen six months ago."

"You a high school graduate?" He sat behind the desk, and motioned me into a chair.

"No, but I have enough credits to take one of those equivalency tests. I have a good grade average, and maybe if I had the chance I could even take the officer's test. You know, the one that qualifies you for O.C.S. even before you go to boot camp."

"Whoo-ee!" he exclaimed, tilting his chair back. "You sure are gung ho about shipping out, aren't you? You ain't in some kind of trouble or something, are you? I mean, you didn't knock over some store or something, did you?"

"No, nothing like that. I . . . well . . . I just want to get away from home for a while. You know, and be a man, I mean, a marine." Slowly his eyes narrowed and he brought his chair down with a vehement thump, in the suddenly quiet room.

"Now listen here," he said slowly, "you ain't trying to skip town 'cause you went out and knocked up some chick, are ya, son? 'Cause if you are, it's no go."

"No—no," I broke in. "Look, it's just that I'm tired of living around here. I've been here since I was ten years old and I'm tired of it. I want a change. Look, I'll even volunteer for Vietnam—right now. You get the paper and I'll sign it."

"Now, this had gone far enough," he said. He stood and turned, so that his back was to me. "I feel I gotta be honest with ya. You're not the kind of man the Marines are looking for. I mean—well—I mean you just *ain't.* That's all there is to it." There was that tone of voice again. He spun around.

"What do you mean?" I asked, trying to seem totally in the dark.

"What I mean, son, is that the corps don't take guys like you—sissies. I know you might not think you are one, but I got a kind of sixth sense about these things, and I can guarantee you, just from talking to you these last few minutes, that I know you ain't mentally or physically equipped to compete in a man's world; and believe you me, the Marine Corps is a man's world."

"But . . ." There wasn't anything to say. I was shocked, at both his words and the gall he had in saying them. How could he say something like that after just a few minutes? I knew I wasn't *that* obviously effeminate, in appearance or in the way I acted. What? . . .

"Okay, all right, I know it don't settle right with you, but that's the way it is and I'm not going to change my mind." Standing up, I felt a tightening in my throat, and a sudden wetness in my eyes. Time to get out of there.

"Son," the sergeant called, softening. "If you're around here at five o'clock this afternoon, maybe I can take you out to dinner or something." It wasn't until a couple of years later that I realized what he was saying. One of the very men I had held as a model for myself had propositioned me.

That evening I talked to Johanna for hours on the telephone, and decided that I would try to stick it out for the remaining few months of school before trying to enlist. And if I tried the navy, I'd get Dad's endorsement, since that was his branch. I went out on the porch and stared out into the darkness for a while. When the screen door squeaked, I didn't even look up.

"What's the matter, Danny boy?" Mom asked, standing behind me. "You seem really disturbed about something. Do you want to tell me about it? Is it Johanna?" I didn't answer her, or even turn my head. It would have been a relief to share what had happened, but I didn't think she wanted to be confronted with my secret again. I loved her, and it wasn't her fault that she couldn't understand, but I wasn't going to change, though I'd have given anything to be able to.

"What happened to the new song you were writing? I haven't seen you pick up the guitar all night."

"Nothing, Mom, nothing. I'm just tired, I guess. Maybe I'm getting the flu or something."

"Let me go get you some aspirin."

"No, that's alright. I think I'll just go in and go to bed."

There was no running away from it. I guess I had been foolish to think that leaving the problem behind would make it vanish. It was within me, and I'd have to deal with it wherever I was. I'd finish school and take it from there.

JUST A CRAZY CONTEST

Saturday morning, April 27, 1968, was the start of one of the most important days in my life. I had the top down as we drove through the clear air. Johanna was quiet, sitting in the seat beside me, as she still hadn't rubbed all the sleep away yet. It was early, not even eight o'clock, and the freeways were still deserted. Like Los Angeles and New York, clear air in San Antonio meant clear of smog, and I breathed deeply and carefully to make the most use of each bit of air, to calm me.

"Are you scared?" Johanna turned to me, and I caught a glimpse of her blue eyes, round and innocent. "I mean are you nervous? Do you want me to drive?" Yeah, I was scared. This was a big moment, and it was my first try in any part of a competition with such high stakes. But driving was draining off some of my nervous energy. We were on the "loop," freeway 410 leading into downtown San Antonio.

"No, I'm not scared," I said, trying to put a tone of masculine confidence into my voice. "Shoot, I'm a little nervous, but it's because of the time of the morning. You know how I get hoarse early in the morning. Well, that's why I'm doing these breathing exercises. My music teacher said they'd help the hoarseness, and calm me down."

Just then a car swerved in front of us and I beeped my horn as I slammed on the brakes to avoid hitting him. As he speeded up, I began screaming and yelling at the driver, although on the freeway, at over 60 miles per hour, I'm sure he couldn't hear me. But that was what I needed to relieve my tension. As we made our way down the exit ramp to Alamo Street, I began to sing.

Johanna, reaching behind the front seat, joined me with a giggle, then settled back into her place with the copy of *Teen Magazine* that had started this dream.

"Super Teen," she read aloud. "That's what it says you are, Danny." I couldn't believe my ears—she was calling me Super Teen even before I'd won the contest. Lately I guess I'd been a little overbearing with the indoctrination, although in the beginning it had certainly been different.

The reason for our trip that morning was a contest. Not just any sort of contest, but, according to the ads in the last five *Teen Magazines,* "the largest teen talent search in history." Winners in the contest would receive a television set, a typewriter, and a Vox guitar. Then, the finalists would win an all-expenses-paid, ten-day trip to Hollywood to appear on an ABC network TV special sponsored by The Singer Company, to compete for a Capitol recording contract, a customized car, and the title of National Champion—Super Teen.

It had all started one evening when I was driving home from Johanna's, with the radio tuned to a popular local rock station.

"Yes, you out there, Super Teen," the announcer's voice told me. "You have a chance right here, today, to make your mark in music. This is your chance to get a recording contract and tons and tons of prizes. Now you've probably been reading about this contest in the national magazines but we here at KONO want to make sure that you know that this contest is for all you super-talents out there, listening right now. All you have to do is send us a tape, that's right, send us a tape. . . ."

Well, it was an interesting thought, a great fantasy, but the odds were just too great. After all, what did I have to back me up? I'd been playing the guitar a little over two years, and I'd only begun to sing a few months before, in Cornbluit's class. How could I even think of such a thing?

About a week later I heard the commercial again, but this time I wasn't alone. "Hey, Danny," Johanna said, "I read about that contest in this month's *Teen*

Magazine. It's really great! Why don't you try out for it?"

If it hadn't been for the trauma Johanna and I had just gone through because of her cheerleader thing, I might have given in right there. We had worked hard on weird jumping routines, and yells and many other things. She was so excited about making the cheerleader squad, that she even infected me with it. But after all that work and dreaming, she had been eliminated in the final competition. No, right then I wasn't about to get myself all fired up over some ridiculous contest.

"Not interested," I said bluntly. "I've had enough disappointments for a while." Johanna just smiled her little, upset smile and turned away. I knew she was still hurt over losing, and maybe I shouldn't have said anything, but somehow it would have found its way to the surface. She knew I was upset over her loss, and I felt better once I'd expressed it.

It wasn't until a week later that I finally decided to enter the contest. One night, having just finished playing at The Lighthouse, the coffee house where I'd been appearing regularly for over a month, I realized that the performance was the best I'd ever done. When Johanna said she wanted to stop at the 7-Eleven for a Coke, I complied instantly, for I wanted to celebrate somehow, without telling her why.

Johanna stopped to look at the magazines when she'd picked out a couple of Cokes, and we both noticed a flier attached to the magazine rack, advertising the contest.

"Wow, this must really be a big one," I said, feeling surprised at the extent to which the contest was being publicized.

"Danny, let's get one and take a look at the entry blank," Johanna said, her voice rising.

"Didn't you say it was advertised in *Teen Magazine*?" I asked.

"Yeah. Let's get one and see what you're going to win." I just laughed, but we bought the magazine.

It was really very simple. I'd filled out an entry blank, made a tape of myself, singing two of my songs, and sent both to the local participating rock station—

a robert e. petersen
production

8490 sunset boulevard
los angeles
california 90069
telephone 657-5100

June 26, 1968

Mr. Daniel O'Connor
.30 Lockhart Lane
San Antonio, Texas 78213

Dear Danny:

We are pleased to advise you that you have been selected
as a finalist to appear on our national TV Special, "Singer
Presents - Superteen -- The Sounds of '68". We will bring
you and a chaperone to Hollywood on August 3. We will
provide you with transportation, room, meals and expenses
while you are in Hollywood. You will be here until August 10.

Please fill out the attached fact sheet, and the measurement
chart and return to us -- pronto. We will also need a full
length shot and a copy of the lyrics.

If you have any questions, please call me collect.

Congratulations!

Robert L. Dellinger
Group Vice President

RLD/jp
Encl.

cc: Jack Carnegie, KONO Radio
    Art Riklin, KONO Radio

KONO. Within a week, one of the d.j.'s called, telling me I'd been selected to compete in the regional tryouts.

"There it is," Johanna shouted, clapping her hands. "You better slow down, Danny, or you'll miss the turn."

"Is that the Pussy Cat theater?"

"No, the one right next to that one." Johanna put her hands on my head and turned it in the proper direction. We both giggled with excitement.

"Braniff flight 314 is now leaving at gate two. All passengers, board please. American flight 223 from San Antonio nonstop to Chicago, all passengers please report to gate five for boarding."

"Have you got the tickets, Mom?"

"Now, don't worry, everything's going to be all right."

"Are you feeling better, Danny?" Johanna smiled tremulously as she offered the cup of water and a packet of aspirins.

I hadn't meant to blow it as badly as I had the night before I had realized that I was going to Hollywood to compete in the finals, and I had realized just exactly what that could mean to me, if I lost, *and* if I won. Somehow winning was more frightening.

Now Mom, Dad, and Johanna were sitting with me on the bench and we were waiting for the plane that would take Mom and me to Hollywood for those finals. We were a silent bunch, and I was miserable. It hadn't hit me during the month after the regional contest. Telephone calls, meetings, even telegrams hadn't fazed me. "You must be meant for the big time, son," Dad had said to me once. "You take it all so calmly."

But going to the top, if that's what this was, hurt, too. There were things I didn't want to face, things I had to do.

"Continental flight 555 nonstop to Los Angeles now boarding at gate 3. Continental flight 555 nonstop . . . "

"That's us," I said, pulling Johanna with me as I stood. "Guess it's time the star and his Mom went off to

Hollywood." I put an arm around Johanna and she reached up to kiss my cheek. Then she whispered, "Don't worry, Danny, I'll never tell anyone. You don't have to worry about that." But I was going to worry. If I hadn't gotten all "Honest John" and told her, I wouldn't be so worried now. And the implications of what I was getting into wouldn't have kept me up all night, vomiting—and vomiting that morning, even once over the side of the car as we sped down the freeway.

I continued to wave to Johanna right up until the time the jet actually left the ground. Once the "no smoking" and the "fasten your seat belt" lights went off, I began looking around.

"Mom, do you think Dad is mad at me?" She had her seat belt off and a cigarette in her mouth. When she'd brought out the matches, she looked up, took the cigarette from her mouth, and spoke.

"Mad at you? Why in the world would he be mad at you? You were just nervous, that's all. Are you feeling better now?"

"Yes," I said, although at that moment I felt, again, the rather unwelcome churning in my stomach.

"Well, here," she said, handing me a little paper bag,"—in case you feel you have to."

"Welcome to Continental flight 555 nonstop to Los Angeles," the captain's voice said. "We'll be cruising at . . . "

I'd forgotten about the sore throat I'd been nursing for a month. We'd consulted two general practitioners and a specialist, all of whom had come to the same conclusion—nerves. A "singer's sore throat" they'd called it. But that hadn't made it go away. When it came time for me to perform, though, it disappeared.

Shortly after I was notified that I was one of the finalists in the contest, a man named Billy Strange called me to ask some questions about the song I was going to sing for the big show. He was the arranger, which surprised me no end; I hadn't known I was going to be recording in such style! I had always done "Imaginary Worlds" with just a guitar backing me up. When

I arrived at the recording studio in Hollywood, however, I was faced with fifteen violins, cellos, trumpets, trombones, flutes, and more. A symphony orchestra was going to play my song!

I watched closely as the conductor tapped the music stand and brought them all to silence. They'd been rehearsing the song, and when he lifted the baton and brought it down, they played the song.

All of those hot, smoggy August days in 1968 are cherished memories. When we arrived, we were chauffeured from one place to another, all around Hollywood. First, there were custom-made costumes to try on, then we made a visit (our first of many) to ABC Studios to hear a lecture on how to behave while on the set. And we did some sighteeing: Disneyland, and a trip through Beverly Hills to see the homes of the stars.

There were over sixty of us, finalists and chaperones, in the three categories—"Male Vocalist," "Female Vocalist," and "Group." It was a lot of people to keep out of trouble for more than ten days.

But everything went smoothly, even the press reception they had for us at a place called The Daisy Club. That night we met the stars who were going to be on the show, Ed Ames and Aretha Franklin, and I spent twenty minutes in the bathroom trying to flatten my cowlick.

"How do I look, Mom."

"No, it's still sticking up in the back," she said. "Better use some of my hair spray."

"Oh, hell!" The blood rushed up in my face. "This damn thing is a pain in the ass." About half the can of spray did the trick.

While we walked down the hall to the elevator, I thought again how lucky I was to be there. Our activities coordinator, a guy named Ed Pazdur, had said we were selected from over 10,000 kids from across the nation. It was too frustrating to try to figure out the odds I'd beaten to get here. Even if I didn't win the contest, which I somehow knew would never happen, and take home that customized car they drove into the studio earlier that day, I certainly couldn't complain.

Mom commented about my aunt, who lived just six blocks from the hotel, as we entered the elevator. We'd visited her that afternoon.

"You know," she said, "your aunt says this hotel is constantly filled with movie stars. She said that one day last year she even saw Rock Hudson getting out of a Rolls-Royce right out there in front. Can you imagine, Rock Hudson!"

Mom seemed to be having even more fun than I was. It was the first time I could ever remember the two of us spending any time alone. Once we had unpacked and settled down, that first night, I thought about telling her why I had been so upset the night before, but once I'd settled into the bed, waiting for her to get out of the bathroom, sleep overtook me, and somehow it didn't seem important enough to fight to stay awake for. She did sense, during the days we were there, that something was wrong, for several times she had told me that if I wanted to talk, she would be willing to listen.

When we left the elevator, we were confronted with the swarm of teenagers in the lobby, who were all very excited about the coming evening. In a couple of minutes, our sheepherder, Ed, told us to go outside and grab the first cab we saw, and then meet at The Daisy Club.

"Ladies and gentlemen," said a man who'd been introduced as the president of The Singer Company, one of the sponsors of the contest, "it is my great pleasure to introduce to you tonight the host of 'The Sounds of '68,' Mr. Ed Ames." I watched as a giant man ascended the steps to the little stage. He was a star, the first I'd seen up close, and I couldn't take my eyes off him as he explained, for the benefit of the press, what the contest and the television show were all about.

"This show," his voice boomed, "is the result of the largest teenage talent search in history. It is the culmination of over nine months of hard work, and it promises to be a spectacular showcase of super teen musical talent." I was awed at what I had just heard. Me, one of the best teen vocalists in the country. Wow!

"And now I'd like to introduce my co-host for the program, Miss Aretha Franklin." After she had spoken a few words, he introduced each of us contestants. When the time came for me to rise, I had become so nervous that when I heard my name I answered, "here" and everyone in the place broke up.

That night I lay awake almost half the night, struck again with the responsibility which had been placed on me. I wouldn't have given any of it up—even being a male at the time—but once home, I knew I'd be a hero, a pseudo-superstar to Johanna, to my friends and to my family. The conversation I'd had with Johanna the night before I left kept echoing in my head.

"I'm a girl," I had told her finally, choking on the words, unable to look her in the eye. "I don't know how to explain it, but all my life I've known something was dreadfully wrong."

"But I don't understand," she said, trying to hide the shock I could see in her eyes. "I just don't understand."

How could I expect her to? Johanna was in love with what she thought was the greatest guy in the world. Who was I to take that illusion from her? She was the first person I had ever cared for. It was hard not to think that I owed it to her, and to myself, to try to forget about this feeling, this sense of wrongness in my life. Maybe, now, finally successful at something, I would be able to change.

Most of the days were busy enough to keep my mind off my personal problems. It took about half a dozen sessions at the recording studio to put the finished tape in the can for the show. We went back and forth between hair stylists and designers for what added up to an eternity of taxicab trips. Outside the cab window, there was a different world from that I'd known in San Antonio, and I watched it eagerly. Finally the day came.

"Good morning, everyone," said a tall gray-haired man wearing black glasses. "Today will be your last day to primp, practice and otherwise 'get your shit together' before the final taping this evening."

The speaker was Bob Dellinger, the producer of the show. He and another man, Tim Kiley, had been my first real contact with Hollywood. They had flown into San Antonio about a week after I had won the regional contest to audition me, and I had found out later that after hearing me live, they had eliminated three other possible choices.

"I know you've all worked hard, and no matter which ones come out on top tonight, to have come this far means none of you are losers."

We stayed at the studio until four o'clock the next morning. It had been a struggle to keep my act together until my moment finally arrived. We had spent four days straight rehearsing for this time and now that it was here it was as though it were all happening for the first time. Most of the day was spent running through the stars' lines. Most of us kids had nothing to do but wait for our scene to come up, so we spent the hours just waiting.

"Okay, kids, this is it," one of the stagehands said. "Get to the makeup room for touch-ups; we're starting the final taping. Good luck!"

I'd been alone for some time. Mom had given up to find a comfortable seat out in the audience. As I walked to the makeup room, I passed the car. Then, I knew I would win it. I couldn't really explain why I thought so, because the guy I was up against was really talented, a fantastic singer.

"All right, quiet on the set," a voice called. "Quiet, we're rolling."

Ed Ames went through a couple of songs, as an opening, then brought in the first entry, a group called Things to Come, from Minnesota. Aretha Franklin followed them singing "Chain, Chain, Chain," the crowd roared.

"Now is the moment you've all been waiting for," Ed said, focusing the attention of the audience on a little paneled section to the right of the stage. "We've assembled a panel of experts to judge our talented teens." And quite a panel it was.

Dick Clark, Mason Williams, Quincy Jones and

Bill Gavin, of the famous Gavin Report, were judging us. As the time passed, I wondered what they were thinking. I did my time on stage in a blur. At about 2:00 A.M. we were sent to the dressing rooms to wait for the judges' results. After a while there was a call to report to the stage for the announcement of the winners. I must have been punchy, because I didn't react until someone pushed me.

"Come on, Danny," Kathy Jackson, one of the female vocalists said. "Don't be scared. Let's go find out who wins the contract."

I hadn't given that much thought. Although impressive, a recording contract with Capitol Records was something like a title—abstract, undefinable. But a customized car, $12,000 worth, done by George Barris, now *that* was a prize. The building was half empty now. Most of the audience had left, since the taping was supposed to have ended three hours ago.

"Places everyone," Tim Kiley said. He pointed to me to move over a little to straighten up the V-shaped formation. "Now, this is it. No matter how surprised you are remember to come up here to Ed, shake hands, receive your trophy and stand to one side." Well, I was pretty surprised.

"It is the decision of our high court of judges that the winner of the title of Best Teenage Male Vocalist, chosen from more than 10,000 kids in fifty states, certainly deserving of the title Super Teen is . . . Danny O'Connor!"

We had just passed the Phoenix city limits and were heading straight for the middle of the five o'clock rush.

"Well, what do you think?" I said, turning to face my mother, who was deeply involved in a television show.

"What do I think about what?" she asked.

"You know," I said, "what do you think about what you're riding in—my new car?" My hunch had been right—I had won, and was now driving home in a customized Firebird loaded with prizes.

"Oh, the car," she said, cocking one eyebrow,

something she always did when she was getting ready to tease. She paused. "Oh, well, the car is okay, I guess, but I think the television reception could be improved a little."

Executive and General Offices
Capitol Records Inc.
The Capitol Tower, Hollywood, California 90028, Telephone (213) HO 2-6252

August 29, 1968

Mr. Daniel Michael O'Connor
??? ??????? ????
??? ???????, ????? ?????

Dear Daniel:

Attached for appropriate signatures and initialing in the spaces indicated
is an original and two copies of an agreement between you and Capitol
Records in accordance with our agreement to sign the winners of the Singer
Superteen Contest.

We are most delighted to welcome you to the Capitol label and sincerely
hope that this will be the beginning of a very fruitful relationship for
all concerned.

If you will be good enough to sign and initial all copies and return
them to me for execution by Capitol, you will be sent a fully executed
copy for your files.

Dave Axelrod, Executive Producer in charge of this particular project,
will be contacting you some time after September 10 in order to arrange
for a producer assignment and to start making recording plans.

Any further correspondence with Capitol should be directed to Mr. Axelrod.

Best wishes for an exciting future.

Sincerely,

CAPITOL RECORDS, INC.

Karl Engemann
General Manager, Artist & Repertoire

KE:cb

Attachments - (3)

cc: Mr. Dave Axelrod

LOST IN A FATHERS'
WAITING ROOM

"Mr. Fairchild. Mr. John Fairchild," a voice called from around the corner. "Please come this way."

The man sitting across from me stood up shakily and strolled very slowly toward the door. When he was gone, I turned back to the small collection of pictures on the wall. It wasn't that they were that interesting or pleasurable, but I was simply too nervous to continue reading the *Esquire* magazine I'd picked up over four and a half hours ago.

Reaching into my pocket, I pulled out the last of my supply of candy bars from the candy dispenser down the hall. It was pretty good, but I'm not sure anything wouldn't have tasted fantastic. It had been a good twelve hours since I'd eaten anything.

"Aaaaacccccchhhhhooooo!" roared the man next to me, shoving what had to be the most overused handkerchief in history to his nose. What's with this guy?—I kept thinking. Why doesn't he just go home and wait for a call? He'd been coughing and sneezing ever since I had arrived and after a couple of hours, I started counting the sneezes out of boredom and disillusionment at having to wait so long. This was his hundred-and-first sneeze, maybe number one-oh-two. It didn't matter.

"Mr. Rodriguez, Mr. Charles Rodriguez," the voice called again, nearer to a monotone than before.

"Yezz, datz be," the man said, pulling the crumpled handkerchief down from his nose long enough to answer.

"Yes, sir. Would you come this way, sir?"

Now it was just me and the snorer. At first, I'd

watched him in utter amazement. He was lying on a couch in the other corner. He would turn and toss, snort a couple of times on one side, then turn and growl like a dog, on the other. He was an older man, mid-fifties, anyway, and by all signs seemed to be an old hand at this.

I glanced at the magazine on my lap again. The title on the cover, "Unwed Mothers Make the Best Wives" had attracted me to it. It seemed to have been written especially for me. After the contest, some nine months ago, I'd been really flying high. Nothing in the world had seemed capable of slowing me down. I had arrived home in triumph with my big, beautiful car and a Capitol contract tucked securely under my arm. Even Dad, who was inclined to be overly pessimistic about most of my ventures had agreed I'd finally made it. I was on my way to becoming a real singing star. Fate, on the other hand, had another kind of plan for my future.

The day the show was to be aired, August 22, 1968, had started quietly enough, although there were to be many firsts—I was even asked to sign a few autographs.

"Wake up, honey," my Mom had called from the kitchen. "Remember, you're supposed to go down to Channel Twelve for the promo this morning."

"Okay." It was warm in bed and I was tired. Even though I wasn't exactly looking forward to doing the talk show that morning, there were certain things that had to be done. My public image counted now. "What time is it, Mom?" I asked as she went by the door.

"About six," she answered, checking her watch. "Better get on the ball if you expect to get down there on time."

Mom was more tolerant toward me now. When the television station had called repeatedly the first day, asking that I come down to make the sixty-second promo spot before the actual program, Mom had seemed to understand that in matters of time and celebrities, one must not always jump at the first hook. That's why I had told her that I was busy working on a new song and that if they wanted me they'd have to wait until the next day, when I had some free time. She had simply nodded her head in agreement and gone back to the phone.

This morning was a lengthy interview on television. I'd had some experience talking to the press at The Daisy Club reception in Hollywood, but this was going to be harder, and I didn't want to blow it. About 7:00 A.M. I got settled in at the station. It was a little frightening, at first. The announcer began his normal introduction of the show, then broke for a commercial. The makeup man was still pottering over me and one of the other hosts reached over me to re-secure the mike they had hung around my neck. With a flash of red and a call "On the air!" I realized I was on my own.

The phone was ringing as I walked in the door and didn't stop for a while. People wanted to talk to me to express their congratulations or surprise at seeing me, little ole Danny, on the television. Later on in the afternoon I heard from Johanna.

"Hello Danny," she said, and I heard a trace of tears in her voice.

"Hi, baby," I said, using the lowest, sexiest voice I could muster. "What did you think of old Dan on the tube? Did I look like a movie star?"

"Danny," she said, "I've got to talk to you right away. It's something I have to talk to you about in person."

"I don't understand. Is there something wrong? Don't you want to go steady anymore?"

That was all I could think of as I hung up the phone and started for my car. In the past week, we'd talked a couple of times about her feelings that I should be free, not tied down to any one person. At first I figured it was because of what I had told her, but she assured me that that had nothing to do with it. She thought that if I expected to be a teenage idol, I couldn't be with one girl all the time. I had assured her, though, that if I wanted to break up I'd tell her. Until that time, which I couldn't foresee in the near future, we'd remain in our present relationship. I thought I'd made it clear, but it must be that again. But why couldn't she talk about it on the telephone?

As I rounded the corner I could see her running down the driveway with tear-filled eyes. Before I could stop the car and get out, she was opening the door on the passenger side and instructing me to drive away from the house.

"Okay," I said, trying to become that authoritative figure girls like when they're upset. "Now, tell me all about it. What's upsetting you so?" She sat in the seat silently, crying for a while. I drove with one hand, trying to watch her and the road for a couple of minutes before she asked me to pull over to the side of the road.

"Danny," she started, then sobbed. "Danny, I'm *pregnant*."

Her announcement put a new light on a decision I had made to go back to California to pursue something I'd heard one of the kids in the contest comment on while we were on one of those field trips. He had said something about a place in Los Angeles where they did sex change operations. The evening before the talk show I had decided to go through with this plan, but I hadn't told anyone yet; I felt it would be much better to wait until the show had aired before I dropped the bombshell.

All the rest of that day we just drove around. Neither of us could find anything to say. After abstaining for so long, we had finally gotten around to having sex. I was frightened at first, for when I reached orgasm, my abdomen felt as if it were coming apart and the pain almost forced me into unconsciousness. This pain lessened after a time, as we tried it again and again.

I thought about suicide that day, but then I thought of Johanna and how she must have felt. That evening, as everyone gathered to watch their local neighborhood sensation, *he* was involved with trying to find a solution to the problem. Her father flatly denied his permission for her to have an abortion. It would have been difficult anyway, for abortion was illegal in Texas at that time. Other options were brought up and tossed away. I had to marry her. It wouldn't be easy, for either of us. We were too young for the responsibility of marriage, let alone the enormous burden of parenthood.

The next few months were spent watching my little dream world crumble. I had to sell my car to support us while I was going to college, and even though the sponsors had claimed a high value for it, all I could get was three thousand dollars. Johanna was going through many different changes too, especially physical ones. She was gaining weight rapidly.

Right from the start, I tried to be honest with her. When we finally set the day for our marriage and were rushed to a justice of the peace by two sets of nervous parents, I told her I'd make my decision to pursue what I felt to be my fate—becoming a girl. She had protested vehemently that day, but at least she knew our arrangement wasn't going to be permanent.

I had begun to dress as a female, too, as often as possible, taking care to keep it within confines of the tiny apartment we had rented. It was hard, I know, for Johanna to relate to a husband who was dressed up like a girl much of the time, but the fact that I dressed as a male whenever we went out seemed somehow to stabilize the situation. My guilt accumulated as Johanna's stomach grew and grew, and the realization that I was going to be a father whether I liked it or not tormented me.

"Mr. O'Connor, Mr. Danny O'Connor," a woman called from the entrance to the waiting room. I fought for consciousness, having dozed off.

"Yes, yes, is it . . ." She didn't let me finish.

"No, it's nothing like that. Your wife is still in the delivery room. But you do have a phone call out at the nurses' station." I pulled myself up from the squeaky leather chair, feeling my shirt sticking to my sweaty back.

As I made my way down the hall to the telephone, I wondered what I would say to Johanna the next time I saw her. I would be a father, and she a mother; there was no doubt about it. How could I tell her I was happy when I wasn't? She knew when I was lying, anyway, and we had talked about my new role a little. Both of us realized I couldn't go on dressing if I were to act the part of father to the new baby.

"Hello," I said, hearing my voice strain from the lack of sleep. It was my parents. I had called them right after Johanna woke me saying she thought her water had broken. Afraid I would do something wrong, I had phoned them immediately to verify my plan of action. Somehow in the past seven or so hours, I had suddenly realized how important this baby was to them. They were going to be grandparents.

"Hi, Danny boy," Mom said. "How're things going? Has she . . ."

"No, she hasn't, yet, but I sure wish she'd hurry up."

After talking to Mom for a while, Dad got on the line and went through his "proud of his son" bit. I thought I was going to cry.

Making my way back to the waiting room, I began rethinking thoughts I'd been having for the past few months. What kind of a father could I ever be? How could a child look up to a father who would probably someday become a girl? Then I began to feel sorry for myself, thinking I'd had a bum break, and if it weren't for the kindness of my heart I'd never have married Johanna. That wasn't true, though. I loved Johanna, and when I found out she was pregnant, although I was in shock for some time, I never doubted my love for her. As time went on, I think my love even increased.

Back in the fathers' waiting room I sat alone and stared at the same pictures, pictures of babies. After checking the magazines, in a vain hope that something new had arrived while I was on the telephone, I sat down on the couch and put my feet on the coffee table. Me, a father, who couldn't even be a man. It was a very scary feeling.

Putting my head down on the arm of the couch, I began to think about my father, and how we were good friends, despite our ups and down through the years. That was something I guess a lot of fathers and sons couldn't say. I remembered spankings—a couple of times he had belted me for doing something bad—and how afterward he would put his arm around me saying, "It hurts me more than it does you."

About to become a father, I felt like a drowning man going under for the third time. Childhood, and the ability to say, "But, I'm just a kid," were fast becoming memories. Adult life, like it or not, was beginning. And I knew it wouldn't help to run away and join the service; that wouldn't change the fact that I had someone who was part of me, my flesh and blood, living on this earth. I couldn't be that inconsiderate of the feelings of an unborn child, an innocent being who hadn't hurt anyone. He was just coming at the wrong time, and that wasn't his fault.

I closed my eyes trying to imagine what my baby was going to look like. Would it be a girl or a boy? I knew for sure it would be light-skinned, with blond hair and blue eyes, for both Johanna and I were blue-eyed blonds. What would it be like to hold the baby in my arms and feel the soft skin against mine? I wondered what Johanna was going through that very moment. Maybe the baby was already born. Maybe it was curled up on her breast. I imagined myself as Johanna. I dreamed it was me having the baby, that I was on the delivery table with my feet in the stirrups, feeling the final bit of pressure as the baby left my womb. It felt so beautiful, so real I even thought I could hear the sound of the baby crying.

"Danny! Hey, Danny, wake up," someone was shaking me out of my sleep. It was Johanna's doctor.

"What is it? Am I going to lose my baby?"

"What? Lose your baby? Listen, everything is all right."

"Johanna," I said, realizing suddenly that if he were here the delivery must be over.

"Your wife is doing fine," he said. "Come on, I've got a surprise for you." At first, I just watched him walk to the door of the waiting room. Then, slowly, I rose and began to walk toward him.

"Come on. Don't be afraid, come on." I could feel beads of perspiration forming on my forehead.

"Am I . . . well, am I . . . I mean," I couldn't find the word, I couldn't say it. "Well, you know am I . . ."

"A father," he said, laughing and patting me on the back. "Yes, congratulations, Danny, you are a fa-

ther." My heart jumped and my head began to spin. It
had finally happened. It wasn't a dream any longer. It
couldn't be rationalized as just a lump in Johanna's
stomach any longer. It . . . I didn't know what I was
father of!

"Well, aren't you going to tell me?" I said, fum-
bling.

"What do you mean?" he asked, teasing.

"You know," I said, a little put out, "is it a boy or
girl?"

"Oh, is that what you wanted to know?" He was
laughing again. "Well, you wait right here and I'll let
you find out for yourself."

The doctor disappeared around the corner. I hated
the suspense, but at the same time felt as though I were
holding on to the last thread of childhood. Quickly the
doctor returned with a nurse who wheeled a small
buggy with a plastic dome.

"Okay, Dad," he said. "Here's your first chance.
Meet your son."

"Did you say son?" I was staring at the baby.

"Congratulations," he said, putting out his hand.

"Thank you." As I returned the handshake, I
pulled my attention away from the buggy. "I wish I had
a cigar or something to give you but I forgot."

Then I bent down over the clear glass dome and
looked at my baby. He was so tiny, I could hardly
imagine him as being a real person. His tiny body was
all wrinkled and red, and his face all scrunched up and
kind of ugly-looking.

"Oh, look at those feet," I said. "Can you believe
those feet?"

We all laughed and the doctor reached over to lift
the dome. Frightened, I looked to him for reassurance.

"Go ahead, touch him. You'd better get used to
it."

Reaching down, I gently touched my finger to his
tiny toes, feeling the softness of his skin. Without warning, the little one let out a sound that resembled a
cabinet door squeaking. Jumping back, I looked at the
doctor in surprise. He returned the dome to its original
position.

"He's a real squeaky one, isn't he?" the doctor said, smiling.

"He's a real squeaky one," I echoed, watching the nurse wheel my son away.

"I'm okay, believe me, I'm just fine," Johanna said.

"Is there anything you want," I said, "candy bars, milk shakes, anything?"

"No, I'm just fine." I sat in the chair next to her bed, holding her hand. Guilt for my earlier feelings mixed with gratitude that both of them were all right.

"Thanks for the flowers, Daddy," Johanna said, pointing to flowers I had had delivered to her room earlier. "I like the name, don't you?"

"You mean, 'Daddy'?" I said, having to force the words out. "Well, sure, I love the name, but it's going to take some getting used to." Johanna squeezed my hand as though realizing the pain with which the statement had come.

"We'll make it," she said, "I know we will, and besides, we have a third person who is ready and willing to help."

"Who?" I asked, puzzled.

"Little Joey," she said. "You know, our son."

The first few weeks were busy for me. We were having finals at college and the baby had gotten his sleeping schedule twisted around, so that he spent half the night crying. When we would finally settle down for the night and start to doze, the cry would come.

At first, it seemed like a joke, something that happened only in the movies, but after more than two weeks of it, both Johanna and I began getting irritable. In utter desperation, we began taking turns sleeping with the baby in the kitchen so that the other could sleep. That worked until his lungs got stronger and his cries permeated the whole place.

As if that weren't enough, my business, the contract with Capitol, was on the rocks. In January, just about three weeks before Johanna delivered, I had recorded four master tapes, but internal problems in Hollywood prevented anyone from giving me a release date for my record. Until the record was released, I couldn't plan any promotion. So I waited, going to school, coming home, and worrying what I would do when the money ran out.

"It's your turn," Johanna said, nudging me. "Get the baby his bottle."

"Oh, no," I said, "not again. I just gave him one a few minutes ago."

"No," she assured me, "that was six hours ago, it's your turn. Now come on, let's be fair. Get up."

I dragged myself up, feeling the cool air on my bare chest and my bare feet as I went padding across the floor over to the other side of the room. He was crying his head off!

"Okay, kid, I'm off to get you some more milk. Hold your horses." I reached into the crib to find the extra bottle. He was much prettier now, since his wrinkles had disappeared and his face had rounded out. He had some hair, now, too, pretty blond hair to match his parents', and blue eyes like ours. His eyes were sparkling with what seemed like pure mischief. Sometimes I think he enjoyed getting us up in the middle of the night.

Rushing off to the kitchen I prepared his formula and poured it into one of those plastic-bag bottles. How a baby changes people, I thought. I'd even changed his diaper a few times. Although I had tried to push that off on Johanna, since I dreaded it, I had managed pretty well. I screwed the top of the bottle on and flipped off the kitchen light before returning to the bedroom, where the baby was really raising hell.

"Please hurry," Johanna said, pulling covers over her head in a desperate attempt to hold on to her sleep.

"I'm coming, I'm coming." I bent over the crib. "Now, there you go, little fellow. Come on, drink it slowly. That's a good boy. Joey, you just go to sleep soon," I whispered, hopefully. Slowly I slipped away, watching him swallowing the milk. Johanna was still trying to get back to sleep.

"I love you," I whispered, pulling the covers over my head so I could join her in her little world. "I love you, Mommy."

"I love you, too, Danny, Daddy."

"What do you think the chances are?" I asked, putting my hand on her tummy.

"What are you talking about?" she asked, putting her hand on top of mine. "What do you mean, 'what are the chances'?"

"—of putting him back there for just one night so we could get some sleep? How about it?" Chuckling, we both drifted back off to sleep.

THE DRAFT BOARD

The room was full of young men of every description: long-haired, short-haired, Mexican, Japanese, Negro, and Caucasian—a true cross section of American society. We all watched as the three people came through a door in single file and took their seats. One was a short, ugly man in his early sixties. He had a scowl on his face. The other man was probably about forty, bald, of about medium height, who gave no sign of warmth or feeling. The third person, a gray-haired woman of indeterminate age, looked like a real bitch. Her hair was done up in tight gray ringlets and her turned-up nose, instead of seeming cute, gave the impression that she felt distaste for those who sat in front of her. I couldn't be sure, but I suspected that the woman was the one who had handled my registration over a year ago, when I turned eighteen.

"May I have your attention," a voice called from the back of the room. "May I have your attention, please." It was a young army officer who had entered the room earlier. "Today is a very important day for you gentlemen. Many of you are here for classification in the draft and, of course, the rest of you are here for testing and induction." He told us about the kinds of tests we would face.

"Now, before we begin any of these tests, we're going to hand our your individual records. You will go up to the desk in the front and pick them up."

My eyes wandered to the woman at the front desk. She seemed to study each man, one by one, as though she were searching for someone. I began to wonder if she was looking for me.

"Abbot, John Abbot, Adams, Albert Adams," the younger, bald man read. He laid out folders as he read the names from them. "Anderson, Bill Anderson. Atwater . . ." Each person got a careful scrutiny from the woman as they walked to the front.

"O'Connor, Danny O'Connor," she said, as soon as it was her turn to read names. I rose, wondering why I had rated first on her list. As I made my way to the front of the room, I noticed a sinister smile cross her lips.

"So, you're Danny O'Connor, huh?" She raised one eyebrow and chuckled.

"Yes, ma'am," I answered, reaching for the folder. "Is there anything wrong?"

"Here's your doctor's letter," she answered, flinging it onto the desk in front of me. "Be sure to get that initialed by every examining station you visit today." Her eyes went back to the list. I picked up the folder and the letter, then tried to walk back to the seat without showing my increasing nervousness. At first, once seated, I wanted to tear up the letter and forget about trying to get out of the draft, but then I remembered my reasons for going to a psychiatrist in the first place.

The bills had been piling up, and with me in college and Johanna in a special class for graduating high school senior girls who'd dropped out because of pregnancy, there didn't seem to be much chance for either of us to go to work. Even though I'd arranged my classes so I could be home in time to take her to class and stay with the baby so we didn't have to pay a sitter, our money was just about exhausted.

"Danny," Johanna had said, one evening as we were going to bed, "why don't you just drop out of college this semester. It's too much for you." I'd been thinking of doing just that, but I hadn't told her, because I was afraid of the draft. Although I'd changed my habit of dressing, now that the baby was here, my feelings hadn't changed. I still felt like a girl, and despite the baby and many superficial reasons for trying to be a man, it just didn't seem to work.

Johanna knew how sensitive I was during the time right after the baby was born, how hard it was for me to adjust to being a father, and she had commented several times that she felt I should get a medical opinion of my problem. Up to that point, I'd shrugged the idea off, saying it seemed unnecessary, to hide my fear of finding out I was insane, or worse.

The next morning, coming out of the building where my English class was held, I paused on the steps to decide what to do with my free period. There was some last-minute research I had to do on a term paper, so I decided to head for the library. What I wanted to do was sleep, or just sit in the sun for a while to relax, but there was too much to do. Too much to do, I told myself—and something snapped. Wheeling around, I headed for the administration building.

"I think it's ridiculous," the woman in front of me was saying, glaring at me over the glasses on the tip of her nose. "You're unaware of the consequences of the decision you've made. If you quit college you'll be drafted, son or no son. It's as plain as that." She was a counselor and I suppose it was her business to tell me those things but it would do no good.

"I've made up my mind," I said. "I'll just have to continue college later." As I walked out of the counseling office I took a deep breath, then sighed in relief. For a minute I could sit in the sun, as I'd wanted to, and not think about anything. There wasn't more than a minute to spare, though. I had to implement my plan immediately. Before I went to my car I located a phone booth to make the call.

"Dr. Evans' office," a woman said.

"Yes," I said, "I'd like to make an appointment."

"What makes you think you're a girl?" he had asked at the outset of one of our many conversations that took place during my half dozen visits.

"I don't *think* I am," I told him, "I *know* it. I'm a girl. There's something inside me, something like another person forcing her way out. I know that person is really me."

"That's ridiculous," he countered. "If there is someone else inside you, who is the person I'm talking to now? Who are you? There are only a dozen or so documented cases of true schizophrenia, and I don't think you're one of them." It was hopeless, for he wouldn't accept what I was telling him, so I agreed with him until he had accumulated enough information to substantiate a letter to the draft board.

"What are you going to write them?" I asked during our last session. "Are you planning on telling them everything I told you?"

"Whatever I write them will remain confidential, but rest assured it will be my medical opinion, and nothing more." He had tried to be reassuring, but this letter worried me.

When the lieutenant had handed out our first test forms and everyone's head was buried in the examination, I opened the letter.

"To whom it may concern," it began. "It is my opinion, after examining the above-mentioned patient on several occasions, that he is suffering from mildly psychotic behavior and has strong tendencies toward suicide brought on by a very severe case of TRANSVESTISM [sic]." What?—I thought. What is he saying? "I thereby recommend that he is not suited for military service." Well, I thought, you came through Doc, and I read the letter over and over, thanking God at the same time.

Hurrying through the test I planned to leave a little earlier so I could show the letter to someone and get out of there. When I approached the lieutenant, though, who was sitting at the desk the board members had used, he turned me down.

"I'm afraid, son, you're just going to have to go through all the examining stations like everyone else here, and whichever station your doctor's excuse pertains to . . . well, take it up with the doctor in charge." I was going to have to go through the rest of the day carrying that letter. The word "transvestism" was all capitalized and underlined. If anyone else saw that I'd be harassed for the rest of the day.

"All right, gentlemen," the lieutenant said, "turn in your tests now if you haven't already, and go out this door and to your left. All of you holding doctors' excuses make sure the doctor in charge sees them and initials them."

"Hey, Danny, hey, wait up." I was afraid to turn around. "Hey, man, what's been happening?" a tall red-haired boy said, rolling his head around, trying to act cool. It was Bill Jackson, whom I had known since fifth grade. Great! There I was carrying around that damn letter with "TRANSVESTISM" sticking out, and trying to hide it from everyone, and up pops an old school chum who would just have to be acutely interested in my doctor's excuse. He took up a place in line directly behind me. "How about it, Dan, you planning on being drafted or you going in as a volunteer?"

"I'm not sure yet," I said laughing nervously. "I prefer not to think of either one right now."

"Say, you're Danny . . . ah . . . Danny O'Connor, aren't you?" said the boy in front of me, sticking out his hand.

"Why yes," I said, shaking the proffered hand. "Why, do I know you from somewhere?"

"Uh, no, but I've been seeing you on a lot of television shows the last couple of months and I think you're just great." Well, it was more like four and a half months, but it was better not to go into it. Besides, that wasn't pleasant thinking right then. I'd received a letter from Capitol.

"Dear Danny," it read, "We are scheduling the releases of your record for April 20, and we'd like you to contact us about a possible record promotion tour."

It sounded fantastic, but unfortunately didn't mean any money, only time spent by me. All the same, I went about getting in touch with the local Capitol promotion man in order to begin lining up radio interviews and television appearances.

It had been fun—almost like being a star again—especially once my record had been released and we had a product to market. I had been on virtually every talk program in the state of Texas at least once, and some twice. Local radio stations had picked up on my record and I'd heard it on the radio. The first time was a marvelous experience that I relived everytime I heard it.

I soon tired of acting like Mr. Teenage Idol and became weary of appearing in public places for fear of some teeny bopper coming up to me. What I was trying to accomplish as a male singing star was of no use any longer. It wasn't, of course, all depressing. One incident in particular always makes me laugh.

After finishing with one of the local teen dance shows in Houston, I had received a call from a disc jockey named Buddy, who had worked in one of the stations in San Antonio. He was pretty excited about seeing me again and told me if I'd come to the station that afternoon to do an interview on his show, he'd guarantee me a week's air play—something no recording artist in his right mind could possibly turn down.

I met him in front of the station as we had planned and he began talking immediately about the promo stunt he was pulling.

"You're a smash, kid! All the girls in Houston have been calling the station requesting your song ever since they heard I saw you on TV, and I informed the jock that's on right now that you'd be here in person to do my show."

"Oh, great!" I said, trying to sound enthusiastic.

"Hey, baby," he said, "you've got to go in there and talk to some of those chicks that've been calling. They're hot for your bod, man! I mean, you could do some super layin' tonight, man. I mean *super*!"

"Hey, man," I said, "I'm married." I held my wedding band up for him to observe. "I don't do shit like that no more." Back to the macho trip, the old school days, I thought. Oh boy!

We made our way through the station, down to the broadcasting studio where another jock was on the air.

"Hey, daddy, this is the man," Buddy said, motioning for the guy to shake my hand. "This is the cat who's been causing all the ruckus around here, baby. This is Danny O'Connor." I shook his hand, but that buildup bothered me.

"Hey man," Buddy said, turning to his friend. "What did that chick call him? You know, the one you talked to for a long time. What did she call him, man?"

"Oh, *that* chick! Yeah, man, after seeing you on the Larry Caine show this morning, man, she told me she thought you was pretty."

"Can you imagine that?" Buddy said, reaching up to pinch my cheek. "You is a pretty boy." With that I broke up, laughing, and I honestly don't think I stopped laughing the whole three hours I was in the station. When Buddy got on the air, we went into our interview right away.

"Tell me, Danny, didn't you just do the Sullivan show last week?" He asked, nodding his head to let me know I was to agree with him.

"That's right," I said, fighting back laughter. "Yeah, I just got back from New York last Friday."

"Oooooooooooeeeeeeeee, you sure do get around! It must pay real good being a new teenage idol, huh, Danny?" I was almost in tears with laughter. He went on asking me ridiculously leading questions, each time shooting the finger at me to get me to laugh harder. Then, each time I tried to answer and couldn't he would bend over my mike, try to imitate my voice, and answer for me. Then we went into the telephone segment.

"Okay, you lucky little chickies out there, this is your big moment, the chance you been waiting for, the chance to talk to Danny O'Connor, the guy you saw on the boob box this morning and who, I might remind you, has a little old record out right now on the Capitol label available at your local record dump. Okay, here goes. First caller, you're on the air!" The telephone lit up like a Christmas tree.

"Hello," a soft voice on the other end of the line said, "Hello, Danny?"

"Yes," I said, trying to make my voice lower and sexier than was naturally possible. "What's your name?"

After upwards of twenty calls I was allowed to say good-bye on the air, but Buddy wouldn't permit me to leave the studio until he could get a relief to take over for him so he could walk me to my car.

When we finally made it to the exit there were about a hundred girls, screaming, tugging at my clothes, and shoving pens and paper into my hands for autographs. Johanna and I had a big laugh about it when I got home.

Not long after that I decided to take Capitol up on their offer to tour with my record. Johanna and the baby, we had decided, would fly to California to stay with her grandparents until I had completed the tour and could join them there. Then I could pick up the pieces of connections I had made in Hollywood the year before during the contest. It wasn't an easy decision to make, to separate from my family, but I knew that if I were to settle my problems one way or the other, I'd better be alone when I did it.

The tour took me through Oklahoma, Missouri, Illinois, Indiana, Kentucky, Tennessee, Arkansas and back to Texas. In each major city, promotion men would join me to escort me to major radio stations to try to get them to play my record. Most of the time I was moving too fast to feel much loneliness, but once back at my parents' house, looking for a way to get to California, it all caught up with me.

I still loved Johanna and the baby a great deal. It had hurt to let them go, but at least I knew that they were being cared for. Then I got something to keep my mind off them—a letter from Uncle Sam.

So, there I was, trapped between a former schoolmate and an interested fan—and I had to show my letter to the doctor.

"What's your name, son?" asked a gruff man with gray hair and a gray moustache. He was scowling.

"Danny O'Connor, sir," I said, handing him the letter, hoping he would keep the contents confidential.

"What are you trying to pull, son?" he growled, ripping one corner of the paper as he handed it back to me. "I'll bet you don't even know what that word means."

"Yes, sir," I finally got the courage to say, "I do know what the word means."

"Just get the hell out of my sight, will you?" He turned to my friend. Next, was a huge community dressing room where we were told to disrobe to underwear. Then it was on to bigger and better things.

"Bend over," one doctor said, after telling about

fifty of us to take off our underwear. "Come on, bend over and spread your cheeks." The treatment we received bothered me a bit, but now it seems almost funny.

"Cough," another doctor yelled, as he placed his fingers.

Then there was the cup.

"Gentlemen," said a young-looking sergeant, holding up a Dixie cup, "you will piss into this cup." We did. As each guy brought his cup to the table, an orderly stuck in a little tab, probably litmus paper, and once the paper had turned a color the same orderly took the cup and emptied it into a huge, full, open barrel next to him. I couldn't help but feel real compassion for that guy.

"Stick one eye at a time on the viewer and read what you see," a tall thin man said. He had just a hint of a lisp in his voice. The next test was a hearing test, then we waited for a visit to the last station, which, I suspected, was a psychiatrist.

Although, so far, I had managed to get each doctor to sign the letter with little undue attention, I knew that this last station was the most serious. My nervousness increased. One person, then another, then another walked into and out of that small room. I was afraid. If I were not excused as a result of the letter I decided to commit suicide. The previous night, even before the physical, I had contemplated suicide, but at the very last moment I had talked myself out of it, deciding it was better to tough it out. And I felt that each time I could face another problem I was becoming stronger—something which proved to be a saving factor in my life.

When it was my turn I walked slowly into the small, narrow room. A desk and a chair filled almost all the available space.

"Hello," the man said. "Do you have anything you want to talk to me about?" He seemed friendly.

"Yes, sir, but I think you should read this letter first." Words were hard to come by. The piece of paper was full of initials, torn a little and battered looking. The young man, of medium height, blond, and blue-eyed, took the letter and started reading immediately, motioning me with one hand to sit down. When he had finished, he got up and shut the door.

"Do you know what this word means?" He spoke softly, and I was thankful for his consideration.

"Yes, sir, but I don't think that's what I am." His eyes widened.

"What do you mean?"

"Well," I said, trying not to feel closed in. "I'm a girl. I know that sounds ridiculous, but I know I'm a girl. Although I'm living as a male right now I had planned to move to California where I hear they perform surgery in cases like mine."

The man glanced through my records quickly. "It says here that you're married and have a son. Does your wife know about the way you feel?" He looked at me, not smiling, not frowning.

"Yes, sir," I answered, feeling the guilt spread through me. "I told her before we were married, but then we found out she was pregnant and . . ."

He had gotten up and was standing at a window. "That's okay," he said, putting a hand on my shoulder, as though realizing the difficulty I had broaching the subject. "Now, I want you to be perfectly honest with me. Your psychiatrist's report indicates you have a severe case of transvestism. You say you're not a transvesitite, you're a woman. Do you dress as a woman, now?"

For some reason, I felt no shame. "Yes, sir," I said, "I always have, ever since I can remember."

"Now I can be honest with you." He sat down and leaned back in the chair. "I've never run across a case like yours in more than eleven years in medicine. It is difficult to conceive of a woman being a man at the same time, but as I look at you I can see your facial structure, skin texture, lack of beard and body hair, and even your voice seem to add up to a genuine gender problem." I watched as he reached into his pocket for a pen.

"I'm going to disqualify you from military service," he said.

"Thank you," I said, over and over again. "Thank you." As I drove home, I rejoiced in my luck. I'd been classified 4-F which meant that I would never be drafted nor could I ever serve in the military. For the first time in my life, I felt as though fate had finally dealt me a good hand.

SING A SONG FOR DANNY

"Are you sure you're going to remember the words to your new song?" Johanna turned to me with a concerned look. "I mean, do you really think you should sing it?" I just smiled at her. Tonight she seemed more worried than I was. We came to a stop at a red light. The car beside us was a Firebird, something like the car I'd won over a year ago. Time had slipped by too fast; I was back in Hollywood, but this time in a '53 Chevy.

I had nothing to complain about, though. The old car had gotten me, my guitars, and most of our belongings through Texas, New Mexico, Arizona and across California to Hollywood.

Once finished at the draft board, I had gone to my parents' house to await the tour, and after the tour I had starting packing, anxious to get to California and Johanna. When they had asked me about the results of my physical, I had told them I'd been failed because of my eyes. Since I'd had trouble with them off and on since I was four, they believed me.

Once the old Chevy was loaded I went to find my mother to say good-bye. She hugged me quickly, then told me, in a worried tone of voice, that she felt something was going to happen to change me. She wouldn't elaborate, but I had the same sort of feeling. I had other reasons for my thoughts, though.

After about four hundred miles of pretty smooth traveling I was stopped by a typical country, down-home, bigoted hick sheriff.

"What are you," he had asked, in a Texas drawl twice as thick as mine, "some kind of hippie draft

dodger?" I knew he was referring to my long hair. It
had been growing for about a year. "Get out of the car
and walk over here to my car," he said, jerking my arm.
"Now! Move it!" I got out as quickly as I could. He
might be a creep, but he was the law.

Once he'd checked my license plate, registration
and identification in a routine check, and had heard
who I was, and where I was going, it was okay.

Through El Paso and halfway across New Mexico
was no problem. Then the same thing happened again.
Once again, after the routine check and a little conversation had taken place I was free to go. It happened
again in California. This time the highway patrolman
told me why. They made it a matter of policy to check
out broken-down-looking, older cars. I resolved never
to cross the country in an old car again.

Once in Hollywood, it had taken Johanna about a
month to find a job and an apartment and to settle in a
little. My contract with Capitol was coming up for re-
newal, but I had decided to go with another company.
That meant negotiation, auditions and more and more
recording sessions. It sounds very attractive, but it was a
lot of work, and there wasn't any money coming right
back to me. It was a quiet time of our life, with little
happening. We did have a nice Christmas that year, Johanna, Joey and I.

Tonight was a big night, though. It was the first
time in Los Angeles I would perform in front of an audience. My producers, Nancy and her husband Phil,
along with Len, who was acting as my business manager, had set up an audition for me.

"There it is," Johanna said as we made our way
down Santa Monica Boulevard and passed a black
building with a big red letter *T* on a sign in front of it.
"There it is, The Troubadour." I'd heard a lot of nice
things about this club. It was known as a stepping stone
for superstars. When I learned that, I had agreed to attend the audition set up for me. It was Monday night,
about ten o'clock. The "hoot"—audition night—had
started.

Turning right on Doheny Drive, I squeezed Johanna's hand and smiled at her obvious excitement. There

was a private parking lot behind the club, where Nancy said I could park the car.

"Can I help you, sir?" a man said, sticking his head inside the open window.

"No, thanks, I'll park it myself." I was afraid to let anyone else drive the old car.

Johanna and I hurried out of the car through the chilly February air. I held my guitar case firmly. There were a lot of bizazrre-looking people around the box office, and I was reminded of my first trip to Hollywood, and of the hundreds of kids on Sunset Strip in 1968. Now, a year and half later, they seemed to be disappearing, which upset me. In a crowd like that I'd be accepted easily.

"You gonna perform?" asked a freaky-looking chick with frizzy, ratty-looking hair, a pimply face and dirty fingernails. She never missed a single chew of her bubble gum.

"Yes." I tried not to seem surprised at her appearance.

"Okay, you're supposed to follow me." I took Johanna by the hand and we followed the girl.

"Hey, wait a minute, where you going, man?" hollered a man in the ticket office. Before I could answer the girl spoke.

"It's okay, Charlie. They're with me." Once inside, she directed us to a right-hand corner of the stage, where a box-like section had been reserved for us by my producers. As we made our way to the table, Johanna squeezed my hand to let me know she was impressed. After a while, Nancy and Phil joined us, with Len and some of their friends. It was great fun until I realized I'd have to leave the party. Then I remembered an experience in Texas.

I had organized a small background band while in college. While it wasn't quite Stan Getz quality, it was certainly sufficient for my purposes, which included small gigs around San Antonio. One time we were hired to perform at a major shopping center. I didn't even know what the occasion was until we had arrived that night. It turned out to be the coronation of a queen of some kind, and I was to do the crowning. After the cer-

emony we had played a couple of my songs. Then, one
of the group suggested we play a tune quite popular at
the time— "Sunny." Once I was singing, a guy in the
crowd yelled out.

"Hey, that guy sounds just like Cher." I tried to
act as though I hadn't heard the comment.

"Yeah," another hollered, "you know you're right.
He even *looks* like Cher!" The whole crowd started
yelling obscenities, so we packed up and left. I would
have forgotten it, but the incident was repeated in some
way or another at about a dozen other engagements.

"Danny," Johanna was shaking me. "You'd better
tune up your guitar. You're supposed to go on at eleven
sharp and the agent who's coming to listen to you is
already up in the balcony, Nancy said." I kissed her and
glanced up at the balcony. There was the bulky outline
of the man I'd met just the week before in a swank Hollywood office. I hadn't thought much of him, but he
had set up the audition, so he must have thought something of me.

There was a tingle in my breasts as I stood up.
Carefully I made my way down a narrow passageway to
the men's room. Graffiti covered the walls. "If she don't
do it, screw it." And another. "Billy, Jack, Joseph,
Johnny, Andy, and Michael are gay. I'll never invite
them to bed again." Laughing, I stood in front of the
urinal and wondered how much longer I'd be able to
tolerate the world of the man. How much longer would
I be able to pull off this role I'd been playing?

Again, my breasts tingled and I thought about my
visit to the doctor just two weeks earlier. That Saturday
morning I had slipped out of bed and left the small
apartment without telling Johanna where I was going. It
was almost ten o'clock and my appointment was for ten.
As I descended the stairs of that old rust-colored building, I wondered where I had parked the car and where
the office was.

Luckily, it was just around the corner. A plump,
blue-eyed man with a slight homosexual lisp greeted
me. He had a handsome face, well tanned.

"Are you Danny O'Connor?" he asked me, shaking my hand.

"Yes, I am." I was a little surprised that he'd waited for me and that I hadn't noticed the lisp in his voice when I talked to him on the phone.

"Oh, well, you're a pretty one, aren't you? I'm Doctor Meyer, the doctor you spoke to yesterday on the phone."

There was no one in the waiting room. "Well, I guess I'm early. Shall I wait a while?"

"No, no. Come right in."

I didn't know exactly what I was getting myself into, but I did know that I was desperate. My friend John, whom I'd met through a correspondence club, had told me about this doctor. John was the first person I'd met whom I felt I had anything in common with. He was a tranvestite, but his brother was a transsexual. We had spent hours discussing our feelings on the subject.

"My friend John has told me a great deal about you, Dr. Meyer," I said, trying to put myself at ease. "I guess I'm only the second patient you've ever seen who was in this condition, huh?"

"Well, yes," he said, turning the stethoscope nervously, "but I've read a great deal on the subject of transsexualism, and I know what you'll need in the way of hormones."

John had told me about Doctor Meyer one evening as I was about to leave his house in the San Fernando Valley, where I had come to visit. Although he suspected the doctor was gay, John had said that he couldn't be sure, and that, in any case, the man was sympathetic and helpful with hormone shots.

"Pull your pants down," said the Doctor, showing me the hypodermic. "Now, this won't hurt."

A couple of days later I started feeling those peculiar itchy feelings in my breasts, and by the end of the first week I'd noticed swellings. By the second week they were obvious. I'd had to wear a vest this evening to cover them.

From the men's room I went to an area just under the balcony, where it seemed relatively quiet, to tune my guitar. The guitar was a new one, a twelve string I'd inherited from a friend who had given up the guitar. When I was done tuning, I checked my watch and realized I had less than fifteen minutes until I was to go on. What if I was heckled again? What if I lost my voice? What if I broke a string?

"Danny O'Connor!" I heard the announcer say my name and I ran up the stairs to the stage.

I began to sing right away and noticed that the rumble in the room died down. This was one of my own songs, "Apple Valley Sally Mule," a country number. It's a very "up" tune, a good number to open with, and I was pretty confident of the range structure. I got a good round of applause when I finished, so I immediately went into another song. This time I heard a couple of wise guys at a table right up front commenting on my voice sounding unmanly, and it blew my whole act. For the remainder of my act I sang very mechanically. Though it was well received, my heart wasn't in it. It had become very important that I impress the two guys in front of me with how masculine I could make my voice sound, and less important that I simply perform and sing well. It wasn't my best.

Sometime later, I figured out why people would so often detect things about me while I was on stage. I was playing a threefold act up there. First, I was playing the act of being a male. Then, there was the act of being a male no one would pick on, and third, the act every performer uses on stage. No wonder I'd been frightened on the stage.

That evening, driving home, I decided it was time to tell Johanna about the doctor, although my conscience was really bothering me.

"Johanna, I have to tell you about a decision I've made. And it's a decision no one can talk me out of."

"What Danny?"

I began the story, starting with the things John had told me. First she chose not to believe me, but finally, as I continued, she broke into tears. It would be months before I made the final break, but I figured she might as well know so she could get used to the idea of losing me. As we talked on, I realized I didn't have to tell everything that one night. She was still triumphant from the evening's performance, and very confused at my words now.

Parking the car in front of the house, I slid over and put my arm around her. What I had just told her was confused with the triumph she felt about the evening's performance.

"I know it's hard to understand, baby," I said after a while, fighting back my own tears, "but it's just that I want you to know what I'm thinking so you can be prepared. That's all—just be prepared."

BREAKING AWAY

I had returned from work an hour ago, and now I awaited Johanna impatiently. Lately things had become tense. My problem was bursting within me. Though I loved Johanna a great deal, I had begun to dread looking into her shining, finely featured face, fearful of her probing eyes.

"Hi, darling. What have you been doing?" she said as she burst into our tiny apartment.

I asked her if she had been thinking of the conversation we had had the other night concerning my striking out on my own. She hesitated, then quickly rushed into the kitchen to begin preparing our dinner. I knew how much the subject must have hurt her, but I also knew that time was of the essence, and I wanted very much to make sure she and the baby were okay before I did something radical.

She returned from the kitchen with a kiss and told me that she was going to retrieve our baby from the babysitter's downstairs and that she needed time to think.

It was a dismal June afternoon and the gray kitchen was no solace as I typed what would be one of the most important declarations of my life. There wasn't much use now in trying to rationalize. I knew it was for real, at last, and though I struggled over each word in the letter, there was no turning back. I was writing to my parents.

I'd practiced a thousand times picking up the telephone, attempting to call them. I remember meditating, which was something I was doing more and more frequently, on just how to broach the subject to a father who worshipped his only son and to a mother who had once said she couldn't live on if her son was ever killed in the war. Although this wasn't war, this was certainly murder. I was murdering myself and living to face the consequences.

There was the obvious, flat out-and-out boom: "I'm changing my sex!" Although there had been flashes of courage I remembered throughout my life, I just couldn't seem to take the blunt approach. My typing was terrible, and though I was typing on the new typewriter I'd won in the contest, it didn't seem to help me finish the letter any faster. I stopped for a minute to answer the telephone. It was my producer. What the hell was she calling me *now* for?

"Danny, we've got a great deal working, and I think you're going to become another Bobby Sherman!"

Why now? . . . after more than seven months of waiting, sweating out disappointment after disappointment! "In a week or two." I'd heard that phrase so many times before that it made me grab at my stomach. Oh, God, why didn't she forget I was alive. I held my breath for a moment, and then, just as if something had taken over my soul I blurted, "I've got something I've got to talk to you about."

"What's that?" she countered.

"Well I'm writing my parents about it now but I've got to do some thinking before I tell you, I just can't talk now."

After I hung up I began to fantasize about telling her and her husband the story of my well-hidden life secret. I began to squirm in my chair, and though I couldn't quite make out the image my mind was projecting, most of what I could see wasn't so great.

Nancy, the woman with whom I'd just spoken, was a slim, beautiful lady. I say "lady" because, during the long readjustment period that lay ahead, she was to be the only person I really wanted to model myself after. She had that grand aura about her, and no matter how she was dressed she commanded respect. With her I knew I would have very little problem breaking the news, but it was her husband Phil who would be the problem.

I could just see him: a short, burly, typical Hollywood music producer, holding up his hand, looking me up and down and saying "Huh, this, *this,* is my star?" It was really kind of funny and I felt a little heartened at the thought of finally bringing something to him that he didn't have an answer for.

I finished the letter to my parents and mailed it, my hands trembling as I put it in the mailbox.

Dear Mom and Dad,

I hope this letter finds you in good health and great prosperity. Believe me, I really hope you all have hit some lucky streaks. Things have started to open up out here, so I've decided to tell you something that has been a real part of Johanna's and my life for the past three years.

I know you're wondering what exactly I'm talking about, so I'll try to get to the point.

Mom, do you remember when I was fourteen and I told you a deep, dark secret of mine? Do you remember how upset you were, and how we both cried about it? I think you also remember all the talks we had, and how I wanted to be changed into a girl, like Christine Jorgensen. Well anyway, I've got to tell you something. I love you all very much—I think you know that. A thing like this could ruin not only a family, but friends and lives. I realize this. I just hope you'll understand what I'm about to tell you.

When Johanna and I got married, it was because I loved her, but not as a normal male loves. It was different. I always took the female role in the sex act and hated the masculine role. I never made love with anyone else before I met Johanna, and when we did it, it was like an experiment. I liked it a lot, but soon learned that one must pay the consequences for such a relationship. I did. Although I love Johanna and my baby, Joey, more than this typewriter can put down, I also have a responsibility as a parent and as human being. I know there is no excuse for what I'm about to tell you, except that it is virtually my only way out.

Mom and Dad, I love you all very much, and it's because I do that I hope you'll find some miracle of understanding in your heart. What I'm trying to get the courage to tell you is that I'm a transsexual—one whose desire it is to become a physical member of the opposite sex—and have been all my life. I have always had an empty feeling—a feeling of incompleteness—inside me. Now, I'm in the process of doing something about it. Let's go back a little bit, so I can explain.

Do you remember the draft board physical I was so nervous about? Well, that was because I had been counseling with a psychiatrist prior to that time, and was to be classified mentally unfit for service. I think now you can see why I was so upset. I was classified as a transvestite, because the shrink didn't know the name to use for what I wanted out of life. It's true I dress a great deal in girls' clothes, but I wanted and still want more. There isn't really any easy way to tell people you love about this. So, if I get foggy, forgive me, for I'm crying, and I want to hurry and get done with this letter before I throw the letter away. I know how I have responsibilities as a father, but unfortunately, if I don't go through with the change, I won't be around to do anything, much less be a father. I've come so close to suicide these last few months I've decided to change—even if I lose everything. Don't get me wrong. I'm not asking for opposite persuasion. Believe me, if you want to persuade me to do anything else, don't bother answering this letter. I've been taking hormones for the last three months and I'm learning about the hardships a woman has to face, chemically. I have developed fairly large-sized breasts and have seen a great deal of change in my skin texture and hip growth.

I've decided—after countless days of just sitting waiting for the right time to die, wondering each day when I got up if I'd have the guts to end it all before the day was over, and, at the same time, realizing that Danny was no more, and that now there was only Canary, the name I call myself—that I want to live.

I'm now planning to move out and get an apartment

alone. I know it isn't right to leave Johanna and the baby, for I owe them a lot, too, but I truly feel I have no choice. I've got to be me, and I think someday the two of them will realize the decision I made was the right one. At least I hope so. I've spent many, many, many hours deciding what course to take regarding the two of them, and I can find no other avenues open. I want Johanna to be able to find another husband as soon as possible, and I don't want little Joey to face the consequences of my downfall as a man.

I'm very happy about the decision I've made, but very, very unhappy at the prospect of hurting those who I love and who love me. Something tells me from inside that I've done the right thing. My doctor recommended that I leave the house, once I become a female full-time, and let Johanna try to forget about me. I know, as you must realize, that I would only be prolonging her misery and mine by staying on.

I'll be calling you all soon, after this letter has had time enough to get to you. For now, there isn't any more I can say to ease the shock, except that I had intended to wait to tell you until after the surgery, which is to be at some indefinite time in the future, but decided you should know the truth.

So, I'll just say I love you a whole lot. I think by now you're had enough surprises for this lifetime.

                              Love,
                              Danny

I was rereading my copy of it when I heard a rap on the door. I hurried to hide the letter. Johanna had just come up from downstairs with our little one and I could feel that same sick feeling embrace me. "Come on in, honey!"

"Danny, have you decided to forget all about this crazy thing of yours about becoming a girl?" she said as she entered. How could I explain to her that it wasn't some crazy idea I'd read and become infatuated with? How could I ever persuade her that the man she married wasn't a man but a girl like her, and that I had already started hormone shots.

"I can't!" I said quickly, for I knew there would

be no more room for another argument this time. "I love you, honey, and the baby, more than you'll ever know. It's just that I'm not a man. I don't know how to explain it, but there is something inside me that has always been there, telling me that this is all wrong. I'm not and never have been a male!"

I could feel those familiar tears streaming down my cheeks, and I hurried out of our one-room apartment. I rushed down the rickety stairs, which I rarely used, preferring to use the antiquated elevator, and into the street.

I could feel the guilt gnawing at my heart, and I couldn't find any justification for what I was doing. Wasn't there anyone out there who understood? Was I always going to be alone like this? Could it be that the things I'd heard from the psychiatrist I'd seen in Texas were really coming true? I remember at our last session he had said, "Go ahead, screw it all up by pursuing this foolish notion of yours of becoming a girl. Go ahead, and I predict you'll not only fail but will ultimately end up committing suicide!" I had choked at the thought.

Now, standing in front of my apartment house, I felt that this time it was going to be different. There was no doubt that people would gather to see my feminine beauty. Gentlemen would marvel at one so flawless, so smooth. I could see myself with long flowing hair, and wearing a beautiful spring dress. How could it be wrong? All I was doing was being my true self, a girl.

"Hey, Dan, what's happening, man!" It was Sam, a middle-aged, dirty-looking man who lived in one of the basement apartments below ours.

"Oh, hi," I said reluctantly.

He was everything I despised in a man. He was a failure, a drunk, and a pervert. I remembered one afternoon when I was walking home from the store he had grabbed me and pulled me down on an old couch which sat pathetically beside a dilapidated service station, across from our apartment. I remember feeling real fear as his hands groped over my body. He began telling me he had been in a mental institution for assaulting a child. I pulled myself free and picked up a nearby bottle. He had leered at me.

"Say, Danny, you got real pretty legs when you wear a dress."

Oh God, it had finally happened. Someone from the apartment had seen me, but why did it have to be this creep?

"What are you talking about?" I replied.

"You know, the other night. Wasn't that you in that brown dress coming out of the front door over there?"

I knew I would have to face him and everyone in the apartment building soon, but I chose to ignore these comments as best I could.

"Hey, Danny, why don't you come clean?" he had said. "You're just another faggot, aren't you?" I knew I would have to get used to talk like that, but it had still hit hard as I threw the bottle away and headed back home. My heart had been pounding. It was a familiar feeling, one I had known many times during my childhood as when I would be attacked by some power hungry kid trying to prove he could conquer that feminine-looking sissy. I was snapped back to reality by Sam's voice.

"Hey, fucker, why you walking away? Maybe you and me, we can get a little whoopie going together! How about it, sweetie? I can swing both ways, baby. How about it, queenie?"

I ran inside and tripped on the first step, falling right on my face. I was scared, embarrassed, but most of all, really concerned that my story would spread through the apartment building on the lips of such a foul man. I felt time closing in on me. I knew I would have to make my break soon. As I opened the paper thin door to our apartment, I felt deeply depressed, knowing that I would again have to face Johanna.

"Danny, I'm sorry." Johanna began. "But I love you so much and the Puppy (a nickname we had given our son) does too. We just don't understand what's happening to our Daddy."

I gasped. There was that word "daddy" again, and everytime she said it, whatever strength I'd accumulated, perished. I knew how much I'd loved my own daddy but no matter what, our little son Joey would never know the warmth and joy of a true father-son relationship.

He was a beautiful little boy. Blond hair, blue eyes, and the most popular baby every place he went. There were times when I'd hold him and dream that he was really *my* baby and that I had carried him and given birth to him. I wondered what it would be like to nurse him like I had seen Johanna do so many times during the first few months after his birth. I remember once holding him to my breast, closing my eyes—and singing him to sleep while Johanna was in the other room sleeping. Although I could not question the fact that I had taken part in the conception of this child, I just couldn't accept the fact that I was his *father*. All I know is that everytime I saw Johanna and the baby, pure, sweet and innocent, I felt hurt and burned.

"Honey," I began, "I have to make my move today."

"What do you mean 'today'?" she responded.

"That creep Sam saw me the other night in a dress and . . ."

"Oh, Danny, please don't do this!" she said, refusing to let me finish.

LITTLE DID THEY KNOW

"Well, Danny, this morning could be a very important one for you," Len was saying. He flashed me a quick smile and turned back to his driving. I nodded, even though he wasn't paying any attention to me, and pushed my dark glasses up firmly.

"Yeah, that's for sure," I said, struggling to keep my voice low. "I guess if he likes some of my songs he might record some of them, huh?" The morning was particularly beautiful, with very little smog. We turned from Doheny into Sunset Boulevard, and I looked out to the right to wait for glimpses of the city far below.

Len was scratching his nose, a habit of his I found oddly reassuring. "Let's hope so," he said. We rode in silence for a while. Just as a matter of reference, I had met Len through Johanna's uncle and aunt back in Texas, and he'd introduced me to the producers I had signed with. For a while I thought about telling him of my plans, but when he'd called me last night and had explained that he had lined up a personal interview and audition for me, I couldn't turn him down.

It was really hard to believe. In the last few days I had begun a break with Johanna and the baby, and had started a whole new way of life. The hurt was getting easier to live with, just like any injury left alone long enough.

Less than seven hours ago, I had gone out in public for the first time alone, as a girl. It was something I'd been putting off for twenty years, and the feeling that I had finally conquered the fear gave me a new vigor and new insights.

As we drove, now, I thought of the hours of driving I had done last night, hoping someone would look at me, some men. When they did, I was ashamed and embarrassed, and although I rationalized my feelings, I was afraid. For the first time in my life I had worried that someone might think I was a boy, quite the opposite of the thoughts I'd had during most of my years growing up. The paradoxes and confusions I would be facing in the next few years had started to assert themselves.

I reached up again to make sure my sunglasses were in place, hoping no one would ask me to take them off. It was really funny, in a way. Last night I had gone out in a dress. This morning I was dressed as a male to meet Pat Boone with Len, and I had to wear these silly sunglasses because I couldn't get my makeup off, no matter what I tried. And for once I was actually enjoying my upcoming role of talented young male recording star because I knew it would be one of the last times I would play it.

"Say," Len said, suddenly, checking his watch, "I forgot that our appointment was postponed for a half hour. Why don't we head for some breakfast?"

"Hey, great," I said, feeling my voice soar up unexpectedly. As we drove down little Santa Monica, I spotted a parking place near a small restaurant and pointed it out to Len.

Something about that area bothered me. The nearest I could figure it was because of the attitude of people around there—they always seemed to have their noses three stories above their bodies, and their personalities out to lunch. Of course, I had bad memories of the area, too. My first job in Los Angeles was right around the corner from our parking place and although I'd cut my hair almost to the nub in order to land it in the first place, I lost the job inside of three weeks. What bugged me about that was sacrificing a year and a half's growth to the ridiculous notion that I should make one last stand at being a man.

As we entered the restaurant I recognized someone I'd worked with in the other place, but the snide look on her face discouraged any unnecessary hellos.

What'll you have?" asked a pretty blond waitress in her early twenties.

"I'll have ham, eggs, and hash browns," I said, hoping I had enough with me to pay for it. While Len gave his order I studied the girl, wondering how I would feel if she were calling me "ma'am" instead of "sir" and saw her in a different way. Now that I could be honest with myself, I found that letting down my armor—my "expected" male behavior—made me see her and other girls as if they were competition rather than prey.

In the past few months I'd also become increasingly more aware of the men around me, and found myself observing Len as he eyed the waitresses with just a touch of lust, and then went on to kid her in a way similar to my customary approach to girls. Watching her walk around the corner in a green and white mini skirt, I thought about the dress I'd worn the night before. It was a velvet dress, black with white trim. I'd also worn it on my first date, about a month ago, with a guy I'd met through the correspondence club for transsexuals.

Sighing, Len and I looked at each other and smiled. "Well," he said, scratching his nose, "I hope you're going to make me a million dollars pretty soon. I'm tired of working on these damn oil wells." Guilt slammed into me. It was a kind of sneaky trick I was pulling, not telling my business people about my problem, but from the beginning I'd suspected they would have been afraid to work with me. Since I'd written over a hundred songs at that time and already had had forty-three of them published, I didn't want to chance business problems. I shrugged mentally.

"Oh, you better believe it," I answered, drawling. Len was a former Texan, tall and lanky, and he loved hearing the "old home sound." We ate our meal quickly and headed on to the Boone house.

"Well, here we are," Len said as we swung into the circular driveway and pulled up by the twin black doors next to some shrubbery. "Now, you want me to tune up your guitar or something before we go in?"

"No, I tuned it at home." I had to smile at his

CANARY:
AN EXTRAORDINARY
TRANSFORMATION

A little boy
who knew too much
about himself.

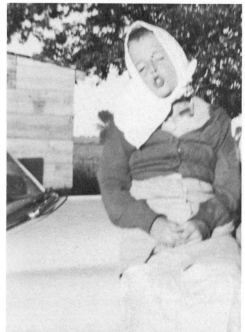

"Dressing"
—summer at
the farm.

First grade and a new awareness: Danny was different.

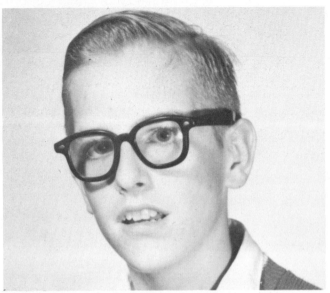

In search of a confidante—twelve years old.

First independence—a motorbike.

Ready for the first prom.

The neighborhood gang.

Between classes
in high school,
1968.

The new "mini" look is in.

Senior graduation picture.

Taken onstage at ABC studios during
prize-winning performance.

One of the prizes Danny received for winning
the contest for best teenage male vocalist.

Danny sings as producer watches
during first recording session.

Swinging out on a record tour.

Disc jockey Bruce Hathaway interviews Danny on KTSA.

Larry Kane interviews Danny for KTRV, Houston.

Danny sings at a U.S.O. show—Brooke Army Hospital.

WMAQ Joe Kaucky, Gerry Maslana, Jim Jefferies,
Danny. One of the many visits across the
country on Capitol Records tour.

Working on lyrics for a new song.

Interviewing Leroy Prinz, WWI flying ace and
Hollywood producer, on the Hollywood Cage Show.

Canary being interviewed on the Merv Griffin Show.

Posing for a fashion layout.

Photo for *Playgirl Advisor*, May 1977.

sudden nervousness. We got out of the car and approached the house.

"Good morning," said the man as he opened the door. "Len, isn't it?"

"That's right," Len said, extending his hand. His nervousness vanished. "And this is the gentleman I talked to your manager about, Danny O'Connor."

"Glad to know you," I said, shaking his hand.

We followed him into the house, down a long hall, then down three steps to a dining room filled with Western furniture. Plaques were hung along the wall facing the door, interspersed with pictures. When he motioned to me, I sat down in a chair with a back that looked like a wagon wheel.

"Why don't you take off your shades, Danny?" he suggested. "It's kind of dark in here, and I'm afraid you won't be able to see." I thought fast.

"Oh, no, I can't. You see, they're prescription and I have to wear them while my regular glasses are being repaired." Pat smiled. We exchanged the traditional amenities about the industry before Len suggested I play a few tunes to let Pat get the feel of what I was doing. From his face, I could tell Pat didn't expect much, but I found his expression, a common one in Hollywood, a challenge. I watched it change as I played.

"Say, that's a real pretty song," he said, when I had finished the first.

"Oh, that's," I paused for effect, "Santa Fe Light," I said, trying to seem professionally disinterested.

"Well, let me get a pencil and paper before you continue," he said, getting up and walking to a small desk, "so I can write down which ones I want to see lead sheets on." It was quiet while he rummaged through a drawer. "You know, Danny," he said, returning to his seat, "you have an interesting voice— countertenor range, I'd say."

For the first time, knowing what he was driving at, I didn't mind this comment on my voice.

"Thank you," I said, "but I can sing lower octaves, too. Here's one I call 'What Do You Say?'" The elasticity in my voice pleased me. The last year or so I'd tried to develop a more masculine singing style, but I'd found, after a while, that I was singing in a kind of falsetto, something women do when they imitate men, so I had abandoned those attempts and decided to work within a comfortable range.

The rest of the morning we went through one song after another, and he commented with a great deal of praise about my songwriting ability. When the meeting adjourned, he thanked us for coming and reminded us to get another appointment to bring him some lead sheets.

I kept thinking how fabulous the whole thing was, and how lucky I was to spend so much time with the star of *Journey to the Center of the Earth,* one of my favorite pictures.

"Well," Len said, as we pulled out of the driveway, "looks like you might have sold him some of your songs, Danny." He headed for my apartment.

"Yes, it sure looks that way," I answered with enthusiasm, which faded rapidly. I had a funny suspicion that I wouldn't be around as Danny long enough to have that next meeting with Mr. Boone.

MALE VS. FEMALE

"Good morning, ma'am," the man behind the counter said. "Can I help you with something?" At first I was conscious of my voice and tried to act as if I had a sore throat.

"I'd like to see someone about applying for welfare," I whispered.

"You'll have to speak up, ma'am," he said, pursing his lips. "It's pretty crowded in here—you'll have to speak up." Because this was the first time I had dressed as a girl in public during daylight hours, I was painfully aware of the crowd in this room, and aware that this place, the welfare office, and this time of morning were busy ones.

"Yes," my voice scattered through a couple octaves. "Well, I'd like to see someone about applying for welfare."

"Will this be for you alone, or do you have any children, ma'am?" the man asked, putting a pen in front of me.

"Yes," and trying to anticipate, I continued, "I have one child."

"And your husband?" he asked, his eyes widening.

"He's no longer with us," I said, trying to seem like a widow, broken-hearted at the loss of a husband. "I'm afraid that's why I'm here, you see. I have nowhere else to turn." The man seemed more concerned now, and I realized I had struck a sympathetic chord.

"Fill this out," he said, handing me the pen and a form. "Put your name here, your child's name here, and the name of your former husband right here. Once you're finished, take the complete form to window 'B', and you'll get someone assigned to your case."

Turning, I sought out an empty chair in a corner. It seemed like there were a thousand people in this waiting room. I'd never dreamed a welfare office could be so crowded. Seating myself, I reached up to check my blond fall, the one I'd bought by hocking a guitar last week. Even though the saleslady had said it was good human hair and a wig to be proud of, I hated having to wear it. My own hair was about shoulder length and didn't quite do. It was my first day, and although I knew I couldn't be expected to change roles completely in the beginning, I wanted to look feminine.

There were many things I hadn't anticipated. Clothing was a complicated matter. I was to wear dresses instead of pants, high-heeled sandals instead of clodhopper boots, and some other articles of clothing, like panties, bras, slips and pantyhose. And then there was makeup, a must for a well-groomed, attractive girl at the time. It was hard to get used to, for although I'd longed my entire life to dress in my proper role, I'd somehow been oblivious to all the details women take for granted as necessary for daily grooming. Trading a T-shirt and Levi's for the new way of dressing took some getting used to.

The *name* blank stumped me. Thinking for a minute, I remembered my early childhood, and weekends with my grandparents. Every Sunday afternoon they would take me to the corner drugstore where I would sit on a stool in the soda fountain area. Friends would wander over to admire their little grandson, gather around, pinch me on the cheek, and request the only song I knew clear through. "Pop! go da weeval," I'd sing, and all of their friends would chuckle warmly.

One time, a stranger watched from her seat at the fountain and smiled at me as I sang. "She's the prettiest little canary I've ever seen," the woman said, reaching over to put a penny in my hand. As she walked away, I turned to my grandparents to check their reaction to the woman's improper gender identitication of me. Although they said nothing, I could tell by their faces that they were a little upset. From that day I always thought of my female self as a bird, a canary.

"Okay, Canary," I said softly, testing the name to myself. "Canary O'Connor . . . no, Connor . . . no, Conn—Canary Conn!" Yes, that suited me perfectly. The rest of the form was easy. Once I had completed it, I double-checked my new name at the top of the page before I deposited the sheet of paper at the proper window. Then I sat down to wait.

"Good morning," the petite young woman said, smiling at me faintly as I finally reached window "B". This had taken an hour, and I pushed back the hair from my cheek to contain my annoyance.

"Good morning," I answered her, too upset to care what my voice sounded like.

"My name's Eileen Finley," she said, motioning for me to follow her down a small hall, noisy with voices from behind closed doors. At one room she stopped and motioned me in. As she closed the door, I took a deep breath. It wasn't going to be easy to tell her my story. "Now," she said, waving me into a chair, "what can we do for you?"

After another deep breath, I began. Her face changed when I came to the part explaining that I was not the distraught mother, but rather the dismayed father.

"Hold on a second," she had said, resting her head on her hands. "You mean you aren't a woman? I . . . can't believe it!" I went on to explain that I had come for Johanna and the baby, in hopes they could receive some financial assistance. She assured me that her office would indeed help the family I was leaving behind, and that they would, for that matter, help me until I could get situated in a job.

Walking to the car, I wrestled with my conscience. I'd been brought up to work, to make my own way, and the idea of welfare didn't sit well. I'd never thought much about the idea of being a welfare recipient. It was something in the same class as bankruptcy or going to the poorhouse—something that never happened to me, to my people. For a while I felt as though I'd hit bottom, but I could also thank God for allowing me some kind of foundation to stand on for a while. As soon as I could, I would find some kind of work, but right now, right now I would try to do just what had to be done.

Once in my car, I began to cry, but they were tears of joy rather than unhappiness. This had been a momentous morning. Not only had I committed myself to dressing as a woman full-time, but I had gone into a crowded welfare office and had received a promise of aid for my wife, my baby and myself.

The bond between Johanna and me was severed now. The previous night we had had what was now a nightly argument. It had been a more bitter one than usual and a lot of the things we said to each other couldn't be easily forgotten.

"Go ahead then," Johanna had screamed at me finally, "go ahead and live your sick life. But don't expect us to be part of it."

Her closing statement had hurt me, but it was a long-awaited acknowledgment that she was ready for the necessary break and that it was now time to make my move.

That morning I'd gotten up a little earlier than usual to choose one of my five dresses and to carefully put myself together before she awoke. It had been relatively easy to slip out unnoticed, but returning was going to be a little different. What would I say to the apartment managers if they saw me dressed as a girl? Sam had seen me and knew, and had probably told everyone who'd been willing to listen, but it would be a far different thing to confront those people. Parking the car, I decided that bold action was the only choice. Quickly, I crossed the street and went into the building. As fast as I could, I climbed the stairs and made my way down the hall. When I passed the managers' apartment, I turned away so all they'd see was the back of my head.

Inside I leaned on the door and almost laughed. I'd made it!

It took me only a few minutes in the still apartment to gather a few possessions. Although I'd told the woman at the welfare office I didn't plan to move out for another week, I suddenly couldn't bear the thought of living there another day and hiding my identity every time I went past the managers' open Dutch door.

Johanna and I spoke only a few words when I returned. We felt, I guess, that it had all been said, and there was nothing I could say to Danny's wife, a person who loved him and hated me for taking him away from her. I was torn with confusion, with conflicting feelings, because I was both the focus of my wife's hate for being a murderer and the murder victim himself, a victim who lived on to face the agony of the grieving widow, my grieving widow.

Less than half an hour later, slipping out the same way I'd slipped in, I was opening the car, and loading stuff into the back. "Well you've done it, kid," I whispered to myself as the engine turned over. "You've done it!"

The entire afternoon was an apartment hunt. Other than a small advance from my music publishers—less than a hundred dollars—and a twenty dollar bill my worker had given me (an advance she felt was warranted in my case), I didn't have any money left at all. It was almost five o'clock before I located a "for rent" sign on what looked like a suitable dwelling in Old Hollywood. Suitable is just a fancier word for cheap-looking. The building was three-stories and certainly old enough, painted a putrid pink outside. Inside, though, it was quite charming. The landlady was Puerto Rican and didn't speak much English. Struggling, I recovered a few words of Spanish.

"Por favor, señora, me gusta . . . to see an apartment you have for rent."

"No comprendo." she said, shaking her head. I tried again. In a few minutes we were winding our way up three flights of stairs—no elevator. Well, that was a good sign—maybe the apartments here wouldn't be too expensive.

Once inside the apartment, I fell in love with it. Nothing fancy, or even mildly chic, it was simply a clean, freshly painted, single apartment with a bed that came out of the wall and very simple furnishings. As I walked through it I began to imagine myself living there.

"How much is it?" I asked, forgetting the language problem.

"*Oh, no comprendo, señorita,*" she said, "no understandie . . ."

"Oh, yes," thinking again, I smiled. "*Cuanto cuesta, esto* . . . how much?"

It took two months to break all ties with Johanna and Joey. When I had settled with my new landlady I returned to the old apartment in the darkening evening and found Johanna, to my surprise, packing.

"I'm going to move to my grandparents' house for a while," she said, keeping her eyes down and continuing to pack. It looked as though she had been crying and she seemed to be in shock. Without a word, I knelt at her side and began helping her. The plan for this break had been made months ago, but the pain of separation was hitting only now. We were both so young, and we had been putting this off for so long. I understood her feelings and I loved her very much; no matter what happened, I hoped she would always remember that. As for me, I could only hope that what I was doing was the right thing for all of us.

We only spoke a few words in the process of packing and during the drive to the San Fernando Valley. As I finished helping her unload, her grandparents returned from what looked like a trip to the store. Before they could get a good look at me, I hurried back to the car and drove away. I didn't look back. I couldn't even cry. I just hurt, something I would be doing for a long time.

"You're alone now," I told myself as I entered the alley leading from my parking lot. "You've got to make it. No matter what anyone thinks of you, you've got to be yourself!"

That night I made a special ceremony of throwing away all my male clothes: every pair of pants, socks, shorts, shoes and every shirt Danny had owned. There was at least four or five years' accumulation. Other than my dresses and other female clothing, I kept only a couple of pieces of jewelry I could use as a female. There was no turning back now. This was a commitment.

After a few days of desperately needed peace, I began to contact all the people who had been involved in Danny's life. Although I'd already sent my parents a letter, our phone had been disconnected, so they weren't able to reach me at all until I called them from a pay booth. Dad was screaming with rage. Mom was crying, fearful that she had not only lost a son, but the right to see her grandson again.

"I'm sorry," I said, over and over. That was the only word that seemed appropriate for the onslaught of "Why?" and "How could you?" coming from the other end of the line. As I hung up the telephone I realized how really alone I was.

My producers were easier. They took it rather calmly. Nancy even spent some time with me, trying to give me some hints about how to dress, how to do my hair, how to use makeup, and more.

Len was pretty disappointed because he'd been counting on something coming out of the visit with Pat Boone. He took my news well though, and like Nancy and Phil, pledged to do what he could to help me in spite of the obvious hardship. None of them were able to do anything, but they did try.

The cardboard person began to come down. It was going to be a long battle to bring my voice under control, and there was little time for training.

Then, too, I had to get a telephone and I didn't know how to explain my change to the telephone company. My financial condition was too tight to allow a new deposit. Standing in the phone booth, I thought fast.

"Well, ma'am, my boss, Danny O'Connor, he said he'd be glad to sign for me if you'd send him the papers."

"No," she said. I didn't like the bitchy tone. "You'll have to tell him he'll have to come down in person to sign the guarantor form." Thanking her, I hung up. After a moment, I dropped another dime in the pay phone and dialed the telephone business office once again. This time I used the lowest voice Danny had ever used.

"Yes, ah, give me the representative for, ah . . ." I rattled off my old number.

"Yes, sir!"

"Miss Schultz speaking. May I help you?"

My voice was straining already. "Yes. I'd like to have a phone installed in an apartment."

"Why, yes, sir," said the woman, sweetly.

"Well, my daughter is in the process of moving, and I want a phone installed in her new apartment. I understand I'll have to sign for it."

"Well, Mr. O'Connor, that'll be no problem," the woman said, nervously. "I'll just send you the forms to fill out and you can mail them back at your convenience." I struggled to keep from laughing as I gave her the name and address of the girl who was to have the phone installed and then threw in a last pitch.

"Thank ya, honey. Now how would you like to go out with a tall, dark, handsome stranger tonight?" I said, using every drop of male hormone I had left.

"Sure, I'm game," the girl at the other end said, giggling. Boy, would she have been surprised!

It didn't happen overnight. Slowly I began to eliminate an entire world from both my conscious and subconscious mind. Even my dreaming had begun to take on an anti-male viewpoint. My concern with gender identity had turned into a continuous trial, with me as the sole judge, a wild, reckless witch-hunt that tried to remove anything that remained in me from the world I'd left behind.

For a couple of months I had some strange experiences in the supermarket trying to sex-categorize foods. For example, on one trip to the neighborhood grocery I spent at least ten minutes in front of the dry cereals trying to decide whether or not to buy a box of Cheerios because of its masculine connotation. Many other commodities, like soaps, shampoos, meats, vegetables, fruits and just about any other item I could conceivably categorize came under my careful scrutiny. On one occasion I remember being embarrassed purchasing several cans of soup with the words "Man Handler" printed on them.

It was as if I had become obsessed with the virtual elimination of everything masculine from my life; as though I were afraid in a tight moment I might step back over the line.

This obsession even carried over to the classification parts of my body according to gender. Feminine parts were loved and admired. Those that weren't as feminine as I felt they should be, I developed a hate for. My hands, I felt, weren't feminine enough, my feet were too large, my nose too long, and so on. Finally, whenever I got home after being out, I was a nervous wreck, wondering what people had thought of me, whether they saw me as male or female. And I got feedback— shades of Rex and the barber shop episode—without making a verbal request for it.

"What are you, a boy or a girl or what?" a stranger had said to me one day as I was walking to my car carrying a grocery bag. That was the first unsolicited comment I had received since I began dressing as a female, and although it didn't seem to bother me at the time, at home I thought about the man's probable reasons for saying what he did, and I cried. It was difficult enough to live this new life and maintain an outward calm; but it was devastating when an experience such as this indicated I was failing. I realize now that there will always be boors who make personal remarks, and they are to be pitied rather than paid attention to. But at that stage, my state of mind made it difficult to ignore any experience which intensified my insecurity.

Was he looking at me, or not? I thought I looked all right. Maybe I'm not standing right. I guess it could be my hair . . . no . . . maybe my hands? That's it! He's looking at my hands. I'm afraid—I want to run! Now the old woman's looking at me. I hate her! She's looking at my feet. Why doesn't she look the other way? Maybe there's nothing wrong with me. Yes, that's it— it's just that I'm nervous. I've got to try to calm myself! There are only two more people ahead of me; why in hell doesn't the doctor hurry up? How can I hide my hands? Oh, he's looking at them again. My hands are part of *me*; I feel sick. Oh, darn it! I'm starting to perspire; I'm scared. Why can't I run? What holds me here? Now everyone's looking at me—I know it! They're all trying to tear me apart. Why can't I shake this feeling? Why am I so frightened? Oh, God, I want to die! I don't want to go on living this way! Please—please let me die right here in the doctor's office! Let me just end it all right now! . . .

"Miss! Miss!" the nurse called from the window not more than four feet in front of me. "You're next. Would you come in, please?"

I would go through this kind of personal agony, it seemed, everytime I'd go out in public. It seemed to come from nowhere. Oh, I had experienced it before, as a male, but only on rare occasions.

"I'm afraid it's only your paranoia," one of the psychologists I'd been seeing at the free clinic said one evening, as I went through the description of what I had felt and continued to feel everytime I found myself in a public place with people all around me.

"That's fine," I said, intentionally looking into his eyes, hoping for some miraculous solution to come booming out of them, "but how do I get rid of these terrible feelings—these feelings that everyone is watching me, that everyone is going to find out? How do I conquer my fear? Is there any way? . . ."

"I'm afraid I really don't know," he said.

Paranoia. At least, now, I had a definition for it. It was a new threat to my sanity—something I'd not anticipated, but that I had to conquer. Sometimes, for days at a time, I would isolate myself in my tiny Hollywood apartment, sometimes even going hungry because of the tremendous fear that had manifested itself within me. Then, suddenly, one day I came to realize that people were only looking at me because *I* was looking at *them*! *They* must have been the ones feeling funny! I began to realize that it wasn't the people around me making me feel odd, but, rather, me, myself who was tearing me apart. As well as the psychological adjustments there were more practical human tasks to be handled.

I had been driving for close to a year without a female driver's license. It did occur to me that I might be stopped by the police for some traffic violation or in a highway patrol vehicle check, but as time passed, the chance of such a thing happening began to seem remote.

Then, one day I looked into my rear view mirror and froze with terror. Behind me, two motorcycle policemen were flashing red lights at me. My first reactions included an urge to ditch the car by the side of the road and run and an impulse to kill myself with one quick swerve of the car into a building or a pole, but these fantasies faded away. I pulled to the shoulder and cut the engine.

The two black-leathered men rounded the back of the car, one approaching me from the left, one from the right. I rolled down my window as the patrolman came to the driver's side.

"Yes, officer," I said, "what did I do wrong? I mean, I can't remember if . . ."

"Oh, miss, you didn't do anything wrong. It's your car. One of your brake lights isn't functioning. May I see your driver's license please?"

"Uh," I said hesitating, "I'm sorry, I didn't hear you."

The man repeated himself, and this time bent down to my window. Before this I had always feared the trip to the Department of Motor Vehicles office with the crowds of people, more than this kind of encounter, but now I realized how serious this could be. Reaching into my purse I pulled out my wallet and plucked out my Texas driver's license in the name of Danny O'Connor to give to him. While I sat there holding my breath the two officers disappeared to the back of the car.

I watched them in my rear view mirror, afraid to turn around. Both men suddenly did a double take as if they hadn't noticed until just then what was shown on the card.

"All right," the policeman said, returning to my window, "what are you trying to pull? You trying to be cute or something?"

"No," I said, shaking visibly. "I'm that person. That is . . . well, I *used* to be him."

"What do you mean, you 'used to be him'?" his

partner asked, opening the door to the passenger's side
to peer in.

"Well, I'm uh . . . a transsexual," I said, hoping
they would be familiar with the word.

"Oh come on!" the man on my left said. "There's
no way you're going to sucker us into believing this
driver's license belongs to you."

What the man meant, although I'm sure he didn't
realize it, was that I had indeed become another person.
Neither of the men believed my story, and in a peculiar
way I began to enjoy their doubt.

"I'm a sex change," I said finally. "I had my operation in Tijuana just a couple of months ago."

"Really?" one officer said, climbing into the car
beside me, as he handed me my driver's license. "Can
you believe this, partner, she's a real trans . . .
trans . . ."

"Transsexual," I said, realizing that I'd finally
caught their interest. "You know, like Christine Jorgensen." That got through to them. I was faced with a del-
uge of questions about just how I came to be who I was.

"I just can't believe you're not a regular girl," the
man to my left said, over and over, as I was answering
the questions of the other. As I thanked them and
waved good-bye a few minutes later, after promising
that I would go down for my female driver's license the
next day, I felt somehow relieved. My attitude toward
policemen had certainly changed.

There were many situations, I found, that changed
with my change of sex, because people dealt with men
and women differently. It was disconcerting for a while
to confront people I had been around as a male. Grocery store clerks, waitresses, postmen and bus drivers all
seemed to be a challenge. Would they recognize me?
Would they notice anything wrong, or off key? And
when I did something I considered distinctly female, I
was even more nervous. Would anyone guess that I
wasn't sure of what I was getting into? But there were
humorous incidents too.

"Yes, may I help you, ma'am?" a tall gray-haired
man who was standing behind the cash register said, as

he finished handing change to a customer in the restaurant.

"Yes sir," I said, trying to keep my nervousness to a casually tapping foot. "I'd like to know where the ladies' room is."

"Oh, yes," the man said, smiling and pointing over my right shoulder. "It's right over there." I thanked the man in my newly acquired soft manner, and hurried off toward the ladies' room. I'd used women's rooms in gas stations, but always when I was alone and when they were empty. This would be the very first time I'd ever gone to a women's restroom in a restaurant.

As I pushed open the door marked "Ladies," I couldn't help but think of the thousands of times I had used the men's room. Since I didn't know what to expect, I decided to walk to the nearest stall and rush in and out as quickly as possible.

But all the stalls were full. I considered going back out but that wouldn't help the pressure on my kidneys. I decided to wait until someone came out. This was my chance to look around. There was one fixture missing—a urinal.

For a moment I forgot where I was. Then, as one of the stalls opened, I was jarred back to my senses to stare straight at a beautiful young blond woman. Startled, I made my way carefully past her into the empty stall, hoping no one would sense anything wrong. I knew what I was—a girl—but I didn't know what other people's responses would be. After years of pretense, I had to learn entirely new attitudes and reactions.

I was in the center stall. Women on both sides were busy.

"Pssssssssssss," went one of my neighbors, relieving herself.

Then the one to the right began making huge bomb-like explosions, something I never imagined a *woman* would do.

"Hey, Teresa," a voice to my left called. "Teresa?"

"What is it, honey?" a voice called from the right of me. "What? Ugh!"

"I'm out of toilet paper, honey. Got any over there?"

If the woman on the right couldn't fill her friend's request, would I be asked to help? I didn't know whether to stay and attempt to empty my bladder, something I'd so far been unable to do, or stand up and pull my clothes back to order.

"Teresa, did you hear me? I asked if you had any . . ."

The woman on the right interrupted her grunts. "Okay, honey, just one second."

Then a roll of toilet paper came from the right stall and rolled directly in front of me, under the divider into the left stall, where a hand reached down to stop the damn thing. The feat so astounded and surprised me I began doing my duty immediately, bringing a moment of truth to the old adage about getting the pee scared out of one.

When the bathroom had been cleared of those two beside me, I ventured out of the security of my stall, somewhat disillusioned about what has often been called the last sanctuary of the American woman.

One other major problem I had to cope with involved the hormonal changes taking place in my body. It was then over six months since I had first contacted my doctor, and the results of the injections he had given me were becoming very obvious. My breasts were developing and I couldn't believe that it was happening. It had taken only two injections to start them blossoming.

Having breasts, of course, was a whole new experience.

Bras took some getting used to, and some movements became more difficult. I can remember rolling over on my tummy in the middle of the night to find, very painfully, that I had moved too quickly. I also noticed a fantastic difference in what had once been my natural movements. Bending, stretching, or just moving were different. There was a different way to stand, to balance. Often times I felt the bra rub across my budding nipples giving me a tickling sensation. I didn't get the chance for several months, though, to find out how really sensuous they could be.

THE FIRST STEP — SURGERY

"Mees Canary Conn, will you step this way pleece?"

As I rose, I clutched my purse in front of me and tried not to sink back down to my seat in fear. It might have been the Mexican food I had had earlier or maybe it was just nerves, but I couldn't help feeling as though I were going to throw up. Following the nurse down a narrow hallway, I tried to focus my eyes on her back and keep my breathing steady.

We came to an open doorway and the nurse motioned me to go on through. The office reassured me. It was that of Dr. Ernesto Lopez, the doctor who was going to perform my first surgery. Journals and magazines were strewn across the nicely hand-carved desk and modern-looking file cabinets. The walls, mostly green brick, were covered with native Mexican art in expensive-looking frames.

When she walked away, I reached inside my purse for my brush, something which had become almost part of my right hand, now that my hair had grown past my shoulders. I began stroking my hair with the brush, and felt it pull slightly against a tangle. Somehow I felt I wasn't dressed well enough, though I'd worn new slacks and a colorful print blouse. The slacks were the only pair I had allowed myself to buy, out of necessity, since the day I had first come out. My blouse, though, was right in tune with the city, Tijuana, Mexico. It had probably been made here.

Wearing the right thing today was important since this was probably the most important event of my life,

so far. Somehow I had waited through those many
months not quite knowing from one day to the next if
I'd ever get enough money together to even contact the
doctors. At least I'd been able to find the doctor's name
and address. My own doctor, and two or three transsexuals had recommended Dr. Lopez. When I had almost
given up, I met a fantastic person who seemed to understand the urgency of my problem.

He was a family man, and had been for over thirty
years. His work record was impeccable and he was
cherished by his employers, an aerospace firm, as one
of their most innovative and successful inventors. Ray
was a couple of inches taller than I, of medium build,
and more than twice my age. We seemed to have a special kind of affection for each other right from the start.
Then, as time passed, he asked me if he could come live
with me. He had already left his family. There was one
catch, though. Finally, he broke down and told me his
story—he wanted to live as a woman.

He had been the older of two children of a war
widow. From early childhood he had worked to help
support his family and had never really had the benefits
of a normal childhood. Something made me feel I
wasn't sure if he was making the right decision. I held
back encouragement for his plans.

I was really aware only of my own problem. The
thought that someone had lived forty-nine years as a
male and had decided, after two marriages and five
kids, that he was a female struck me as incredible. But
we did decide to move in together and to relocate out of
Hollywood to the town of La Puente in the San Gabriel
Valley. Not long after we moved he told me of his plan
to help finance my operation.

At first I was overjoyed, but guilt rapidly overtook
me. After living with the person, seeing him go out to
work in the morning dressed as a man, seeing him come
home dressed the same way and then don women's clothing, I began to have more questions. It wasn't my
place to make value judgments on his or anyone's else's
life, but I couldn't help it. Something was very wrong,
and I didn't know what to do about it.

Ray had made a deal with me and another male-to-female transsexual, a girl named Josie, that if we would go down to a doctor named Lopez in Tijuana with him, he would pay for our operations. It was a miracle dropping out of the sky, but the thought of this man, a fantastically nice person with everything going for him, having his sex changed, began to haunt me. At first I tried not to think about it. Then, as the time for our first joint trip to Tijuana to visit the doctor came, I decided to talk to Josie about my feelings.

She was, of course, in agreement with my feelings, but after discussing the feasibility of our getting the operation through other channels, we decided to leave the matter to time to let it work itself out. Time, however, didn't seem to help.

After we had seen the doctor a couple more times and dates had been set for our prospective surgeries, I was torn apart with guilt. I couldn't seem to shake the feeling that I should try to discourage my financier, even at the risk of losing the backing for my first operation. I decided to call my attorney to discuss the problem.

"He's a grown-up man and a lot more mature than you or Josie," he had said in his gravelly telephone voice.

"I know." I was twenty-one and had a lot to learn. "But I just can't shake the feeling that if he goes through with this operation he'll have made a terrible mistake!"

The controversy was still going on inside my head the morning I was to leave for Tijuana. Putting my arms around Ray, I kissed him to thank him for the money for the operation, although I wanted to run out of the house without saying good-bye. Smiling, I even managed to compliment him on the nightgown he wore, saying I felt it made him look very feminine. That was a damned lie!

It was my lawyer friend who graciously offered to drive me down to Tijuana that morning. He was a sort of roly-poly guy who constantly told jokes he collected from his clients.

"Hi." he had said as I entered his big Cadillac, "Boy, do I have a good one for you this morning!"

"Yeah?" I said. I was not really feeling like any jokes, but I didn't want to hurt his feelings. "What's the big one today?"

"I just heard it from a doctor friend of mine, really great!" he chuckled. "Do you know the medical word for hemorrhoids?"

"No," I said, again trying to show interest. "What is it?"

"Anal tonsils!" he said, breaking into a belly laugh. I forced a smile. Boy, I thought, all I need this morning is jokes about misplaced appendages.

"Good morning, Mees Conn," said a voice behind me.

"Oh, good morning Dr. Lopez," I said, smiling faintly at the short, round-faced, elderly man seating himself behind his desk.

"Now, how are you feelin' today?" he said, his somewhat comical accent becoming more apparent. His face became concerned as I told him of my queasy feeling.

"It's not that uncommon," he said, reaching over to touch my hand. "You know thees operation is a beeg, beeg moment in your life. Now don't you worry none, we gonna take real good care of you." He then escorted me to an examining room adjacent to his little office and asked me to strip. The tile floor was very cold on my feet and I climbed gratefully onto the examining table. As I lay there waiting for the doctor, I glanced around the room. It was even more modern than my personal doctor's office in Hollywood.

The nurse came in carrying three full hypodermics. "Pleece roll over on your *estómago,* ah . . . stomach," she said, motioning with one hand. I did as she told me and tried to relax, as the first of what would be countless injections was shot into me. These were antibiotics given in preparation for the operation and the recovery period. After she had finished, I just lay there a while, listening to the doctor, who had come and gone, sputtering phrases in rapid-fire Spanish, much too fast for my brain to decipher. My head seemed to be the center for a swarm of buzzing bees and I kept whispering to myself, "It's beginning, it's finally beginning, Canary, what you've always dreamed of. . . ."

"Mees Conn?" The young brown-eyed nurse was standing next to the table. "You can put back your clothes as soon as you feel strong enough."

Thanking her, I began dressing. I couldn't help but wonder what the next few days would hold. How much pain would be involved? It was my first time in any kind of hospital situation and I had millions of questions, but I hadn't thought of them before, and now there wasn't enough time to get them answered.

"Okay, Mees Conn," the doctor said, returning to the room. I faced him bravely in my clothes, clutching my purse in front of me again. "I want you to go weeth thees man." He turned to motion to a little broken-down-looking Mexican man. "He weel take you to the hospital you weel be staying at, and I weel join you there thees evenin'." I gathered up my things, handed my small suitcase to my escort, and headed down the marble stairs of Dr. Lopez's office building to the street.

It was a beautiful day. The Mexican sky was crystal clear and, other than a little February wind, a reminder it was still wintertime, it would have been hard to tell this was not a day in August.

As we made our way down Eighth Street to Revolution Boulevard I caught a glimpse of the hustling and bustling little metropolis; the real Tijuana's taxis honking their horns, the rattle of engines on the bumpy street, and the cab driver's hustling.

"*Buenas tardes, señorita,*" a handsome Mexican man said as we passed him.

"*Hola, bonita, hola!*" cried a group of teenage boys from their '53 Chevy. *That* brought back memories.

This kind of attention I had first thought was meant to demean me, to upset me, and of course, I'd immediately associated it with the kind of attention I had received all through school. Then as I began to realize that, most of the time, the "hi there, sweetheart" or the "oooooh, baby" was simply a stranger's compliment, an unsolicited comment on my beauty. That day, however, I was barely concerned about passing comments, believe me!

"Quiere usted tomar el camión, señorita?" the man next to me said. At first I didn't know what the man was saying and tried a series of overused *turista* Spanish words to try to convey my confusion.

"No comprendo—comprendes—comprendemos—" I said, trying to conjugate the verb "understand" to its proper person. "I'm sorry, I no understand."

Somehow or other I managed to convey my ignorance to him, and he summoned a taxi for us, bound for the Caliente Race Track. I'd heard the driver say to one of the other passengers, "The taxis there run up and down one street picking up passengers like a minibus service for Caliente," and that was all I'd needed. I began to think I was en route to a white slave market to be sold—something I'd heard wasn't that uncommon in this part of Mexico. Not ten minutes after we had started our journey, the taxi stopped and the little man nudged me and motioned for me to get out. Sure enough, we had made it to the race track.

That would have been fine for a vacation, but I really wasn't in the mood for mistakes, even honest ones, and if that creepy old man thought I was going to the races with him in order to get to the hospital, he was sadly mistaken.

"Dónde está el hospital? . . . Where is the hospital?" I said, hoping that my original statement was decipherable.

"Allá," the man said, pointing across the street down a dirt road to a green building. I had begun to have serious misgivings. Maybe what my mother had told me the evening before, when I had talked to her long distance, was true.

"I have an odd feeling that something is going to go wrong," she had said. "I don't want you to go down there. If you must go through with this thing, at least have it done here in the United States." I hadn't argued with her, even though I had tried desperately—without success—to find a doctor in Los Angeles who would do this kind of operation.

"Don't worry, Mom," I had said with a phony

confidence in my voice. "I'm sure that everything down there will be first class."

Well, there might have been a better description of the hospital I'd just entered. Oh, structurally, the building was new enough, but as I was to learn in those next few days, a hospital is more than a building.

"Good morning, Mees Conn," a young nurse said, as I struggled to adjust to the curtains she had just opened. Other than a brief visit from the doctor the evening before, I'd been left virtually alone for my first twelve hours in the hospital. The room had a television in it, something every hospital patient learns to value above all else, and I had used my share of juice the night before trying to get my mind off what lay ahead.

"Oh, no," I said, as a tray was placed in front of me by a fat old Mexican woman. "This must be some kind of mistake." The door was closing quietly before I could repeat myself, and the woman had vanished. I stared in disbelief at the meal in front of me. There was a cup of coffee, a glass of some thick kind of fruit juice and a bowl of an unnameable mush. As I ate, slowly, I began thinking of my life so far, on this last day before the operation that would begin a great change in me.

I thought of Johanna and the baby. The love I had for them was still there, and I missed them. For almost six months, I had managed to separate myself from them, which was hard at first, for I knew Johanna's new telephone number, and the apartment she had found back in Hollywood was only twenty minutes from where I was living. Some evenings, I'd drive back into town, cruise slowly in front of their apartment building, and roll the window down, hoping I would hear the sounds of either one of them. I never saw or heard them.

I began to wonder at the irony of my life. It was February and the first February since I'd met Johanna that we wouldn't be together to celebrate her birthday. My baby's birthday was two days after Johanna's. This would be his second. The thought that I would never see either one of them again burned, deeply, but I realized, for all our sakes, I had to stay away. They deserved a new life as well as I did and with that objective, I maintained my isolation.

For almost two months after I had broken up with Johanna, I hadn't heard from my family. This gave us all time to cool down after some of the things that were said in my last call to them. Since that call, Mom had come around, and was even calling me Canary and referring to me in conversation as "she" and "her." I knew what a big adjustment it must have been for her, and I appreciated her patronage, more than she could ever have realized. Dad, however, was a little less willing to call me anything but "What I named you, damn it!"

He would often refer to me as Dan, but after I sent a picture of my new self to them, even nail-hard Dad came around. I listened with peculiar fascination as they described various people's responses after finding out.

"Well, Vincent said he just couldn't believe it," my mother would say, "but he reminded us that he had commented several times about Danny being an odd sort of a kid." It really surprised me how many friends of the family, relatives, etc., had at one time or other commented to my parents about either my physical appearance or a feeling they had had about something different about me, something they couldn't seem to identify.

Until I got my Christmas package from home I wasn't really sure I had convinced my parents that I was not turning back and that I was really going ahead with the operation. They had sent me everything, in that package, makeup, nightgowns, jewelry, a personalized cookbook with my Mom's own recipe for fudge, and more in a supreme declaration of their love and support of their new daughter. My two sisters had even gotten into the habit of calling me their "new sister" in phone calls and letters.

My career was on shaky ground, since it had taken me months and months to teach myself a natural singing voice, one without the frills of masculinity and mechanicalness. At first it seemed almost impossible. After all, how could I ever expect to sing again? I had once been the best teen-age *male* vocalist in the country. It seemed to me that only a first-class fool would attempt what I was trying, but whether it was my hardheadedness, my fear of total failure in music, or an artistic ego, I managed somehow to pull together a voice which many people said, at the time, was more commercial than the voice I'd left behind as a male.

There were days and weeks of just plain "letting go" when I sang. Sometimes I would sound like a man, but as I began to realize my true identity, that of being a person absent of artificialities, things began to change subtly. I was getting hoarse less and less, something I had had problems with as a male singer. And my songwriting even changed in gender.

Instead of love songs to girls, I was writing about an imaginary Prince Charming, and I had even set about changing lyrics to some of my earlier songs. Musically, I felt I'd accomplished the impossible, and though I still had much to learn, I was confident I'd achieved the degree of professionalism I felt necessary in order to pursue my career.

"I'm going to geev you a strong slipin' peel, Mees Conn," a tall, slim Mexican man was saying as he stood over me. "Now, you are not going to remember anything, so you'll just have a pleasant sleep." It was the end of the long first day, and as the anesthesiologist walked out of the room I began to face the realization that part of me would be gone this time tomorrow, and I would be in pain, something I had not experienced yet. No more television right now, I thought. I lay as still as I could and waited for the sleeping pill to take effect. Dinner sat untouched on my side table. I couldn't see that I would miss a cup of Jell-O, a small glass of apricot nectar and a slice of toast.

"*Medicina para Usted,*" a short, dumpy nurse said as she came through the door. She poured water into a glass, and I wondered how the hospital was able to keep so many different nurses on duty. I hadn't seen any face more than twice during the past day and a half. Lying back, I hoped the pill would work quickly, but I was out of luck.

Trying not to think about it, I put my hand down between my legs. My genitals felt different now—as if they weren't even there. I had a small penis and testes to begin with, and after I had begun to take hormone pills and shots, they had become even smaller. I thought of the first time Johanna and I had had sex and the pain I had experienced with my first orgasm. Then I went even further back, to the second grade, remembering a kick between the legs and that terrible throbbing. Was that the kind of pain I would have to go through?

My heart pounded at the thought, and I placed my hand on my breast for comfort. I thought of all the times in the past months I'd been afraid to go out because my male parts were still intact. When the doctor first examined me, my embarrassment colored me deeply, and even this evening, just a few hours ago, I had felt the same kind of embarrassment when the nurse shaved me.

"Take all clothes off," the young nurse had said. "Panties, gown, all off. I'm going to shave." I hadn't expected something like this, although I had expected many strangers.

"Spread your legs," she said, as she covered my pubic area with half a bar of soap. As I felt her first swipe with the razor across the inside of my right thigh, I started shaking and her grim face contorted into a sneer. I battled for calm.

When she had finished with her prepping, I lay in the bed fighting for my feminine pride, lost at having to expose my male parts, and fortunately it wasn't long before the pill began to take effect.

It was still dark when they woke me. The operation was scheduled for 9:00 A.M., but there seemed to be a number of things they had to do beforehand. I was still hazy, sleepy from the sleeping pill.

*Someone was lifting me, I thought, but I wasn't sure—not of anything, not even that I was alive. My eyes fought their way **open** and I saw doctors and nurses, or at least people in white clothing, wheeling me down a hall. Although I tried to raise myself they shoved me back down. "Am I dead?" I tried to ask, over and over, but I wasn't sure the words were coming out.*

"*Lay down,*" *a man yelled at me.* "*Lay down.*" *They didn't seem to understand, I was still awake and there was red stuff all over my legs. Someone put something into my arm and it hurt.*

"*Lay down,*" *the man yelled again.* "*Lay down.*" *Yes, Dr. Lopez, I recognize him. They want me to lie down, but I feel awake and I feel afraid and there is something in his hand. A knife. I can feel it, cutting into me.*

...AND THEN I BUCKLED
MY SEAT BELT

"Please fasten your seat belt, ma'am," a voice said. I turned and saw a beautiful blond stewardess smiling at me.

"Oh, I'm sorry," I said, realizing I'd been off in a dream world. The past three months since my release from the hospital in Tijuana had become somewhat cloudy, now, and that was exactly as I preferred it. Up to now I had succeeded in blocking out my memory of the teriffic pain I'd felt when waking for the first time after surgery. There were still signs, however, of the toll the operation had taken on me—both physically and emotionally.

I'd discovered something about myself during my stay in the hospital—I had an extremely low tolerance to drugs. In the first few days after the operation I had become addicted to the pain killers they gave me. Until the sixth day, I hadn't realized they weren't helping, but instead, increasing my pain. When I mentioned this to the doctor, we guessed that I was hooked. On top of everything else, I had to go through withdrawal, something quite rare with such a short period of addiction.

In addition to problems with the drugs, I had a catheter going from my bladder, through my penis (left intact by the first operative procedure) into a plastic bag which collected the urine. The installation was meant to keep me immobile while the area was healing.

Because it was inserted improperly, however, I had a lot of unnecessary pain which it took a week to realize was out of the ordinary. Of course, there was the legitimate, expected pain of the operation, too.

My first look at the result of the operation was upsetting. For a couple of days I wasn't in any mood to look, although the doctor and his nurses had checked the area each morning. One quick look revealed a gory mass of stitches and blood which reminded me of something from a monster movie. Now, three months later, the original gash-like wound had taken its proper form. There seemed to be a formation of the outer lips of the vagina, the *labia majora*. Standing in front of a mirror at home I remember thinking that now I was even more a freak, with both a penis and a partially constructed vagina, than I had been *before* the operation.

Now I concerned myself with the problem of getting money for the second stage operation. Finding another benefactor was more difficult than I had expected. The doctor said I would be ready for the second stage ninety days after the first stage, but the fee, $3,500.00, would have to be paid first.

As the captain's voice came through the loud-speaker, I grabbed one of the airline publications tucked in the pocket of the seat in front of me to try to get my mind off what was behind me, in Los Angeles, and what lay ahead of me in San Antonio. Someone leaned over me a minute later.

"Would you like something from the bar?" the stewardess asked me. Although I wasn't much of a drinker, I felt it wouldn't hurt to relax myself a little before seeing my parents.

"Give me a double Bloody Mary," I said, smiling. Holding the magazine in my lap, I turned back to the vista below me. Going home hadn't been in my plans, because the simple problems of everyday living were complex enough. Meeting my parents as a female seemed just a fantasy, one of many I had had since the operation.

The problem with my roommate had been brewing all along, I guess. Ray, now Rachel, had become hostile to me, and I had decided to find another roommate. She was probably justified in her feelings toward me, for it seemed only natural that a person who had waited almost fifty years to make a decision as grave as a sex change, would feel some resentment for someone who had made it thirty years earlier. Also, she was still working her job as a male and coming home to dress as a female, even after the first surgery. I guess that would have driven anyone a little batty.

Josie, the only other transsexual I knew at the time, had become increasingly aware of my problem with Rachel and had offered me a place to stay with her in the San Fernando Valley until I got a new place.

She was still living with her former wife, who, realizing that her former husband had had his genitals partially cut off, had tried to commit suicide. As things became worse in La Puente, though, I decided it would be easier to deal with Josie's situation than with Rachel's hostility, even though I liked and admired her.

One other problem was with a girl—yes, a girl—who had fallen in love with me. Her name was Jill, and she had been a nun in the Catholic church. I had met Jill through my lawyer, at his office; I often spent a great deal of time there, not only for legal advice, but also to make contacts with the people my lawyer knew. The visit on which I had met Jill had been one of the most confusing.

"Send Canary in," came the voice through the squawk box. Usually I did not wait long, but today, a Monday, had been very busy. People lined both sides of the corridor-like waiting room, and some had begun to grumble. Charlie, unlike many attorneys, was very lax about his appointment schedule. He had everyone scheduled for the same time, then they would wander in late, or wait their turn. Although this would seem to eliminate many prospective clients, people simply waited. Indicative of the kind of attorney he was, was the fact that, of four cases up before the Supreme Court, he had won three!

"Hi, Canary," Charlie said, holding up a tape in one hand, and clutching the telephone to his ear with the other.

With a smile and a wave I took the tape from him and sat down in one of the plush, black leather chairs. I'd almost given up on it. This was a tape of a couple of my songs, made for a writer friend who was working on a movie script. He had taken them to MGM and that was the last I'd heard from him.

"Well, you've finally gotten your first chance," Charlie said, as he hung up the phone.

"What do you mean?" I asked anxiously.

"That was your friend Marv at MGM, and he says you're set to go into a session next week at their main studio and lay down a demo sound track for the movie. MGM is footing the bill."

"Wow!" There weren't any words to explain the tumble of feelings he had unleashed. This was my first time recording as a female, after nine months of practice, and I had finally reached the point where I could record as a girl without anyone knowing the true story.

"Now," Charlie continued, "the arranger is working his ass off to get the charts ready for the session. All you have to do is keep your little bird's voice in shape."

Despite an expertise in criminal law, Charlie made up for his lack of musical experience at that time with raw enthusiasm. He was new at playing manager for me.

"Tweet, tweet!" I said, giggling as he put his hand over his eyes and tossed his head back in disbelief.

"Oh, yes," he said, raising his hands to brush over the top of his head, "I almost forgot."

"Forgot what?" I asked hopefully.

"There's a girl who's interested in meeting you, a musician," he said, turning his wrist to look at his watch. "Okay, she should be done with the deposition by now. Let's go into the library, huh? What say?" I didn't know how to tell him gently that I was in no mood to meet anyone. Rachel had come home from work unexpectedly that morning complaining about the kind of pressure she was under, and had told me she didn't think she could continue in her job. One thing led to another and somehow we had gotten into an argument about a domestic problem. When I had gone flying out the door, I was in an old dress and wearing shoes that were scuffed and unpolished.

"Charlie, couldn't we wait? Some other time?" I pleaded with him. "I'm . . . well, I'm not dressed . . ."

"Don't be silly! She's dressed casually, too. Come on, Canary, no one cares how you're dressed."

That I could take issue with. Everyone who had met me at Charlie's office had been told about me, and up to that day I was always carefully dressed and made up, trying to give the impression of being "Superwoman."

"Oh, I've heard so much about you," the girl said, opening her eyes wide. That was the beginning.

We had plans for a simple luncheon date the next afternoon, something that sounded very innocent. But I couldn't shake the way she had looked at me with her liquid brown eyes, up and down, sort of awe-struck, and the way her hand had touched mine a bit more warmly than I was used to in normal woman-to-woman conversation. Her manner of dress, too, was unconventional, for she was wearing men's shoes, Levi jeans, and a man's Levi jacket; her hair was cut in a short, almost masculine haircut.

The next day at lunch she confessed to me.

"You know, Canary," she had said, "I'm not afraid to talk to you."

I glanced around the small Hollywood restaurant she had chosen for signs that someone had noticed her hand on my knee in a manner no one had used since I had begun dressing as a female.

"I feel I can talk to you, too," I said. She didn't seem to notice my discomfort.

"What I'm trying to say," she continued, rubbing my knee, "is that I'm attracted to you, I mean, more than just friends, you know?"

"Well, not exactly," I said, as her hand found its way up my leg a bit.

"What I'm trying to tell you is that I'd like to take you on a date."

I was flabbergasted! After the painful operation I had undergone just about a month before to be able to have a normal sexual relationship with a male, I was being asked out on my first date by a girl! For a while I just sat there, toying with my food. I hadn't really dated up to that time and everytime the chance had come up, I had declined politely, fearful that my secret would be discovered. And I was lonely since I had left Johanna. Sometimes I woke in the middle of the night to realize I had been talking to Johanna in a dream. In the worst times, I felt I would have to be alone the rest of my life.

I had needed time to think about Jill's offer, for although I had plans and dreams, I wanted to take stock of my situation. She didn't push me.

After a long time I broke the silence. "Sure," I had said finally, "I'll go out with you." Eagerly she had smiled at me, and we had made plans for the following Saturday evening. I had hinted clearly that my financial condition would not allow Dutch dating, or treating, but she had ignored me.

"I'll be at your house at seven thirty sharp!" she had called as she drove off in her Volkswagen. For the rest of the week I didn't see her or hear from her.

My upcoming recording session took up most of my time. I had written another song just the week before which I wanted to get into the session, so I spent hours singing and rewriting. Before I realized it, the week was up and she had arrived.

"Check the old watch," she said, pointing to her wrist as I climbed into the bug beside her. "How's that for timing?" I laughed in answer, as we roared toward the San Bernardino Freeway and, beyond that, Hollywood.

Stealing a glance at her, I noticed for the first time that she was beautiful. Her face was a pretty arrangement of features, lightly tanned, and her hair shone a jet black common to women of her Italian heritage. In the evening light I noticed how lovely she was and wondered why she hadn't worn something other than her Levis to accentuate that beauty. We had ridden without speaking, the radio up loud, until she pulled into a parking lot close to the intersection of Melrose and La Brea.

"Well, here we are," she said, and flashed me another one of those dazzling smiles. We left the car and as we began walking, she took my hand, which confused me. It was unusual for me to feel embarrassed to hold hands with a girl, but I had had no practice at holding hands with men. Regardless of my physical changes, I still had Danny's memories.

There was a small restaurant sign, barely visible

from the sidewalk, next to a door, which we headed for. "This restaurant has the greatest food in Los Angeles," Jill said, "and it's the gathering point for all the high-class gay people in Los Angeles." I looked up at the blue neon sign. "David's" it said.

My only other contact with the gay world, up to that time, had been a club I had joined after reading their ad in the *Free Press*. The T.A.O. advertised itself as "a transsexual action organization" but turned out to be a gathering place for a bunch of drag queens who were mostly interested in running pink flags up poles and picketing college campuses as well as having sex with anyone who walked by, male or female. It was a fiasco.

"Can we help you, girls?" a mild-mannered, somewhat affected man asked.

"Yes," Jill said, her voice a full octave below the one she had used in the car. "I have a reservation." When he had confirmed the reservations, the man escorted us to a little table through a crowd of what seemed to be sighing effeminate men. I hadn't been in such a crowd for a while and the paranoia was strong.

"Do I look all right?" I asked, turning to Jill. "I mean, do I look like . . . "

"Don't be silly," she said, putting her arm over my shoulder and confirming her part as male, or "butch," in the relationship. "You're the most realistic transsexual I've ever seen. If you weren't I wouldn't be taking you out, now would I?" It seemed dumb to have brought it up.

After a minute a thin, tall gay man greeted us. He was our waiter. He took our order in an exaggerated feminine fashion and I had to bite my lip to keep from laughing as he sashayed away.

"Have you noticed anything peculiar about this place?" Jill whispered in my ear, letting her lips touch my hair briefly.

"I've noticed a few things," I said cautiously, moving away from her, because I was a little uptight about our touching. "You've got an adding machine roll? I'll make you a list." She joined my laughter, then went on to point out we were the only two women in the entire place. Gay women, lesbians, normally didn't show up at the place until some hours later.

"Why?" I asked, wondering why she would take me there if she had known we would be the only girls. She smiled slyly.

"Well, I just wanted to have you all to myself, without another chick checking you out. And besides, by the time we're done with dinner, it'll be time to meander on over to the Bacchanal. You know, the place I told you about." She had mentioned it on our lunch date. It was one of the most popular girls' bars in town.

"Do they have a band there?" I asked, sipping my Black Russian. Jill had ordered it for me, as a guaranteed relaxer.

"Yes," she replied, acting as though she were getting turned on by my innocence. "And all the girls dance together, just like a normal club except . . . "

The waiter arrived with our steaks and I ordered another Black Russian, enunciating the words as clearly as I could through the haze of alcohol. I had begun to like Jill very much. Not only was she well-read and well-educated, but she also seemed masterfully understanding of my situation. She commented at one point, that there was a friend of hers, a really loaded one, who might back my second operation, but she hadn't mentioned it again.

"Will that be all, girls?" our waiter asked as he materialized with the check.

"Yes, that's fine," Jill said, putting her arm around my shoulder. She pulled out a credit card and signed for our dinner. The times I had been in her situation, playing the male to Johanna and to others, came back to me, and I remembered how much I had resented my role, the feeling of mandatory dominance, and suddenly I wondered why a person born a normal female would openly welcome such a role. It wasn't the only thing I was to wonder that night.

"May I see your I.D.'s please," a man asked as we entered the Bacchanal, or Bach, as I would come to call it.

After a momentary hesitation—I still had Danny's

Texas driver's license, since I had stalled about getting a new one as Canary—I pulled out the card and handed it to him. His eyes opened wide.

"This is a male's driver's license. This says Danny O'Connor," his voice squeaked. "What are you trying to pull?" It wasn't my first dubious response to my identification. It had happened before whenever I had tried to cash a check or open a bank account.

"It's hers," Jill cut in. "She's still a male, at least partially. She's just had her surgery."

"Well, well," he said, holding the flashlight up to my face, then shutting it off suddenly. "You're the prettiest one I've ever seen. Don't that beat all!"

We went over to the bar and Jill introduced me to Jimmy, the bartender. We gave him my purse and went off to find a table. The band was on break, but would be starting again in a few minutes. In the meantime, I had a lot of bizarre sights to get used to. One person, a giant, looked like a man except for the rather obvious bumps in her black motorcycle jacket. Her hair, black like Jill's, was cut in a more obviously masculine fashion, and her face was pocked. Her hands and feet, which were big, made her seem almost ape-like.

I nudged Jill, who was telling the waitress to bring us two beers. "Who's that?"

She finished talking to the waitress and turned to me, putting her hand on my shoulder. "Who's who?"

"That one, over there," I said, trying to point discreetly.

"That's Grady," she said, with a touch of irritation. "Why? You want her to come over and join us?"

"No," I hurried to soothe her, "I just noticed how much she looks like a man is all. No thanks!"

"Yeah," she said, appeased. "I guess she's about the most real-looking of all of us in here. She even shipped a big black guy out of here one night. He had bullied his way past Joe and refused to leave."

"Are you kidding?" I said. I'd never heard of such a thing.

"Oh, yeah, she's a mean mother, or maybe I should say daddy, just in case she's listening. She always manages to get into some kind of knock-down drag-out here at least once a weekend."

Laurie, our waitress, returned with the beers, and set the bottles in front of us. "Say, Jill," she said, as she took the money from my date. "Grady said to tell you she thinks your taste is improving."

"How's that?" Jill asked as she accepted her change.

"She said that your new lady here," a gesture with her chin towards me, "is a real fox and you'd better keep your eyes on her or . . ."

"Tell her to fuck off! And if she tries anything I'll kick her ass!"

I was shocked! I'd never heard girls talk to each other that way and I began to pretend in my newly acquired prim fashion, that I'd never heard that kind of language before.

"That bitch," Jill muttered as I turned to her when Laurie walked away. Possessively, she put her hand over mine. "Who does she think she is, anyway?"

"Jill!" I said, trying to sound shocked, and to forget the knowledge I had had of those words as a male.

"What?" she said, innocently. "Oh, my language, you mean."

"Yeah," I said, trying to maintain my new position. Then I copped out. "I don't give a fuck what you say, Jill." We both began to laugh and then talk about our mutual worries.

"I don't understand one thing, though," I said.

"What's that?" Jill asked, catching my serious tone, and removing her hand as though readying for an attack.

"Why you were so harsh on Grady, I mean, for paying both you and me a compliment."

"Oh—that bother you?" she said, returning her hand to its position over mine. "That's just dyke talk. It's the kind of language and mannerisms accepted between me and my friends."

"You mean Grady is your *friend*?"

"Sure, I'll prove it." Before I could protest, she had called Grady, standing at the bar, to us. As the lumbering woman approached us I marveled at her bulk. I'd never seen a woman so large.

"Hi, Jill!" the woman said, her voice a soprano, as she patted Jill on the back and pulled up a chair, sitting defiantly close to me.

"Did you get my message?" Grady said. "I mean, about your girl?"

"Canary," Jill said, "this is Grady. The meanest bastard in all of L.A."

"Oh," Grady responded, sliding her chair even closer, and putting an arm around my shoulder as she took my free hand and kissed it. "You're a sweet one, honey. How about leavin' old Jill and coming home with Grady, beautiful. I'll show you a time you never imagined in your fondest dreams!"

The band began to play and Jill took it as a signal to jerk me to my feet and toss a finger at the woman who had just propositioned me. "Come on, baby," she said, "before this horny bitch starts drooling on herself." With the band, the quiet bar had come to life. Dozens of couples, all female, crowded the floor around us. At first I tried to sneak peeks around and over my shoulder, but the pace was too fast to get a clear focus of any couple.

The evening went quickly, dancing and returning to the table occasionally to meet some of Jill's friends as they wandered in. Some were secretaries, and there were even mothers and members of the P.T.A. Some were dopers, hustlers, and some were just plain creeps.

In the small hours of the morning, we made our way back to my house at a slower pace, with the radio somewhat lower. We'd had too many dances and too many drinks. Jill reached over when she had stopped in front of my house and kissed me on the cheek.

"Thanks," she said, her gentle eyes watching me.

"For what? I should be the one thanking you but, you didn't give me . . ."

"No, don't. I'm the one to thank you—for gambling, you know? For coming with me tonight when you had no idea what was going on. Besides, I'd pay for a hundred dinners anyday just to have you sitting there beside me." She turned off the car motor and I let her kiss me. Her soft lips against mine confused me, but I was shocked too. They were like many other lips I had kissed, more times than I cared to remember. What a switch! It was hard to put it all together.

Every spare minute of the next week went to practice for my first recording session as a female. When the day of the session had finally arrived I performed with grace, I must say. Not only had I sung at least as well as I had as a male, but I had impressed a Las Vegas booking agent who'd just happened to pass through the studio.

"Listen, I can book you with a new singing group I've got playing at the main lounge at The Sahara. They need a strong girl singer, and I think your voice is just what they've been looking for." For a moment I almost said yes, but luckily I caught myself. If he found out about me he would change his mind.

"No," I said, reluctantly, "I have to stay here in Los Angeles to pursue my career."

For a while that was how it went. I would receive many offers but would make rejections quickly; or, if I decided to think about it, they found out about me from the many people in the recording community who were familiar with my story.

The sound engineer commended me on the smooth, professional quality of my voice once. He didn't realize at the time the impact on me of what he was saying. He hadn't suspected one thing about me. He had simply accepted me as a pro girl singer, with no questions, no funny looks, nothing—total, utter, unquestioning acceptance!

The night of the session I decided to meet Jill for a drink. She was excited to see me again and couldn't keep her hands off me.

"When do I get to hear the tape?"

"I won't have a final copy 'til tomorrow," I said, "but you just wait and see. You're going to be surprised." She had never had a chance to hear me sing. When we had talked about it, I had played down my talent so she would be more impressed—an old trick of mine.

"Hey," I said, changing the subject. "I think I'm

going to move to my girl friend's house in the Valley.
I'm still having trouble with Rachel, my roommate,
and . . . you know?"

"Well," her head bent away from me. "Would you
still like to get together—and go out, I mean?"

"Oh, of course. Sure. I had a blast the other night,
and the Valley is only a few minutes on the freeway
from Hollywood. We'll still be able to see a lot of each
other."

After she had left the bar I realized the impact of
my new relationship. I was now in a couple almost identical to the one my wife and I had been in, but I was
now playing the role my wife had played and Jill was
playing the part of Danny. She was trying to be something she wasn't, a male, and I was feeling the kind of
confusion Johanna must have felt.

Jill had discussed her feelings about being a female
with me. She disliked anything female in herself and
tried to wear masculine clothing and, in every other way
possible, to eliminate the word "female" in reference to
herself. It was ironic, for I could have even coached her
a little on the role she was trying to play.

It all seemed so phony to me. I couldn't fall in love
like that. I would have no future. And she hadn't been
honest with me about her past. I kept wanting to ask
her about her experiences in the convent as a nun, but
she never even gave me an inkling that Charlie had told
me the truth about her that day we met. But, that wasn't
something I thought Charlie would get confused.

The next few weeks were busy with the move and
settling into Josie and Sherrie's house. They had managed to stay calm for a couple of days and not fight.
Josie wavered back and forth, first playing a pseudo-
sister role, then taking the dominant husband role.

Josie was pretty tall, a couple of inches taller than
I, and her build was that of a heavy woman. She once
had had a tremendously muscle-bound figure, at first it
had been hard to pass as a female, but she had succeeded, even to the point of dating a couple of times.
Sherrie, on the other hand, was short, petite and soft-
looking. Her face was round and gentle, and she had
dark brown hair like her husband's.

Josie would say, "We're just like sisters," over and over each day, but when it came time to fix dinner or to do a household chore, the role would change.

"Sherrie," she would say, her voice dropping a register, "get in there and wash the dishes, damn it!" At first it was easier to ignore the role change, but after a while I noticed each change becoming more and more distinct, as though Josie were truly two separate people. Then I began to wonder about myself. Was that the way I really was? Could it be that I was that obvious about my changing personalities?

Then I remembered the psychiatric examination I was required to have before I could have my first surgery. At the same time, the welfare office had contacted me. It seemed their office required psychiatric testing, too, and it would have to be done before I could be put on the rolls. Fearing starvation, unable to find work, and glad of an opportunity to take care of two problems at the same time, I called the office the welfare people had recommended. Where Josie had been tested almost a month before me and was easily qualified for A.T.D.—Aid to the Totally Disabled—I did not have the same results.

When I went into the cold office building a few blocks from the welfare office on Beverly Boulevard I was petrified. The nurse showed me into an empty office and assured me I wouldn't have to wait very long for Dr. Daly. When the doctor arrived we exchanged amenities and then he put me through a very thorough word association test. The man seemed peculiarly fascinated with my appearance and my reaction to words concerning beauty. After an hour of this, he asked me to briefly tell my life story.

"I feel I've got to be honest with you," the doctor said about halfway through my story. "I don't feel you're the least bit incapable of handling your circumstances either emotionally or mentally." Instead of saying anything, I cocked my head and stared at him. "Now don't act dumb," he said, his voice rising with anger. "I know and you know that you're as sane and as intelligent as I am. For that reason I'm going to recommend that you not be put on the A.T.D. program."

Although I was angry at first, now I could see why the doctor would recommend Josie for the program and not me. She was in a dangerous position, mentally and emotionally.

Jill, in the meantime, had been coming over regularly on Saturday evenings and on and off during the weekdays. After a couple more dates, I decided that being a lesbian was not what I wanted and that I would have to try some other way to find friends. It wasn't easy to tell Jill, for I am not the sort to strike down a friendship quickly.

"I'm going to watch my program, Sherrie, and if you try to turn the channel I'll knock the hell out of you!" Josie would scream at her cowering "wife." Josie rarely left the house, letting Sherrie support her and provide for her needs and desires; she spent her days smoking cigarettes and watching television, her two favorite pastimes.

"I'm going to kill you!" Josie was screaming in the other end of their two room apartment. "I'm going to pay you back." I jumped up from the couch and ran into the small bedroom where fists were flying.

"You'll never get the operation finished—I won't let you!" Sherrie was screaming, as she pulled out chunks of Josie's hair.

"You'll pay for that, you'll pay for that!" Josie yelled. I moved in to break up the quarrel, something I've since learned is a pretty dumb thing to do in a fight between husband and wife, even if the husband is a girl. Before I could get between them, Josie planted her foot in Sherrie's stomach and sent her to the floor with her hands to her abdomen, screaming. Josie, realizing what she had done, began screaming. I stood there confused.

Josie ran out of the room and I took off after her. The bathroom door slammed.

"Josie, come out." My voice broke in two tones. "I know what you're trying to do, but just come out and we'll talk about it."

"I won't! I won't! I'm going to slash my wrists! I don't want to live any longer—it's all for nothing! I've killed the one I love most!" By this time Sherrie had recovered miraculously and stood by me.

"What's she doing in there?" Sherrie asked, her eyes widening. "Josie, this is Sherrie. I'm okay. Come out." They screamed at each other through the door and I began to figure out how to open the door.

The first problem was that the door was put on backwards, opening out instead of in, and the hinges were embedded in the wall. There was no way I could get them separated, even with a hammer and screwdriver. For a moment I considered calling the police, but, imagining their response to the situation, I discarded that idea.

"Canary, you've got to do something!" Sherrie screamed at me. "Please, you've got to do something." Oh, so Josie's wife of over seven years was demanding that *I* save the day? I was getting angry over the whole situation. I would save the day, all right.

Now, sitting here twirling an empty glass, I was aware that what I would be facing in Texas was going to be as complex and demanding as what I had left in Los Angeles. My parents, again, for the first time in over two and a half years—and I was wearing a dress. I caught the stewardess as she went by.

"May I have another?" I asked.

Reaching down I pulled my sandal off and pushed Sherrie out of the way. It was one of those moments I find difficult to describe accurately. All I really remembered is placing my foot against the panel which had been used to construct the door and giving it a swift kick.

Josie screamed. Sherrie screamed. And I began to cry. My foot had disappeared into the door, sending parts of the middle section of the door into the bathroom. Other than the stream of tears, I was unaffected, so I pulled my foot back through and reached inside the newly made hole to unlock the door.

"Hello, Mom?" I said. I'd decided to call her that evening from a pay phone. The operation, the hostility with Ray/Rachel, Josie and Sherrie, and this new situation with Jill had taken their toll.

"Yes, hi, baby," my mother said lightly.

"I'm afraid I'm about to go under and I don't think I can hang on much longer." We talked for a while and my Dad went to the neighbors to use their phone and call my grandparents to borrow money for my plane ticket.

"Okay," Mom said finally, "everything's set. Now, you be a big girl and hold on until tomorrow, when you come home."

HI, DAD! I GUESS
I'VE CHANGED...HUH!

"Ladies and gentlemen," the voice said over the loudspeaker, "we are now approaching San Antonio Airport. Please fasten your seat belts and observe the 'no smoking' signs until we have touched down."

This was it. There was no turning back now. Quickly I pulled my makeup case out of my purse and did a quick touch-up. Then I began tugging at my pantyhose, trying not to be too conspicuous, since they had worked themselves uncomfortably low. The crotch had sunk to a point about even with the hemline of my dress. The window showed me a view of the city I had grown up in as a boy. I wondered how she would receive me, now that I was no longer her native *son*. As the plane descended, I slapped some perfume on and built up my sagging lashes with more mascara.

"Wooo!" I said aloud, feeling the sudden rush of the two Bloody Marys. Realizing what I'd just done, I looked around me, then suddenly out the window, until I felt it was safe to resume my primping.

A bump dissolved all my built-up courage. The people all around me got up, reaching for their bags and lined up in the aisle for the front exit. Standing up, I gave my pantyhose one last subtle tug, guarded by the seat, and stepped into the aisle. When I said good-bye to the stewardess and turned to the open doorway and the stairs I again felt a mean jolt from the alcohol. With my head down, I walked down the stairs and towards the terminal. I was afraid to look up until I heard my sister Janet's voice.

"Canary, Canary! We're over here! Canary!" My parents and my sisters were waving frantically for my attention. For a moment, I ignored them and tried to figure out what I'd say when I first greeted them. After a minute, I decided to show some recognition, so I raised my hand and waved. I wanted to shout, but I was afraid that my voice wouldn't sound right. Good old paranoia came skulking back.

"Hello, baby," my Dad said, giving me a self-conscious hug.

I was then passed to my mother, then to Dee, then to Janet with the same reaction. I wanted to cry, then to laugh, then to cry again. Standing back for a minute, I tried to get my eyes to focus. The alcohol or the Texas sun was blurring them. I kept opening and closing my eyes; Mom said later I looked like I was in shock.

As we made our way down the airport terminal toward the luggage claim, my dad kept repeating how pretty he thought I was. "This is my daughter, she's pretty, she's not a 'he' at all. She's pretty!"

"Hush!" Mom had said, putting her hand over his mouth. "As far as anyone is going to know, Canary has always been our daughter." Janet came up to me and commented how much she and I looked like sisters. We walked side by side, comparing notes. As we were passing one of the ticket lines, a herd of soldiers saw us and started a series of wolf whistles and catcalls. It was really rather cute. After all, Mom and Dad were with us. I remember turning to Dad to seek his approval but he was blank-faced and, I'm sure, totally confused.

"Does that happen often?" my mother asked as Dad went for my baggage.

"Just once in a while," I said, trying to act overly humble about my appearance. I took the guitar case from Dad.

"Let me take that for ya, beautiful," a tall, dark air force lieutenant said, grabbing the case from me. My parents were open-mouthed.

"How long you going to be here?" he asked, his brown eyes flashing lust, but gentleness too.

"I don't believe I know your name," I said, turning

to him as we walked through the exit to the passenger loading area.

"Bill Waters," he said. "And I almost feel as if I know you."

"Why's that?" I asked, looking at him in wonderment.

"I watched you on the plane. I was right across the aisle from you."

"Oh?" I said, wishing I could remember. "Well, how about that!"

"Do you know this young man?" my father broke in, stepping toward us protectively.

"Ah, no sir," the man answered before I could say anything. "That is,—well—she—well, we were on the same plane together, sir, and . . . well, my name's Bill Waters."

The man stuck his hand out and shook hands with my father. It was fascinating; the pickup couldn't have happened at a more opportune time, since those first few minutes with my family were vital. My sister was looking at me in a way she had never done before. I detected a hint of jealousy in her eyes, although she had no reason to be. She was one of the most popular girls in her high school class. Grabbing her hand, I pulled her forward in an almost brotherly fashion.

"This is my sister Janet," I said to the handsome stranger, who turned away from shaking hands with my mother.

"Hello, Janet," the man said. Janet was almost swooning. My diversion didn't work, though. Bill's eyes came back to me, then to my father.

"Sir," the lieutenant said, "with your, and your wife's, permission I'd like to come calling on your daughter."

Dad's face went pale, almost to a snowy white, and Mom now looked as though she were in shock. "Well . . . Ah . . . I think so," Dad said, recovering, and turning to my mother for agreement. "You know I was once in the service myself. Sure, it's fine with us. That is, it's up to Canary." I watched my father set down my bags and cross to the parked cars. Mom, Janet, Dee and I waited at the curb.

"So, that's your name, Canary. I just knew you would have a beautiful name, and it's so different."

"That's not even the half of it," I said impulsively, and we all laughed. I could see Bill didn't understand the joke, but he didn't want to be left out. As the laughter subsided he pulled out a well worn black book and a pencil, and asked for my number.

"Canary, what are you doing tomorrow evening?" he said, his drawl stretching each word. "I mean . . . that is, would you like to go out with me?" I almost said no, for the man had an uncanny confidence about him, but I decided to give it a try, almost as thanks for the unwitting impression he had helped create. Neither he nor my family had to know it was my first date with a man.

"Sure, I'd love to," I said, flashing my eyes at him in a smile heretofore practiced only on male cashiers and gas station attendants. Dad pulled up in our green Ford, the one he had brought me to the airport in over two years before to compete as a male in the Capitol contest. Bill and I talked for a minute while Dad put the luggage in the trunk, then the men opened the doors for us ladies.

"Seven be alright?" Bill asked as we were pulling away.

"That's fine," I said, waving back to him.

There was a shocked silence in the car. Understand, my father had just witnessed his son come home as a pretty girl, and not ten minutes after her arrival, be propositioned by a serviceman, the kind of man he always had a lot of respect for, the kind of man he had wanted *me* to become. My mother had greeted her son from Los Angeles, who was now a woman that looked very much like she had when she was younger. Although my hair was blond, my facial features were closer to hers than were Janet's or Dee Dee's. My sisters must have been the most shocked. Janet had been so proud of her brother, looking up to him through countless failures. When I had won the singing contest and come back a pseudo-star her love and admiration had changed to hero worship. I wondered what she was thinking of me now.

"Danny," she was saying, "—oh, I'm sorry—
Canary, you're beautiful! I never thought you'd turn
out like this. I'd imagined something different." Mom
turned around in her seat.

"Honey," she said, grabbing my hand, "you're
more of a daughter than I expected and now it's hard to
believe you were anything but a girl."

"Well, she sure as hell didn't take long to start running them boys, did she?" Dad said, and the car roared
with laughter.

As we made our way home, each talked about
their first response to me. Dad kept talking about my
voice and how feminine it sounded. "But you sound just
like a girl," he'd say, "I don't understand how you do it.
I mean, you don't talk like you used to talk at all. You
don't even have a Southern accent anymore. You sound
like some damn Yankee."

"What do you mean, I sound like a 'damn Yankee'," I asked, leaning forward and biting him on the
shoulder, a teasing act which seemed quite natural. I
realized later that that was the first time I'd ever
touched my father in such a warm way.

As I sat back, we all were quiet for a minute with
surprise at my emotional outburst.

At home, we spent most of our first day in the
living room, talking about the phenomenal changes I
had been through. For the first time I realized what an
effect my sex change had on my world. Before, I hadn't
thought about individual responses to my change, but
there were obvious differences.

"Oh, Vincent and his wife said they weren't that
surprised about the whole thing; they always suspected
something about you," Dad spoke up.

"You know, son—I'm sorry—Canary, there were
many comments made about you in one way or another
throughout the years that I chose to ignore. I guess it
was safer, easier to accept that way. If I had taken them
all seriously I would have begun to think those things
about you myself. As it is though, everything worked
out anyway, huh?"

They would continue to make mistakes, that is,
"title errors" as I called them, for the first couple of

days. It was only natural, for I had lived with these people almost eighteen years as a male. Although my physical appearance had changed, there was something very
important I was learning. It's the intellectual and emotional self most people communicate to and from. If it
weren't for the change, I guess I'd never have had the
opportunity to discover that. There was also something
else of grave importance I was starting to realize.

When my parents spoke of me as Danny, it was in
the past. I began to wonder what it would be like to be
him again, walking through the house with my hands in
my pockets, trying to play the big man. I wondered
what it would be like to be called "sir" on the telephone
again, or "Mr." instead of "Miss." I began to think, as I
looked about this house I'd grown up in, that this was
the house I had died in. It was as though I had died and
come back to pick up the pieces, like in a movie. My
parents continued to reflect on what had been, who
used to be, what was no more.

This first day home was my first chance to relate
to my family as I'd always wanted to. When Mom took
me on a tour of the house to point out changes, it all
seemed different. Danny's room, the room I had spent
so many aeons in, seemed empty of sorrow, and as she
explained the moves she had made with the furniture, I
simply shrugged and said it was pretty. That night, after
Janet had fallen asleep, I crept down the little hallway
to my old room.

At first, I was frightened as I stood there. I began
to feel guilt for taking away the life of one so dear to
the people I was staying with. Then, I realized that if I
had killed him, myself, or at least what used to be me, I
still had all his memories buzzing through my head. It
confused me. How could I say I'd killed myself and
then stay around to see the consequences? This was
something I was going to have to come to grips with.
Memories were flooding in on me. It was in that small
room that I had begun playing guitar. Coming home
from my first lesson, I had been discouraged and annoyed by the instructor's attitude. I had spent what
seemed to be a lifetime in that room, practicing that
first guitar and learning, learning more every day. I had

written my first song there, "Spit Twice and Curse the
Ground I Walk On." I remember spending hours just
laughing at the lyrics. The song that had won me the
contest was conceived and written on that bed. And,
thinking of the bed, I remembered Johanna.

How I longed for her company that evening. It had
been over two years since we had spent the night in that
room, together. We had lain in the bed and made love,
had shared our growing love. I wondered where she was
that evening. I wondered if she thought of me as often
as I did of her. Pain I had thought long since taken care
of, came back. For a minute I held my breath. I thought
I heard her voice calling to me, whispering her love for
Danny, the Danny I had killed. A fear of the dark was
taking over me. It was time to return to my sisters'
room.

"Wake up, girl," Dad said, bending down to kiss
me on my cheek, a gesture I took as another sign of his
growing acceptance. "Come on now, time for breakfast,
and guess what it is!"

"Bacon, eggs, and hash browns," I said. "And I
didn't even have to guess."

As I jumped out of bed the nightgown fell down
over my nude legs. Dad looked kind of funny, but he
didn't say anything. I knew he was surprised at seeing
me, once his son, in such a thing and I remembered that
night long ago when someone had discovered me sleeping in a nightgown. My hair dropped around my shoulders, almost to the middle of my back. Grabbing my
father, I hugged him.

"Good morning, Daddy," I said, softly at first,
then again, more positively. "Good morning, Daddy." I
knew Janet was watching.

"Good morning, honey," he said, trying to catch
his breath.

Then I went into the kitchen, where my mother
was already busy setting the table. "How'd you sleep?"
she asked, turning her eyes to me long enough to see the
dark circles under my eyes. I thought of telling her of
the countless memories which haunted me.

"Fine," I said, smiling at her. "I haven't slept that
soundly in a long time." After breakfast, when Dad had

gone off to work, I started feeling like I was on trial again. Now I thought no more of wearing women's clothes than I ever had about donning a T-shirt and jockey shorts. It must have been a strain on my family though, and Mom spoke up after a while.

"Let's go shopping today and get you some new clothes," she said, over our second cup of coffee. "We'll take Janet's car."

"Doesn't Janet need her car to go to work?"

"You guys can take me, besides, you do need some new clothes. I was looking at the stuff we unpacked, and, well . . ." She was right. Because I'd been so broke, many times I'd purchased things that didn't always fit or some things of poor quality.

"Okay," I said, trying not to seem too excited at the prospect of my first shopping trip with my mother, as a female.

When we dropped Janet off, Mom turned to me. "Where would you like to go, Canary?" For a moment I wasn't sure. There were a vast number of shopping centers readily accessible, all of which I had visited as a male.

"How about North Star Mall?" I said, feeling my stomach churn with the excitement.

"Now, you sure? I mean, aren't you afraid of seeing people you know there, after all . . ." I knew what she meant. I'd spent a year employed at the grocery store there, and this would be a sort of test of myself and my appearance. If no one noticed, or recognized me, what more proof could I ask?

"I'm sure," I said. "I've been dreaming about this return visit for some time." Watching with fascination, I greeted each once-familiar sight silently, and almost jumped with excitement when I saw the mall.

"Look, look, Mom." I pointed to a roly-poly black-haired man who walked around our car into the parking lot. "Don't you recognize him, Mom? That's Nick, the creep!" Mom simply nodded. She must have been very aware of the likelihood of a scene if someone recognized me as a former male, someone they had once known, dressed as a female. But I was very confident, and this was a dreamland, a fantastic journey no one knew about but me.

The sun was hot and blinding. I suggested we go into the grocery store I had once worked in, but Mom was almost too nervous to agree. As I took her on a tour of the store and passed this one and that one I used to know, none of them giving me a second look, she began to relax. Nick passed us as we were walking out and never batted an eye.

"Can you believe it?" I said, turning to my mother and clenching my fists in excitement. "Can you believe what's happening? Isn't it fantastic . . ." Mom gave me a faint, ironic smile. Nick had hated me, picked on me the entire year I worked in the grocery store.

"He didn't even look our way," she giggled. "I told you, you look like another person!" We walked down the shaded walkway and passed a barber shop where I'd once had a haircut. The barber was still working there. I wanted to wave as I went past.

"What do you think, Mom?" I asked, grabbing a handful of hair and tossing it over my shoulder.

"I don't understand," she said.

"You know," I said, trying to fight back the laughter, "do you think I need a haircut?" We encountered people I had once known as Danny all along the mall. There were two girls I'd known all through high school coming out of a shoe store. Another girl, one I had dated, passed right in front of me. A couple of guys I'd played football with didn't even recognize me. The best encounter was one that almost happened in a small restaurant. It was a French-style restaurant situated in the middle of one side of the mall, and I had chosen it for the view of people who passed.

"I'll have a ham on rye," I said, smiling at the brunette waitress. She had gone with one of my high school buddies. Then I froze. I didn't want to seem too obvious, but I wanted to let my mother in on what was happening.

"Mom," I said, leaning over to one corner of the table between us. "Mom, look, but don't make yourself obvious." She turned her head just long enough to catch

a look at the girl who had just entered and sat down. It
was Penny Price, a beautiful green-eyed brunette who
had once had a crush on Danny. Off and on, we had
dated for a year, and she had been over at our house
many times. At first, I wanted to walk up and introduce
myself as Danny's cousin, but after a moment of consideration I decided that would be pushing my luck a little
too far.

"Would you like to leave, Canary?" Mom asked
softly, reaching up to push a piece of my hair back from
my forehead.

"Are you kidding?" I said, smiling back at her. "I
wouldn't miss this experience for anything in the world.
Besides, it's good for my ego." Other than Johanna,
Penny had been the only other girl I'd become mildly
intimate with. She sat not ten feet from me, and didn't
notice. Again, I toyed with the idea of going up to her,
introducing myself as Danny's stepsister, but it would be
too much.

When we were served Mom and I had a general
gossipy sort of conversation. I began to hope, even
though I'm sure my mother felt just the opposite, that
Penny would come over and say hello to Mom, but it
never happened. When we got up to pay our bill, she
never even glanced at us. We spent the afternoon traips-
ing in and out of dress shops. It finally got to the point
where I decided I'd scream if I had to try on another
piece of clothing.

"What time was that nice young man going to call
you?" Mom asked as we climbed in the car.

"What young man?"

"Didn't you make a date with that lieutenant
what's-his-name?" She looked confused. "At the airport."

"Bill Waters. I'd forgotten."

He called at about ten minutes to seven. I was in
the bedroom tugging a dress down over my hips when
the phone rang. Everyone else had gone into the front
room to watch TV and wait for me to model my new
clothes.

"Canary," Dad called, "it's for you." The new

dress gave me confidence. It was a red and white print, dotted, and I had a new pair of suede boots.

"I'll be right there, Dad. I'm coming." After a final struggle with the zipper, I ran to the hall extension.

"Hello," I said, in my sexiest, most seductive feminine voice.

"Well . . . hello. Guess who this is."

"Is he tall? Does he wear uniforms at airports? Is he in the air force?"

"Yup, that's me. Now I'll bet you don't even remember my name, but I do yours."

"You wrote it down!" I said petulantly. Of course I remembered his name, but I didn't want to let him know he'd made any kind of impression on me. As we talked, I felt an ironic sense of understanding. I was able to sense this man's male drive, his lines, and his intonations.

"Yes," I said, "I'd love to go out tonight. No, silly, I don't need three hours to get dressed. Why don't we make it at eight? Okay. Fine. Now, here's the address. Write it down."

My role as female in the relationship fascinated me. This man would come when I was ready for him to pick me up, he would ask me where I wanted to go, and he would thank me for it! I rushed to the front room to tell my family.

"Well," Dad said, his face flushed and smiling, "don't just keep us waiting. How about it, are you going out or not?"

"Yes. I'm expecting him at eight o'clock." Their faces lit up, then Janet's crumpled.

"Eight o'clock! That's when Tom's supposed to get here!" Tom was one of her many high school sweethearts. He was one of the guys I'd stood in front of to "scope out" for my little sister. It had only been about three years since I had done that for Tom. Now he was my sister's unofficial fiancé. I wondered if he would slip and use an incorrect pronoun or something, maybe accidentally call me Danny.

"Janet, can't you call him and have him come a little later?"

She nodded and ran to the telephone in the hall to try to reach him. I hurried back into the bedroom to get ready. A minute after eight the doorbell rang. Janet had just come in the room to apologize for her failure to locate Tom.

"It's okay," I had said, hugging her. "It's just that I didn't want him and the rest of you to be uncomfortable, that's all." We heard Tom's voice and Janet ran to the front door.

"Tom, where have you been?" she said. "I've called all over town to try to find you. Canary's got a date tonight and he should be here . . ."

"Yeah, that must be the guy who pulled up here right after I did. See, he's there, crossing the lawn." I stood in the hall with my heart jumping and my stomach turning with excitement and with fear. This was like a scene from a play. In the other room, the supporting cast waited.

Mom was the mother of a son *and* a daughter as well as part-time confidante to the protagonist. She had seen her son grow up, begin dating girls, fall in love, become an overnight success in show business, marry of necessity, father a child, and finally, choose to be a girl and turn into one!

My father, who often served as the antagonist in the boy's years growing up, had indeed witnessed a dramatic transformation—that of a son into a daughter. He'd seen a boy not quite like other little boys, grow up among constant threats of trouble in school, a boy who made him proud when he got to dating girls and even, at times, brought those girls home to show off for his Dad. A boy who somehow won some crazy singing show and wouldn't get into anything solid or reliable, something with a future, something his father could be proud of him for. His son had knocked up a girl and had to marry, but that was okay. After all, his son gave him his first grandchild. And then Dad had to watch his son, dead, come back to him as a girl.

Janet was the sister of a boy whom she had worshiped. He was a brother who always had a lot of neat guys around, friends who would tease her and include her in their pranks. He was a helpful brother who would often talk to her for hours on end about the solution to her problems. Her brother had somehow faded into the maze of stardom, marriage, and fatherhood—none of which she could really understand. Then her brother wrote a letter to her telling of his intentions to become her *sister*, and take away the brother she loved.

"Canary," Dad yelled. "Lieutenant Waters is here."

He was just the kind of guy I needed for my first date. We had dinner at a beautiful Mexican restaurant and I disguised the shaking of my hands as best I could and drank a couple of Margaritas to loosen up. His eyes sparkled as he told a corny serviceman's joke and somehow, I laughed. He'd been pretty curious when everyone had given him an intensive once-over, but Super-Lieutenant Bill Waters, as he often referred to himself, was a gas. Nothing seemed to bother him for long that evening.

"Do you want to dance?" he asked, placing a hand over mine. I remembered Jill. That brought me out of my worries about my appearance.

"Sure," I said, not realizing what I'd let myself in for. I'd never danced as a girl with a *man* before. Although I'd turned "American Band Stand" on at home and danced alone in front of the television, this was something different. I started to tell him my food hadn't settled yet, then the band started and we were surrounded by swirling bodies. Trying to imitate the girls around me, I danced, and peeked once at my date. He was smiling in my direction. As we made our way back to our table after the dance, I fought to catch my breath and feared to speak because I was sure my voice would distort to a lower tone.

"Hey, you dance really groovy," Bill said as we sat down. He covered my hand with his again. His eyes, looking straight into mine when I looked up, made me tingle, a new feeling. "You know, you're beautiful, Canary. I mean really beautiful. If we hadn't been on that airplane together, I'd never have met you and we wouldn't be here now."

"Thank you," I said, smiling with relief and flashing my eyes at him. How had I pulled the dancing off? "I haven't danced . . . well, it's been a while."

"What's wrong?" he asked abruptly, frowning.

"Why, what do you mean?" I waited for the worst.

"I don't know. I can't really put my finger on it, but there seems to be something upsetting you." He rubbed the back of his hand against my cheek. "Can't you tell me about it? Maybe it would do some good."

"Oh, I'm sorry, I'm still a little tired from the trip. You know how it is."

"You're a living doll," he muttered, leaning over to kiss my cheek, then my lips. I was in shock. This was my first real kiss! Somehow I was expecting bells to ring and angels to come rushing down from heaven. That's how my fantasies had gone. But mostly, I was relieved I didn't have a problem with facial hair, a problem many transsexuals had. What little I had had was gone now, via electrolysis: a painful process that involved putting a needle inside each hair follicle and burning the root.

The band struck up a super rock number and the young lieutenant grabbed my hand and pulled me to the middle of the dance floor. When I'd almost gotten my act down, I saw someone, and nearly went into shock again. I couldn't be sure, at first. All I saw was a black beard on a tall man, but as the man swirled around I lost all doubt. It was Bruce Hathaway, a very well-known local disc jockey, host of a local teen dance show. Just a couple of years ago I had starred on his program for two weeks in a row to promote my new record. I'd even signed autographs. Now I was dancing less than two feet away and he didn't even blink an eye. My partner moved close.

"Isn't that Bruce Hathaway?" he asked, motioning to the man.

"Yes," I said, realizing the situation I was in. The person who had once introduced me as San Antonio's own, the man who'd gotten me a big write-up in the local paper, that man was walking with his date to a table in the corner of the room. We left the club not long after that at my suggestion.

"Where to now?" Bill asked as he opened the door of his rented car. It was a little after twelve.

"How about if we just ride around for a while?"

"Okay, where do you want to go? Any good parking spots around here? I mean, with a good view?"

"Well, that wasn't what I had in mind," I said. His face fell.

"Then, what?" I pointed to a road and said I wanted to swing by my old school, just up that road.

For about an hour we drove around the high school, talking about ourselves. I had to be careful, for one slip, one reference to myself as a cool guy, or a stud, and my cover was blown. Somehow I felt calm though, and I didn't make slips, even when I was lying about my entire past.

"I was a cheerleader for two years."

"I thought so. I had a feeling you were a special kind of girl, and of course, you wanting to come by the school kind of gave you away." I laughed and tried to think things a former cheerleader would think. What would this poor man think if he knew the truth? What would I do if he tried to rape me—me with male and female organs? It went well, though.

"I'll be leaving tomorrow," he said, sliding across the seat after he parked the car in front of my house. I could feel the weight of his body as his arms went over my shoulders and pulled me forward.

"You're really beautiful," he whispered, placing his lips over mine and his tongue between my teeth. At first I lay back, hoping his arms would stay right where they were. As his tongue began to probe I felt those tingly feelings again, and I began to feel submissive. I began to want him, but at the same time, fear him.

"I think I'd better go in," I said, hoping I wouldn't hurt his feelings. As I walked into the door, I began to feel very depressed. I'd wanted to go all the way, something I'm sure most twenty-one-year-old girls wanted, and I couldn't. It wasn't fair. His kiss was so different from those I'd shared with Johanna, with other girls. He had a musty taste, a sour, masculine taste, but it was a kiss that excited me more than I could ever remember feeling. There was going to be a lot of anxiety in me if I planned to date before the second operation. Walking across the front room, I shut off the one lamp and felt my way to the empty bed where I would pass a second sleepless night.

Dad came in early, full of questions.

"Well, let's hear it. What happened? How was your date last night?" He hounded me until I told him, and my mother and sister had gathered around to hear. My account of the night before was bringing back the excitement I'd slept away.

"And then . . ." I broke off just as I had come to the conclusion of my date.

"Go ahead," Janet said, almost screaming. "Come on. What happened? You know—did he—I mean— well, did he kiss you?"

I looked at my family, Mom showing confused anticipation, Dad, unwilling to hear, but patient, and curious enough, and my sister, an incurable romanticist, bouncing on the bed in her excitement.

"And then he kissed me," I said, feeling a flush cross my face.

It was a strange moment. I was standing before my family, a group of people who had seen me become a husband, a father just two years before, and I was telling them of my experiences as a woman. Instead of feeling uneasy, embarrassed or even ashamed of myself, I was happy, and I was starting to feel contentment.

There was still a long way to go, I knew that. This trip home, the time with my family was a time to regroup my forces. I had to prepare myself for the task of earning and saving money for my second operation. My parents had helped me so much in that short time, but I couldn't stay there, because I couldn't develop as I needed to in a place with so many old memories. Whatever might come, I had found new strength to try my luck in Los Angeles again.

JOBS, JOBS, JOBS

"I'm afraid your work experience isn't quite what we're looking for, ma'am, I'm sorry." That was it. As I walked out of the employment agency, I swore I was never going to tell the truth on another application as long as I lived.

A month ago, I'd returned from my parents' house. I remember feeling that no one and nothing in the world could hold me down that evening, as I got off the Greyhound bus in Hollywood. Oh, it had been hard, leaving my parents just when I'd gotten used to having a family again, but the overwhelming burden caused by not having the change completed, and the thought that my only skill, in music, would go down the drain drove me back.

The first few nights back in town I spent at the "Studio Club," also known as the Hollywood YWCA. It was a gas for the first couple of days. I caught glimpses of what it would be like to have been a girl in boarding school. The woman in charge treated me like a virgin, and went to the extreme of having me write down where I was going and the time of my return every time I left the building. Little did she know!

It was fun, that first time I spent in exclusively female facilities, and I have to say, a little astonishing.

For one thing, there were no private bathrooms, but rather a series of four giant rooms along the hallways, all with cold brick floors and two toilets, two sinks, and one shower stall. Because the doors to the stalls were taken off, probably to reduce lesbian activity, I preferred to sponge bathe.

After those first couple of days I found an apartment building about a block away. It wasn't what I'd hoped for, but the place could be paid for weekly, and that was a lucky break for me. I was down to thirty dollars of the money my parents had given me in an envelope with instructions not to open it until the bus started out. What they'd given me and what I had saved had amounted to only a little over eighty dollars to start with, so I wasn't in much of a bargaining position.

The day I paid my first week's rent, I moved my three suitcases and my guitar into the new place, counted the three dollars my new landlady had given me in change, and went out looking for a job. I'd been doing a lot of job-hunting for five days, and no luck. Today, though, I spotted a "help wanted" sign in a dry cleaner's a block from where I was living.

"Sure," the little man said, smiling, "I'll put you to work today."

The job paid about sixty dollars a week clear and everything was fine until the man who had hired me, the manager, was fired. It just wasn't the same. The new man wasn't interested in helping me at all, and my normal sentimental attitude asserted itself. I walked off the job two days later, and, although the rent was paid for another week, I was left with about as much money as I'd walked in with.

I had to make some drastic moves. Before that day, I'd never had the courage to lie on an application or to a prospective employer, but it was time to learn. Walking down Hollywood Boulevard, I paused a moment in front of a bookstore. It was time to figure out what I wanted to be. There was a book in one corner of the store window, *The Secretary's Handbook,* and it started me on a plan of action.

"That's what I'll be," I said, as I began walking again. Typing wasn't a good point of mine, but I'd had a half a semester of it in the seventh grade and I knew if I had to, I could come across.

Not long after that, I was off on my first job interview as a prospective secretary. Stopping at the first nice-looking employment agency, I'd followed through with my plan. Necessity and fear have always been my strongest motivators, and that day I was over-endowed with both.

"You've written here," a short, gray-haired lady said, "that you've only had one previous job."

"Yes," I answered, realizing it had been ingenious to put down Charlie's law firm, since he would back me up in anything I said. "Yes, I was with the firm three years, ever since I got out of high school." I knew as I walked out of the office building I'd cinched it.

"Yes," the man at the employment office said, "she called not more than ten minutes ago. And yes, my dear, you have the job."

The job itself would have been easy enough, but I'd lost my car to the sheriff's office when I left it parked around the corner from Josie's house. It had been towed away. To get to the job at eight sharp, I had to take two buses, the first leaving at 6:30 A.M. To this day I haven't figured out whether the freeway traffic or the Southern California "rapid" transit system is more tiring. My back had become a problem while enjoying 130 degree heat in the dry cleaner's during the month of July. My doctor told me the combination of hard bus benches, lack of sleep, improper diet, a flagrant kidney infection and body shock from the operation, five months past, combined to produce extreme pain and partial paralysis.

Despite my physical problems, the first few weeks I spent as a secretary were really enlightening. I also learned a great deal about myself and how others would relate to me when they didn't know my secret. My job was a combination switchboard operator, receptionist, and private secretary for anyone who needed my services. I'd settled in right away and made friends with everyone. It was a good boost for my ego to act as receptionist and switchboard operator for such a big insurance company. After all, if they had known, or even suspected, anything odd about me—especially that I had once been a male—they never would have hired me, much less put me in a position to greet all their customers.

Breaks and lunch in the lounge were great fun and very educational. The room was always full of gossiping females at those times, and I really joined in with gusto. Making friends was one thing, but becoming close friends was something else. I had to be careful about whom I socialized with off the job. I knew I was different, and if I became too personal with anyone I knew at work I might slip and tell my story. That would be job number two down the drain.

After about a month, however, I'd made friends with three of my co-workers, and set up a little social schedule, meeting this one at first break, that one at lunch. We even had a standing Friday afternoon date to go out at lunch, a treat because most of us preferred to bring our lunch or buy off the truck that came in the morning, and eat lunch in the lounge at noon four days a week to save money.

There were new things to learn about being a female employee. At the dry cleaner's I'd been allowed to wear slacks, for anything else would have been ridiculous. This job was different. I was required to wear dresses every day. At first this was pleasurable, but after a while (like anything else I felt forced into) I soon grew to resent it.

"Oh, these damn pantyhose. I hate them!" I must have said, at least a thousand times. Among other problems facing the average working girl was the secretary's dilemma, running a pair of hose every day.

A female employee, I began to learn, held more responsibility than I had realized. Besides the requirements of dress, I was expected to serve coffee to the execs and kowtow every time they barked. At first, I felt rebellious, but after I saw I was the only woman in the office who felt her independence threatened, I decided I'd better get used to this aspect of the female world— second-class citizenship.

Boredom crept into the everyday routine. I got tired of catching the bus to work, working every day, all day, and catching the bus home. There was a dating service advertising in the *Free Press,* and I was considering it.

One day, at ten minutes to five, I got off the bus mad. All day I'd had problems with my supervisor, an older woman who suddenly took a dislike to me. There'd been a terrible incident on the bus when a group of blacks decided to start a rumble. The bus driver had to stop and call the police but it took ten minutes for the squad car to arrive, and those ten minutes were hellish. Well, I told myself, at least now it's over. As I turned the final corner to my street I decided to call the agency.

After my first date with the young lieutenant at home, I'd dated continuously, even returning to the night club we'd gone to alone, something I'd never have done before dating him. I'd become very popular, and one man wanted to marry me, even if it meant moving to California. Besides the fact that I didn't love him, I hadn't told him a thing about me, so I declined.

"No, we're absolutely free to women," the girl who answered the phone told me.

"Do you mean you don't have any kind of entrance fee?" I asked, remembering several phone calls before this one to people who had quoted exorbitant membership fees.

"No," the woman repeated, "and we even pay our girls ten, sometimes fifteen dollars for each date they go on."

Hanging up, I planned what to wear to my appointment the next day. This was just what I needed, I thought. There would be an abundance of dates, the girl said, all ready to do the town.

The next day at work seemed to drag more slowly than usual, as my anticipation of the coming evening grew. My recurring backache was almost forgotten as I put up the night lines and came out from behind the switchboard, signaling the end of the day. We all lined up at the elevator.

First, I caught the same bus I took each night, but then I transferred to a northbound bus. Even this minor change in routine was welcome. At Hollywood Boulevard I got off and walked about two blocks east of Highland. It was about ten minutes to six. The sign on the door said:

Opening the door, I was confronted with a mass of gaudy tomato decorations. A young-looking girl sat behind the reception desk.

"Hello," she said, in a sort of superior tone. My throat clenched in a spasm, and I was afraid I'd sound wrong. I just looked at the girl.

"Can I help you?" she asked, her face wrinkling in surprise.

"Yes," I said, happy at the sound my voice made. "I'm the girl who called yesterday. My name's Canary. I believe I was supposed to see Phyllis."

"Oh, so you're Canary," the girl said, her face lightening a little. "Hey, you know, that's a cute name. Is that really your name, or? . . ."

"No, it's my name all right," I said, trying to hide a flash of resentment. "Is Phyllis in?" The girl picked up the phone, tomato red, and dialed the next office.

"She'll be right out," the girl said, replacing the phone, "and in the meantime, I'll give you this application you have to fill out." Sitting down in a tomato red chair, I started on the questionnaire. Before I'd finished, a woman walked out of the inner office. She looked like one of the Bacchanal gang.

"You Canary?" She must have been using her best effort to produce low tones.

"Yes, I'm Canary." I didn't let any surprise show.

"I'm Phil," she said, extending her hand and I stood to shake it. Though she tried to squeeze my hand, my own was larger than hers and her efforts were in vain. We turned and she led me into her office.

"Have you ever dated with any kind of agency before?"

"No."

"Well," she said, "just so you'll know, this ain't no shlock joint. You'll be treated real nice here. The guys choose you by a photograph we take right here." She gestured to one corner where a Polaroid camera rested on a chair. The corner had been set up with a white sheet draped behind the chair.

"Now then, you don't have to go to bed with any of the guys, and if we catch you, you're out of the club." She went on to tell me, while she took my picture, that I would be expected to go out with whoever chose me, and I would be paid fifteen dollars for the ugly ones. Though I didn't tell her, I couldn't have cared less what they looked like. I was interested only in going out. After a long time cooped up in my little world, it would be nice to get out. As our meeting came to an end, I realized I'd have to catch a bus home in the dark, and I decided to call a taxi.

"Don't be silly," she said, her eyes reflecting her lust. "I'll take you home." Although I protested, the prospect of saving taxi fare lured me.

Phyllis, who preferred "Phil," turned out to be a pretty nice person, and we had a pleasant ride. I ignored her repeated hints and went upstairs with the admonition to stay by the phone the next evening. Although I didn't see how any guy would choose me from the ugly photograph they'd taken of me, next evening, I sat on the couch, reading a magazine and waiting for a TV dinner to heat. It was seven o'clock, and I was a little tired from the routine at work.

The phone rang.

"Canary?"

"Yes."

"I've got a gentleman here," Phyllis' voice told me, "and he'd like to take you out. Will you be available tonight?" Wondering why she would ask me this after our conversation yesterday, I answered affirmatively. "Great. That's fantastic. We'll expect you here at eight o'clock." There was a buzzing in my ear—she had hung up.

Calling a cab, I yanked the TV dinner out and wondered about the guy. Phil hadn't described him, and I didn't know how to dress. I chose a green print dress my sister had given me and checked my slip when the taxi honked. After a run down the stairs, I jumped into the waiting cab, gave him the address, and settled back for a minute.

"Canary," Phyllis said as I walked through the agency door, "this is your date." I had expected Sir

Lancelot or at least Prince Valiant. Instead, he was short, balding, and resembled Porky Pig. He was really ugly and I nearly cringed at the thought of dating him.

"Hello," he said, smiling.

"This is Alex," Phyllis interjected, her face carefully composed. Walking forward, I took his outstretched hand.

"Hello, Alex," I said, guilty at my original impression. Phyllis' eyes lit up in amazement and Alex squeezed my hand. "How are you?"

"Ready to go, baby," Alex said.

My first date was one of my finest. He was funny, always cracking one liners about Polacks, and since he was Polish, they were even funnier. First we had dinner in a well-known steak house in the San Fernando Valley and then we found a movie. Although he wasn't the best-looking man I've met, I was beginning to realize first impressions weren't all they are built up to be. As we pulled up in front of my apartment, I was ashamed at the thought of my first classification.

"Good night," my date said, kissing me lightly. I waved and said good night as I walked through the entrance to my building. It had been a good evening, and I was content, for the moment.

During the next week I didn't hear from the Tomato Patch, but I was having a great deal of back pain and had to take off a couple of days from work to have it checked out. Despite my financial condition, I decided to find out what was causing the pain.

"I'm afraid I can't find a thing wrong with you," the doctor told me. "I've checked you thoroughly and even the X rays don't show anything." Frustration struck me and I started to cry. Then, feeling as though something had taken me over, I began to hallucinate, and my train of thoughts scattered like marbles dropped from a bag. Later I learned I spent seven and a half hours at the doctor's office having my first nervous breakdown.

But, as always, I knew it was up to me to pull myself back together. There was no time in my life to have a nervous breakdown. Josie had given me a lift to the doctor's office, so she took me home when I was done.

During the ride to my apartment, I huddled in the front seat, trying to figure out how to communicate with the person next to me. It didn't seem to matter. As far as she was concerned I was in pain from my back problem.

"You've got to stop this," I said aloud as I let myself into the empty apartment. Talking to myself, I tried to assert some sort of rational thinking process into the confusion I felt. It was okay to feel sorry for myself; there was no one else to feel sympathy or understanding for me right now. No friends, no relatives, no one else would pull me out of this. Out of the fog came a burst of sudden anger.

"Fuck you, world!" I screamed. "Fuck you! I won't give up! I'll never give up!" Tonight was a night for a good drunk, I decided, and I grabbed my purse. As I pulled the apartment door shut behind me someone hollered at me.

"Hey, hook! What you doing out here in the dark all alone?" I froze when I realized what the man had called me. "Hook" was short for "hooker," something I definitely wasn't. He was looking for trouble.

"Hey, honey, maybe you'd like to show me your merchandise? Who knows, maybe I might just be a customer," the voice called again.

It was odd how something always seemed to happen to take my mind off my own troubles. As I was about to fight my way out of my first nervous breakdown with a pint of something to flood the sorrows I felt, all of a sudden, out of nowhere, a freak shows up.

"You don't want to talk to me, huh? Well, I'm going to show you, whore! . . ." That was all I needed. Wheeling, I faced the man. At first, I couldn't make him out in the dim light, but when I could pick out his features, I felt a stomach-turning revulsion. His face was unshaven and his hair hung in dirty strings around his shoulders. There was a putrified odor coming from him, and his eyes bugged out as though he were on some kind of speed. As I sensed him preparing to lunge at me, I tensed my body. For once I was faced with a sicky who didn't scare me. I was too damn mad at the world right then.

"Come here, you son of a bitch!" I screamed, coiling the strap of my leather purse tightly in my right hand.

"Uh, sure, you little bitch," the man grunted, raising his hands as though he wanted to catch me around the throat. As he came at me, I let my purse fly as fast and as hard as I could take it through the air to the side of his head. Danny had always laughed at the idea of a woman hitting a man with her purse, but that purse was a very practical weapon.

Half the contents of my purse had been strewn over the sidewalk, but the first blow had landed well, and before I could hit him again, my would-be attacker had disappeared into the darkness. I wasted no time worrying about him. After gathering up what had dropped from my purse, I ran the rest of the way to the liquor store and once there, I caught a cab straight home. I didn't want to push my luck.

About a week later I was called into the office I'd been hired at.

"I'm afraid you're just too ill to continue here," the personnel director began. My tears cut her off. It must have been embarrassing for the poor woman. I made my way back to my desk in tears and stopped only as I waited for a bus. At first I was sure she fired me because I was a transsexual, although I couldn't figure out how she knew, but later I realized my appearance was fine, but my emotional makeup was slipping.

At home, I took stock of my situation. I had enough money for two months' rent, and a back which was almost at the point of giving out. While I tried to figure out what I could do, the phone rang.

"Canary, this is Phyllis. You are available tonight—good," she said, before I'd gotten further than "hello." I tried to interrupt her, but she kept talking. "I have a young man here, Canary; his name is Frank. He'd like to say hello to you." As I began my protest, a low, sexy masculine voice came on the line.

"Hello. Is this Canary?"

"Yes," I said, "but I was about to tell Phyllis I don't feel well this evening."

"Oh, that's too bad," he said. "But you know, I bet if you just decided to go out for a little snack with me this evening, you'll probably feel a whole lot better." His sympathetic tone was causing me to weaken. "Now," he continued. "What do you say? Will you give me a chance? How about it?"

"Okay," I said, feeling relieved that someone would care enough to want to go out with me in my condition, sight unseen.

"What time do you want to meet?" I asked him. We set it up for seven o'clock, and though I had last-minute qualms, the added prospect of ten dollars for the date helped me.

"Oh, here's Canary," Phyllis said, as I stood in her office doorway. "Canary, this is your date tonight." I gazed in awe at the beautiful hunk of man who stood before me. He was young, I'd say close to my age, and blue-eyed. At first I thought of a basketball player; he was tall, about six-five and thin, with short hair that showed as blond. By the time we'd exchanged amenities and gotten to the elevator, I'd realized I was really turned on by this guy.

"Now see," he said, in that low voice, "aren't you glad you decided to come along? I'll bet you're feeling better already."

"Well, maybe," I said, trying to keep my feminine mystique, newly acquired and very rough around the edges.

"Ahhh, come on," he said, cracking a big smile and putting an arm around my shoulder. "I don't know anything about whatever's upsetting you, but I'll guarantee you you'll feel better about it before the night is over." It felt good, that arm around my shoulder. His prediction proved to be true.

By the time we were settled in at the Captain's Table, a swank restaurant on Restaurant Row, I was laughing so hard I'd indeed forgotten my troubles.

"Where you from, Canary?" he asked, laying an arm across my shoulder as the waiter cleared our dishes away.

"Texas," I said, taking care to put myself on automatic lie thereafter.

"Texas," he said, slumping in his chair, moving his face distortedly and affecting a swagger, as though trying to imitate a drunken cowboy. "What them men like down thar in Texas? I min, is they as good as us California boys?"

"Wha . . . sure, suh," I said, drawling. "Why, back in Texas we got some fine, mighty fine men." Then I suppressed a chuckle at the thought of Danny having been one of those men.

"You go to college back there?" he said, his face clearing, sobering.

"Yes, Southern Methodist University."

"Bachelor's?" he asked, cocking an eyebrow.

"Master's," I answered, feeling the prestige of my imaginary world.

"You know," he said, leaning his elbows on the table in front of him and lowering his head to look at me with his hypnotic blue eyes, "I just knew there was something special about you. Even when we talked on the phone I sensed you had a high degree of intelligence."

"Why, thank you," I said, feeling my ego soar, "I guess I do all right for an old high school cheerleader."

"Oh, were you really? I've always had a fixation for cheerleaders." I turned my head and fluttered my eyes.

"Is that so?" I said.

"Yes, I don't know what it is, but I've gone with a cheerleader of one kind or another since my high school days. I was in basketball, you know." He fascinated me. In the car we had talked about his college days. He was a former USC basketball star and turned accountant after school for a major West Coast firm. If it had been possible for me to be a cheerleader at my old high school, what would it have been like walking arm and arm with a basketball star through the halls, the other kids ooohing and ahhhing?

"Were you a cheerleader in college?" he asked.

"No. It took up too much of my time, you know."

"Oh, sure," he said, emptying his water glass in one gulp. Then he slid over next to me. "May I be the one-millionth to tell you you're one of the most beautiful girls in the world?" Reaching up, I stroked his cheek, feeling the heavy beard against my softened fingers. What would it be like to have sex with this man? Would I ever be able to enjoy his body the way I'd heard girls talking about their dates? Most of all, I wondered if I would see him tomorrow.

As we walked from the restaurant, he held me close to him. I could feel the warmth of his body through his thin sports jacket. A new feeling, warm and protected, like a little girl being held by her daddy, took over for a couple of minutes. It was hard to understand; I'd only met this man a couple hours before.

The rest of the evening went beautifully. We went on to a discotheque, dancing for a couple of hours, then found an all-night horror movie. I remember clinging to his arm in the movie whenever something scary happened, and at the same time remembering the times I'd been in his position.

On the way home, in the early morning, I began to feel distraught at the possibility of never seeing this man again. Plotting, I tried to figure a way I might continue seeing him—and not through the agency.

"You know," he said, as we were making our way down Santa Monica Boulevard toward Vine, "I sure would like to see you, I mean without going through the agency, you know?"

"This is it," I said, pointing to my street, avoiding his questions. It was a relief. All my plans were unnecessary. When he had brought the car to a stop in the driveway, I answered him.

"Sure, I'd love to see you again."

"Fantastic," he said, sliding close to me after he shut the engine off. He put his hand on my cheek, stroking it gently, and kissed my forehead. I began to feel what I was to know later as instant infatuation. I closed my eyes and saw us a married couple. It would be beautiful if he knew the whole story about me. He reached down and touched my knee. Tingles darted through it.

"You know, lady cheerleader," he said, finding his way up my leg, "I'll bet you're fantastic in bed."

"Well," I said, trying to get back down to a reality

level, "I'm okay, I guess." I put my hand on his as it slid further up my leg. My body began to soar with ecstasy.

I wanted him. I wanted sex. And his hand was near the danger zone, the area that prevented me from having what I wanted. I began to feel sick.

"Please don't," I said, pushing his hand back to my knee.

"What's wrong, did I do something wrong?" He jumped back and I saw a torment on his face in the haze of the moonlight.

"No, it's just that . . ."

"I don't turn you on, is that it?"

"No! It's not that at all." I searched for excuses. "It's just that I can't have sex tonight, and I don't want to get both of us all excited and, well . . . you know."

"Well, what's wrong?" he asked, his breathing becoming shallow, his face defensive.

"It's just one of those girl things," I said, hoping he would leave it at that. I didn't want to tell him the truth, but it would almost be a relief to do it.

"You mean you've got your period," he said, his voice calming.

"No, that's not exactly it."

"Then what is it?" he asked, sliding back across the seat. I began to feel the pressure of the truth; I wanted to level with this stranger and maybe gain a friend, maybe a lover.

"Do you really want to hear the story?" I asked, moving toward the door a little, subtly, so he wouldn't notice. If he didn't like what I said, I wanted to have an escape ready.

"Yes," he said, seriously. "Please. I like you very much and I would like to know."

"Okay," I said, feeling my stomach muscles tighten. "It's not easy to tell you this, I mean I don't tell anyone. You see, well . . . you've heard of things, I mean operations that change people's sexes? I mean . . ."

"You're kidding," he said, his mouth dropping open in shock. "You're . . ."

"I'm a sex change, a transsexual. I used to be a man. I've had one stage of the surgery already, but . . ."

"You're mean you're a dude. That's why you can't have sex. You're still a male down there."

"Not exactly," I said, feeling shame at the way he'd put it. "I'm not a guy, I'm a female, but I just have to have one more operation before I can have sex."

We talked for a long time after that. He was obviously in shock, but at the same time full of interest. When I said good-bye to him, I knew it would be for good, but somehow I wasn't as hurt as I thought I'd be.

As I waved good-bye I wondered what had driven me to tell him. He hadn't suspected anything. I believed him when he promised he'd never tell the people at the Tomato Patch, but just the same, it was time to find another agency.

"Well, this is a rather different kind of job than you're used to, I'm sure," she said, her face wrinkling into a smile.

"Look," I said, remembering I'd been unemployed longer than my budget could stand. "I'll take it, as long as it pays minimum wage." The job was listed with the employment agency as that of a packer in a warehouse of pornographic materials. It wasn't what I'd hoped for, but I couldn't afford to be choosy.

"Come on in, honey," said the man I was to know as Hal. "Have you ever had any experience in the pornography field?"

"No," I said, wondering exactly what he meant.

"Well," he said, his face taking on a serious look. "I'm the kind of man who don't believe in fooling around." Pulling a ring of keys from his pocket, he motioned for me to follow him. I began to wonder, as we walked through a series of doors, if this was the right kind of job. I didn't know what I was letting myself in for.

"Here we are," he said, his voice full of pride. "These are our best, the greatest selection." I couldn't help laughing. I'd never seen so many dildos in my entire life.

In a week I'd managed to get my giggling down to a couple of times a day. It was funny, at first, to handle hundreds of imitation penises. I was an experiment: the first girl they'd ever hired to work in their warehouse.

"You're not using your imagination," Hal said one day when I'd spent four hours sorting and cataloging new devices we'd just received. "You've got to be creative. Make me a series of display boards, and I want to see every dick we got on them." It seemed a funny way to show off creative genius, but I set to work displaying the commerciality of the new items. The firm had just received a new device which, through a combination of heat and plastic sheeting, would seal anything in plastic, within a five-second cycle. Hal was experimenting with it as I labeled.

"PAC Hard Rubber Dick, size eight," I'd say aloud.

"PAC Hard Rubber Dick, size eight," he'd echo as he'd take the newly assembled package and seal it in plastic.

It took Hal and the new owner about a week to decide I'd have to have sex with them to keep my job. I remember the day clearly. Shortly after I'd arrived at work, I set about counting and separating a new shipment. I'd never seen so many French ticklers and vibrators in my whole life. Hal and the new owner walked by and heard me mumble.

"Here," Hal said, his hand brushing my rear end, "let me help you with that." I turned, half angry, half surprised that he would get behind me without my noticing.

"Thanks," I said, trying to work my way past the two men.

"Here, here, where does this little lady think she's going?" the tall man said, starting a hint of fear in me.

"Excuse me," I said, trying to get past them, using a little more of my greatly faded strength.

"Hold on now, honey," Hal said, running his hand up and down my stomach, each run getting a little lower. "Joe and me, well, we've been talking. We just think you ought to be a little more friendly, you understand?" I pulled his hand away. Looking at the man he called Joe, I wasn't so sure of myself anymore.

"Yes, that's right, you've got to be a little more respectful of your bosses' wishes," the tall guy said, reaching for me. I slapped his hand and realized I was locked in the place, and rape was imminent.

"What's the matter with you, you fucking whore!" Hal screamed. "We aren't good enough for you? How about that Joe, not good enough for this bitch. Maybe we should show her just how good we are!"

"Okay," I screamed, trying to stall them. "If we're going to do anything, at least have the decency to take me into the office where we can all be comfortable."

"Now you're coming around, honey," Joe said, reaching for my breast, but not holding it long enough to realize it was mostly padding.

We made our way back to a clear area, and my mind worked frantically. I could run, but Hal had the keys to two of the three doors I'd have to use. I could murder the men with the knife I carried in my pocket to open packages, but that would cause more trouble. I could tell them my story, put myself at their mercy, but that would mean more trouble, most likely. Hal grabbed my arm as we entered the office.

"You know how to give head, honey," he said, trying to force my head down with the other hand. Jumping back, I felt anger fill me, not mine, but Danny's, and I felt a degradation.

"Drop dead, you son of a bitch!" I said, my voice lowering. Both of the men jumped in surprise. I wasn't the nice, shy girl they'd threatened, and they didn't know I'd had some practice in confrontations of this nature.

"Come on Joe, let's show this bitch who's boss," Hal said, recovering from his shock. Hal lunged forward and grabbed my blouse, ripping it so that one sleeve came off in his hand. In panic, I grabbed a letter opener and held it to them.

"Back off! Back off, or I'll use this." Their eyes were full of fear and ungratified lust.

"Now, come on, honey, we were just fooling around," Joe said, whining.

"Yeah, sure honey, I didn't mean to rip your blouse like that. We were just clowning around—no harm intended."

"You have one choice," I screamed. "Get out of here and leave me alone or I call the police."

"No need to do anything drastic," the big man said. "We'll leave right now, right, Hal? Let's just leave her alone and everything will be okay."

"Sure," Hal said. He made his way to the doors and called out, "The doors are unlocked, honey." Walking out of the office, I kept the letter opener in my hand. They couldn't afford any trouble that might bring the police to this secret warehouse. "Now," Hal said as I left, "get the hell out and don't bother coming back tomorrow!" Grabbing my purse to me, I wondered if I really would have driven the letter opener into one of them, and took a breath of the clean air.

I had to get right back to the unemployment office, but I was a mess. My slacks were dirty from the warehouse and my blouse sleeve in tatters. I got on a bus to Santa Monica and Highland, then looked for a dress shop.

When I had purchased a brown corduroy skirt and blouse set and some pantyhose I went to the service station and changed, fixed my hair and reapplied makeup.

"What kind of work are you looking for?" the middle-aged woman asked, pushing her huge glasses back on her tiny nose.

"Anything," I said, then corrected myself. "That is anything but another job in a dildo factory." The woman laughed and her glasses slid to the end of her nose.

"What?" she said, pushing them up again.

"Nothing," I said, "just one of those crazy situations I let myself into."

The next couple of months were spent in and out of more jobs than I like to remember. Some lasted only a day or two, others a matter of hours. I'd taken on another dating agency, too, and through it I had one of the most frightening experiences of my life.

THE DATE

The phone rang only minutes after I'd gotten in the door. It was another phone call from the new dating agency I'd just joined. Although I'd taken my sweet time about getting up the courage to contact this agency it seemed as though they were using me for all their dates. In the fourteen days I'd been with them I had dated every night.

Jan, who was my contact with the agency, had a lightly accented voice which was as familiar to me now as someone of my own family. She was a pretty Swedish girl, blond with light blue eyes, typically Scandinavian features.

"Guess who this is, little bird," she opened.

"Oh, Jan," I said, crossly, "don't tell me you have another one? Can't I please have just one evening to go to sleep?" All day long, today over eight hours' worth, I slaved as a personal waitress—also known as a private secretary—to a big insurance executive.

"Well," Jan answered me, "all of the other girls are either unavailable or already out. I'm depending on you, kid. Besides, Dietrich says you'll be getting paid for your dates this week."

Dietrich was the owner, a short brunette, thirty-five, whose manner closely resembled that of a man. She was loud, obnoxious and terribly overbearing, with a bark like a dog. She greeted the girls when they first arrived at the dating agency to meet their escort, as a precaution for both parties, who then had the right to refuse the other, and made it very clear in this encoun-

223

ter that she was head man of this very profitable business.

"Ugh! What time is my date tonight?" I asked.

"It'll be at eight o'clock, so you'll have to get going," she answered.

I glanced at my watch and gasped—it was 7:30! I wasn't ready at all, and I'd have to call a taxi, as I hadn't gotten a car yet.

"This is a rerun of last night, Jan," I laughed. "Tell the guy I'll be about ten minutes late." As I hung up the phone, I pulled my feet from the pillows I'd propped them up on and hurried in to shower and to change. While I chose a light cotton dress and white sandals, I called a cab. I used to spend hours and hours worrying about my bodily proportions and how they stood in comparison to those of a normal female, but since I'd begun dating through this agency that had almost ceased.

My hair was now mid-back length, long enough to caress my bare shoulders and breasts when I sat, nude, playing the guitar, singing. Sometimes, with my eyes closed, I would worry suddenly that this was all a dream, that I would wake up in a room somewhere, with my hair short again, and someone calling me Danny. The taxi honked, bringing me back to my senses, as I stood in front of the mirror.

As I descended the stairs, I had a momentary feeling that something was wrong, something I couldn't quite put my finger on, but *something*. Shaking it off, I decided to think about the money. Jan had said I'd be getting paid. We were paid twenty dollars per date and this was my fourteenth date. I climbed into the cab, spouted the address at him, and reached for a mirror from my handbag.

Looking into a mirror for a once-over always seemed to calm me down. As a little boy, I was prone to dream and fantasize about how things might be or could have been. As a young woman, things were no different, but at that moment I was anticipating the very worst. This fantasy was a common one, though. Dietrich and the man I was supposed to date would be standing together as I entered the agency. Dietrich would smile, motioning me forward and indicating to the man that I was the girl for him. Normal procedure, but then the man would turn into a raging maniac and scream—"That's what you call your prettiest girl? Can't you see that her face is too long and her eye is crossed and her legs are too muscular and her fingers are mannish looking? You expect me to pay money to go out with that? You've got to be kidding! That looks like a man."

"Yes, you know, you're right," Dietrich would reply. "She is ugly and looks terribly male. Her nose is awfully masculine. I don't see how I could ever have thought she was a girl. She's pathetic. That's not a boy, or a girl, it's an 'it'." I would shudder, and imagine myself with a pistol in my hand, shooting both of them to pay for what they had said. When I had shot them, I would have to run, for the police would be after me.

"Miss! Miss!" the taxi driver was exasperated. "Come on, that's two dollars even. I've got other calls to get to. You sick or something?"

"I'm sorry," I muttered, but I didn't really give a damn. I paid the man, then got out and took a deep breath, getting into my act, getting ready to deal with the evening.

The agency consisted of two offices inside a dilapidated building, and was indicated by a small sign hung crookedly over the reception office door in the narrow hallway. It was almost impossible to find if you didn't have directions. The door creaked as I opened it, alerting everyone in the room to my arrival. Faces turned toward me as I walked in.

The men fixed their intense stares on me, covering me with searching glances that made my skin crawl. There were always four or five seedy-looking characters hanging around, who seemed to be waiting for a free date or something. I thought about Dietrich's speech to me when I signed up with the agency about running a clean, respectable agency, not a pimping hall, and her indication that vice cops were always hanging around.

Jan looked up from her desk and greeted me with a smile and "good evening."

"Where's the lucky man?" I whispered to Jan as I bent over her desk, extending my hand as if showing her the ring on my hand. She extended a finger to a huge, tall man in the corner.

"There, that one. His name is Jimmy." I swirled around carefully and got a look at him as the door behind Jan swung open and Dietrich stood in the doorway, motioning to me to enter. Each time I went into that office, I had to try not to laugh. It was a jumbled assortment of crazy items and odd posters, with a rusty sword on the wall behind her desk. Dietrich slouched in a strongly masculine way, with one hand in the front pocket of her Levi's. For the two weeks I'd been going there, she had been wearing the same pair of denims, and they still had some sort of food stain on the left knee.

"Well, honey, you've got a good one tonight," she said, smiling. I should have suspected something was wrong then, for I was spared her prostitution lecture for the first time. "He's one of my steadier customers, so you just take good care of him." I wondered what that meant.

"Well," I asked, "what does he do for a living?"

"Oh, he's got some mean, tough job somewhere as a security guard or something," she said. The thought of any sort of law enforcement person frightened me, because I had a great deal to lose by getting in trouble with the police. It was only eight months after the completion of the first of a series of two operations it took to complete the sex change and I had the sex organs of both male and female. Up to this point I'd never been discovered by even the most clever of maneuvers. I'd questioned other transsexuals who had had trouble with the police and I had no desire whatsoever to test their stories personally.

Dietrich was leading me out the door back to the waiting room. Jan motioned to Jimmy to come forward to meet his date. Both of us, Jimmy and I, were obviously nervous. Dietrich always acted as though she were the mother of the women and the men were nice young schoolboys on their first date.

"Now, children, have fun," she said, "and drive carefully. Remember, this could be the first of a lifetime of dates." She continued, but I'd heard the speech before, so I studied Jimmy. He was tall, thickly built and hairy. His brows were thick, dark brown and his eyes almost black. The hair on his head was also dark brown, and his hairline receded just a little. With his heavy, but closely trimmed beard, he resembled every picture I'd ever seen of a caveman. There was something different, something disquieting about him that I couldn't pinpoint. It wasn't until later in the evening that I found out what it was.

As we left the agency, he put his hand on my shoulder, squeezing a bit too hard, and began steering me in his direction. I struggled politely to move away, but his grip was steady. Just as I was about to protest, he let go. There didn't seem to be a car parked in front, so I asked if he had one. He pointed, wordlessly, to a gray, battered Ford down the street a little, with a faded emblem on the door. I guessed that it had once been a police car or some kind of official vehicle. The seats were torn, and, as I got in I noticed a musty smell as if the car had been stored somewhere.

As he was rounding the car to enter on the driver's side, I noticed a badge pinned to the visor above his seat. "San Francisco Police Department" was written in fancy script around the badge. This guy must have been a cop once and did something to get thrown off the force. But why did he still have a police car?

When he got in, he spoke his first words to me. "You know, I picked your picture out of all the pictures in the agency because you look like a good sport." Big deal, I thought. That was nothing new, or great. But just what did he mean by good sport, I asked.

"Well, I really want us to just have a quiet evening. Maybe just a little wine and some hamburgers, and then I'll explain what I mean." I figured I'd just let that remark pass, although something in his words was beginning to scare me. He looked slightly strange, but that didn't have to mean anything. Sometimes people told me I seemed a little weird, but it didn't really put me off.

Looking back, I can understand what they must have sensed in me. There are few people in the world who can hide a mental anguish twenty-four hours a day.

Although I'd spent some nineteen years practicing it, I'm sure it came through at times. I was new, too, at the small gestures and attitudes of a woman. Sometimes I just didn't know what to do and I couldn't quite hide my indecision.

"Faggot!" What? I struggled with everything I had to keep my face composed, to avoid responding to his comment. I knew I wasn't a homosexual, but some uptight men found it impossible to rationalize me and my situation. "Faggot!" he said again, nodding his head forward. This time I almost giggled with relief. A swishy, gay guy was crossing the street, stepping carefully through the crosswalk. "You know," he continued, "those queers are all over this place. I never saw so many sissies in my life. It's too bad we couldn't round them all up and . . . " Oh, no, I thought.

"Where do you plan on going for dinner?" I interrupted.

"Uh, well, how about Tiny Naylor's?" He seemed surprised that I'd cut him off. Okay, I thought, deciding to play this one solemnly. Early in my short dating career I learned to become the type of girl the guy wanted. Not only did this virtually insure the success of the date, but it often stalled the need for a pass at the end of the date. I gambled, but I usually won.

We made a right turn onto La Brea Boulevard, on our way to the restaurant. I remembered meeting at Tiny Naylor's with a group of music producers. A couple of times I had brought my wife there to treat her to their great banana splits. Tiny Naylor's, on the corner of La Brea and Sunset, was a centrally located place frequented by Hollywood teenagers, by big shots in the entertainment industry, and by Hollywood police. How ironic that I was there with a man, after having been there so often with my wife, and none of the waitresses recognized me as a woman. After we got settled, I turned to Jimmy. There was something I had to do, especially at this restaurant.

"May I be excused?" I requested. After having been to the men's room in this place so many times, I was going to the ladies' room this time. What a ridiculous accomplishment, I thought as I crossed the parking lot, but how satisfying. And no one would ever know but me.

I'd been to a ladies' room before, but at times the action took on special significance. As I entered, I noticed a huge woman, probably in her late thirties, standing in front of one of the sinks, holding something in her hand. I hurried by her into a stall. For some reason I didn't realize what she was holding until I'd closed the stall door behind me. It was a sap, a leather pouch filled with buck shot, and used in much the same way a blackjack is used. Silently, I sat and wondered what would happen when I came out. Was she interested in robbery? Danny had never had a fear of anyone female; he was too busy warding off male assaults. Canary had never had to deal with situations like this. She, I, wasn't really afraid of anyone yet, and I'd not developed the sort of sixth sense women have of recognizing situations and people who threaten them.

I must have spent ten minutes waiting for the woman to leave. Two rather small feet maintained their position patiently. That crazy woman was going to try something! Okay, I planned my defense. If she hit me she would be using one arm, so I would use my large leather purse as a blocking shield. There wasn't much room in the place, so I was going to have to move rapidly to get out the door quickly. If I needed to scare her, I had a pocket knife in my purse to ward off trouble, but I didn't want to have to use it. I didn't want to stab anyone.

With a burst of courage, I opened the stall door and confronted the woman with a glare. She was leaning against the wall, with one hand tucked behind her. That was the hand to watch. Her arms were large and muscular, and her eyes halfway closed, as though she were trying to look tough. Slowly, I moved past her, breathing carefully, watching her as my hand found the doorknob.

She was a girl, I was a girl. I never realized women treated each other violently. No one ever told me about it. I'd seen movies about women in prison. The door wouldn't open. It was locked. As I fumbled with it, my hands began to perspire. Just as I found the lock, she

made her move. I froze just long enough to let her bring
the blackjack across my left shoulder. Because I was
five or six inches taller, she couldn't reach my head.
And there was still muscle left in my shoulders from my
days as a male. I unlocked the door, flung it open, and
took two steps through the tiny lounge. I ran through
the second door and slammed it as hard as I could. For
a minute I stood just outside the door, trying to catch
my breath. A patrol car had pulled up, and two policemen, who must have just been starting their break, got
out. I went over to them.

"What's the problem, Miss?"

I didn't know what to tell him. The relief made me
start to cry. "There's a woman in there, and she's got a
sap." I was holding my shoulder. The policeman looked
carefully at me and asked if I was hurt. If I told him I
had been attacked, I'd have had to identify myself and
make some kind of statement, perhaps appear at a trial.
The only identification I had was a driver's license issued to Danny from Texas. This would cause me more
trouble than the pain in my shoulder.

"No," I said, "but I caught my arm on the door as
I ran out. . . ."

"Okay, Miss," he answered, and walked back to
the car. He and a couple other officers conferred before
one of them radioed for a policewoman. I told the police I'd be inside if they needed me.

Jimmy looked up at me oddly. "I thought you'd
cut out on me."

"Let's go, Jimmy. I'll tell you about it as soon as
we get out of here." As we rolled out of Tiny Naylor's,
I looked over at the policemen waiting for the answer to
their radio call. The woman in the restroom was probably awaiting another victim. Was she going to be surprised!

I'd been conquered by a female, by fear of a female. There was still a trace of male ego in me, and there
was a trace of shame at the memory of the confrontation.
I'd been fooling myself a long time about super-powered
strength. I might have been able to beat bullies, but perhaps my true self, my female nature, had been the stronger
all along, as I had believed. If I'd been raised as a female,

there wouldn't be this division in me. I would understand my female self better.

Jimmy was muttering something about Mexican food, but I told him I wasn't hungry and began an edited version of what had happened.

"She was a loony lesbian," he suggested, when I had finished. "We used to bust them all the time when I was in San Francisco. Just like I said, all them damn faggots are alike. No good for nothing but taking up space in public restrooms, assaulting children, going to jail, and believe you me, I busted hundreds of them slimy bast . . ."

"Is that all you can talk about? What about Frisco? Did you used to work there or something? Is that your badge? I know zero about you."

"Uh, yeah," he answered. "You see, I was on the force up there for almost twenty years. Just nine months until my retirement from that hell hole and some lousy effing queer fouled it all up!" He stopped, and seemed to be thinking.

"Well," I said, "don't stop now. What did that queer, I mean, homosexual, do to you to foul you up on the force?" He grumbled a couple of times, but I now considered that part of his vocabulary.

"Well, you see, I was working vice right outside the Wharf. Me and my partner were working a series of public restrooms up there and had made a lot of arrests. I was up for my last promotion, which meant a lot more money toward my retirement, and was really rousting them queens right and left.

"One evening we had been staked out in this lousy restroom oh, two or three hours, and these two dudes come in, see? One of them was a big lummox almost as big as me and the other was a little swish about your size. You know, I just can't figure them big fags out. They got all the brawn of a man. No doubt about what they are, but they turn queer. Crazy, huh? Anyhow, this big one comes in and leans up against the wall to do his duty, see? Course, I couldn't expect you to know much about the layout of a men's bathroom, could I now, little lady?" I nodded my head and tried to seem puzzled. "You git the picture, though, huh?" I nodded. For the first time, I noticed this man had a mouth full of broken teeth. He was really enjoying the story. Everytime he said the word "faggot" or "queer" his eyes lit up.

"Well, anyway, this big guy is just finishing up and I spy the little bastard coming in. The big guy turns as soon as he hears the footsteps and nods to the runt. Well, soon as they started their perversion, we busted 'em. The big guy, he was real calm, but the little guy, he's got to make it rough on himself. He takes a swing at me. Now this is the little guy, see? He's so weak he couldn't whip a noodle and he's swinging on me. Nineteen years on the force and this little fag has to take a swing at me." He hesitated for a moment as though catching his breath.

"What happened to the little guy?" I asked after a minute.

"Uh, I just kept thinking that little fag had touched me. He'd laid his filthy hands on me. I just started hitting him, pounding him, and pretty soon my partner let go of the big guy to come pull me off, but I couldn't stop. You see, that punk had no right. He should have known not to touch me. He *deserved* to die. They had no right to take me off the force because of a fag!" He stopped, then looked at me. "Ah, let's talk about something else. Let's find a restaurant and have something to eat."

I was out with a murderer, in the same car, and he wanted to eat! I should have refused to go out with him when I first suspected something. I didn't know quite what to do. Now, I probably could have gone to a restaurant, then made my escape, but right then, I just wanted to get away from him.

"I don't really feel like eating," I told him. "That incident in the restroom back there, well, it kind of upset me. How about making the date for some other time?"

"What do you mean?" he asked, turning to me. There was a kind of irritated look on his face. He seemed to be getting angry. How quickly could I get him to take me back to the agency?

Slowly, I stretched the muscles in my stomach, and tried to keep the ache and the nausea from rising. Taking a deep breath, I continued my request. "I have a stomachache. I guess it's from all the excitement back at the restaurant," I said. "You know, I just don't feel like going out anymore."

"You're scared of me, aren't you?" He was almost grinning. "You want to go home, huh? Well, listen here, baby, I paid Dietrich a fortune just to take you out. No deal. You're going to stay with me until I tell you different!"

Well, he was right, I was scared of him, but for more reason than he suspected. If something happened and he found out about me, I just might be his next victim. No one in Hollywood even knew if I were alive from one day to the next, except the people on my new day job. Since I'd only been there four days, they'd just think I skipped out. This man could kill me and get away with it. I had to maneuver him into letting me take a taxi home.

"I have an idea," I said, trying to be calm, pleasant. It was quarter to ten. If I called right away Dietrich might be able to fix him up with someone before they closed. I relayed this to him.

"Oh, yeah, okay." He seemed easily persuaded. "Look, my house is just around the corner here. Why don't we stop there and you can use the telephone and save time?" I hesitated, suspecting something, but unsure of how to move next. He was going too quickly for me to get out of the car, and there was always the possibility that he had nothing planned. After all, I consoled myself suddenly, Dietrich had said he was one of her steady customers. At Fairfax and Third he took a quick left. We zoomed down a side street right away and he pulled into a driveway which led to a broken-down house.

"Well, this is what I call home," he said, carefully. "Let's go!"

"Can't you call Dietrich? She knows you much better than she does me and after all, you're a steady customer, she'll probably fix you right up." I hoped he couldn't detect the quiver of fear in my voice. He smiled, slyly.

"Ah, come on, I'm not gonna try anything. It's just

if you don't talk to her she'll think something's wrong. You know how women are." He had murdered someone, but he was free, so probably he was exonerated of blame. I was a girl who was once a boy, and I probably didn't always get my signals straight. I smiled, shakily.

"You're right. I'm sorry. I'll go with you."

He opened his door and got out. By the time I had composed myself he was at my side, and helped me out. Despite myself, I was pleased. At the top of some small cement stairs he pulled open a raggedy torn screen door and fumbled for his keys. When he had the door open, he motioned for me to enter first.

The house had a musty odor, just as his car had. It seemed as neglected as the car was, and certainly was as thoughtlessly chosen. All I could see was a water bed and a couple of chairs. When he flipped the lights on, I jumped.

"Where's the telephone?" I asked. He began looking around under dirty clothes as if searching for the cord. I started to help him, and realized as I lifted and moved clothing that almost everything was black. I stumbled over something, and decided I had found the cord, but bent to uncover a coil of rope. Shrugging, I gave up.

"Did you find it?" I muttered, looking up. Jimmy was gone. "Did you find the telephone, Jimmy?" I called. Still no answer. My heart began pounding wildly, and I started for the front door. There was a grumble from the other room.

"Yes, here it is. Come on in here. It's looped around a table," he yelled. Something in his voice terrified me. I started to run for the door, and the lights went out, plunging the room into darkness. There wasn't any light in the room, not even a crack from under the door. I froze. Fear had taken over my body. Frantically, I tried to find the door. Part of me wanted to scream, but the rest counseled silence. I could hear my heels clicking on the floor. And I couldn't find the door. I was totally disoriented.

"Jimmy, there's something wrong. I'm not the girl you're looking for! This is some kind of mistake. Dietrich knows I'm out with you, and if something happens, she's going to report it." A series of giggles and moans answered me.

"Jimmy, turn on the light and take me back. I'm tired of this silly game. I want to go home." Tears were streaming down my face, and my voice quivered. Extending my arms, I continued my search for the door.

"So, you're afraid of little Jimmy, huh? You think maybe he's going to hurt you? You think maybe you can get away from him, huh?" I found the door! There was no knob, no handle, no latch that I could find. I could find a keyhole, though. This was the kind of door you had to open with a key, like a door my grandmother had on one of her closets. The lights went on. I blinked back the sudden blindness. Then I couldn't believe what I saw.

Across the room I could see a man dressed in a black jacket wearing stockings, a garter belt and high heels. His lips were exaggerated with lipstick; rouge covered his entire face, except for the beard and moustache. My first impulse was to laugh.

"Darling, now this little boy is going to punish you." He was lisping now, not whining. "You see he's just like you. He's a woman too." No! This man certainly wasn't a transsexual. I began searching for a weapon.

He lunged at me. As his hands went around my throat, I thought of the pocket knife in my purse, but too late. I drove my hands into the sides of his arms, violently, and jumped away when his hold was broken. Stumbling, I jumped onto a chair, but before I could get over it he had my ankles and was pulling me down. Again his hands went about my neck. I was choking now. His hands were squeezing the life from my body.

Bringing his brilliant face close to mine, he laughed and muttered at me. "Die! Die! Die!" I panicked and waved my arms wildly at him, hitting him wherever I could. One finger seemed to strike his eye, for he screamed immediately and let go of me. I could breathe again, short, careful sobs of valuable air. Coughing and choking, I began to scream. He backed away from me, with a frightened, puzzled look on his face. My scream faded and my throat closed and I be-

gan choking, then I coughed the tightness out and began
screaming again.

Jimmy was scrambling around the room, trying to
find articles of men's clothing he could pull on. He
would disappear into the other room to put one piece
on and remove a part of his costume. I don't remember
him leaving. Hours passed in a blur of tears and pain
and choking.

When I awoke the room was pitch dark again.
I could hear no sounds of my attacker, but outside
there were comforting sounds of morning. Carefully I
stood, stretching the sore and painful muscles, trying to
figure out where the door was. When I found it, it was
still locked, but that didn't bother me this morning. Me-
thodically I made my way to the nearest window and,
bracing myself, put my right foot throughout it. Splin-
ters of glass flew into my legs and caught on the tattered pantyhose, but I was too angry and anxious to get
out of the place into the light to care about hose or a
little bit of blood. I kicked the glass again and again,
until there was room for me to crawl through.

The old Ford was gone. A "for sale" sign looked
as though it had been hastily replaced. Shaking my head,
I began to walk towards Fairfax. My watch was gone,
but it seemed early. I berated myself. How could I have
been such a fool? When I came to a bus stop, I sat down.
Moments later a big yellow and white bus came by. There
weren't many people on it.

"That'll be thirty, uh . . . what? . . . " The bus
driver looked up suddenly. Glancing at his big mirror, I
confirmed for myself what had caused his shock. One
eye was blackened, blood stains marked my mouth and
my neck was black and blue. Shaking, I started to faint.
The bus driver leaped up and led me to the seat behind
him. As he sat me down, I realized I'd left my purse in
the empty house.

"My purse has been stolen and I don't have any
money," I whispered, noticing how hard it was to talk.

"Want me to call the police for you?"

"No, but thank you. If I can get to Vine, I'll get a
cab from there." He nodded and resumed his seat. I
thought about going to the police then considered the

problems I'd have with the medical report when the doctor discovered I was half male, half female. I didn't want to go on record as being a drag queen prostitute. It would be easier to stay clear of people for a couple of weeks, live off my hoarded savings for the next operation, and wait. I tried to ignore the stares of surprised commuters.

When we reached Vine the driver got out of his seat and helped me down, offering again to call the police for me. There was a gas station on the corner, and the station manager saw me coming. He opened the ladies' room and helped me to it. Declining his offer to call the police, I washed my face, and removed my tattered pantyhose. Then I crossed the street to a cab.

The driver helped me up the stairs to my small apartment and the manager, a lady of fifty or so ran up to greet me. She didn't seem to want to believe her eyes.

"I was in a car accident," I told her, spontaneously.

"Do you have your keys? I noticed you don't have your purse. Here, let me open the door for you."

The small apartment, with its torn carpet and tattered curtains, never seemed lovelier. It was home. I paid the driver, chased the manager out, and settled for some sleep.

Dietrich had crossed me. She knew the guy was a sadist, but he had probably paid her enough to silence her conscience. She could keep the money. I wasn't ever going there again. The Dietrichs of the world could have this round and I wasn't going to fight the next one until tomorrow, if I could get some sleep. I did, eventually.

But I had learned, in one night, a lesson that girls who grow up *girls* learn over a long period. They develop an ability to gauge character and sense things about men from having dated boys, then teen-agers, then men. They develop a sixth sense which enables them to say "no" before it's trouble time. I was learning by trial and error—a very inefficient way to learn, and sometimes a very dangerous way. But I was learning. Boy, was I learning!

WHAT DO YOU THINK
YOU ARE — HUMAN?

"Well, you're not the only patient here," the nurse said, twisting her face into a smirk. Turning, I took my seat again and stared around me at the others in this reception area. Desperation was the only thing that kept me here. Last time I had come, I'd waited six hours to see a psychiatrist for fifteen minutes.

In the few weeks since my experience with Dietrich's agency, I had begun to have attacks of paranoia, and they increased in frequency and intensity. Sometimes I awoke in the middle of the night to feel that fiend's hands on my neck, choking the life from me. And now I was not only afraid of men, I was afraid of women. Dietrich had set me up, and she was responsible for my close shave with death. There was no one to trust; I needed help if I were to stop this sinking feeling of depression.

It wasn't as though I thought anyone but I could have a more valid insight into my problems and their solution, but my friend Jerry at the unemployment office had suggested some help for me. He had given me the name of the hospital, and a suggestion to talk to some people there.

After what seemed like my weekly trip to the unemployment office one day, I had stopped for lunch at a little snack bar across the street. I was on my eleventh job through the agency, and I guess Jerry, my counselor's supervisor, had taken an interest in my situation.

"Aren't you that girl who's setting all kinds of records in our office?" he asked, coming up from behind me to take the empty stool beside me. First I was shocked, then I recognized his face.

"Oh," I said, "you've been reading the headlines." We both laughed and he introduced himself as the supervisor of the unit I was assigned to. Jerry was a handsome Oriental from Hawaii, a friendly man. We hit it off right away. Within fifteen minutes he had asked me for a date, and noted my hesitation.

"I know there's something wrong inside; you need to talk to someone," he said, in the lull in our conversation after his question. "I don't want you to think I'm too forward, but I have a feeling you've lost your ability to feel. I'd like to help you."

"It might be a little too late for that," I said, surprised at the words coming out of my mouth.

"Wouldn't you just give me a break? You and I know that someone who goes through a job a week must have something bothering her, and sooner or later, it'll have to make itself known." Suddenly I felt like Danny, who wanted someone's shoulder to cry on, who wanted just one friend to confide in, someone who could feel the hurt and the pain.

"Look," he said, putting a friendly hand on my shoulder, "there's no rush. Would it be all right if I called you tomorrow to see if maybe you've had enough time to think about it?"

"Sure," I said, taking care not to volunteer my phone number. As we got up and walked to the cash register, he plucked my bill out of my hand without a word.

"Thank you," I said, heading for the bus stop. "I didn't intend, you know . . . I mean to have you . . ."

"Don't be silly," he said, his brown eyes gazing into mine, "I was the one taking your time, remember. And I enjoyed our conversation, really."

After our discussion, I didn't see Jerry or the unemployment office for over a month. I had almost set a new record for me. Somehow I was too embarrassed to go back. By following up on a series of job openings they'd given me, I had landed a fairly good position with an overseas shipping outfit on Melrose Avenue. At first it went smoothly, and I worked long enough to look forward to a pay raise, but problems came up again.

"What are you doing after work honey?" it always started. "Come on in, close the door. Take a little break." Or—"Say, you know, you really have a nice set of legs." These lines were so standard, I wondered that they thought me innocent enough to fall for them. I'd turn these guys down, and the inevitable right-hand woman would take me aside, within a few hours or a few days.

"I'm sorry, Canary, dear, I'm afraid we'll have to let you go." It ceased to matter anymore. I began to really enjoy lying my way into a new job every week, and my methods, devised to get me a job on the first visit, pleased me. At first, I'd been afraid to tell a fib. My morals kept me losing the better jobs, and ending up with the losers. After five jobs or so, the truth became clear.

"It says here you're twenty-seven," someone would say, "but you don't even look twenty-one."

"Thank you," I'd say, tossing my nose subtly in the air and my hair over one shoulder. Employers paid more to women in their late twenties.

"Oh," the interviewer would continue, "you've only had two jobs." More than two jobs gave a prospective employer insecure feelings, and besides, they took too damn long to "print neatly."

" 'Office manager,' hmmmm!" would be the next comment. Eyes would widen. Well, it wasn't always office manager. Sometimes I'd decide to be an economics specialist, or a management consultant specialist, or my favorite—personnel director. The real secret to landing a job, I learned, was to tell them anything, everything they wanted to hear. For instance, one interview was for an assistant's position for a Beverly Hills stock exchange salesperson.

"We don't have applications in this job," the balding middle-aged man said. "We go primarily by personality, confidence, and background." I remember smiling assuredly, something that pleased every prospective employer, and geared myself for the barrage of bullshit.

"Ever sold before?" the man asked, shifting his

eyes quickly toward mine, hoping to catch me off guard.

"Oh, yes," I said, keeping my voice calm, even-toned, assured. "I handled the sales force for Mini-Cam Mining Equipment, out of Houston, for four years just after I graduated from college." The company was non-existent, but important-sounding, something even stock-brokers don't question.

"You got your degree, your bachelor's, there in Houston, did you?"

"Master's. I majored in psychology with a minor in business management."

"What are you looking for in the way of salary?"

"Well," a hint of humility, now, "I'm new here in town, and I realize I'm new in this particular business. So, I'd be willing to take whatever you could offer with the understanding, of course, that it would be a tempo-rary salary, that is, until I could prove my worth to the company—in clear profits."

He bought it, unsuspecting, and I was hired on the spot. May I say that the five days I worked there were among the most satisfying of my business career? I walked into the unemployment office shaking my head at my adventures.

"Canary, come on over," he said waving to get my attention. Smiling, I waved to Jerry in answer and made my way from the line of people through the maze of desks. I must say, I thought, I've begun to have a little pull around the old place. As I reached Jerry, he greeted me like a long-lost friend.

"You must have been giving it the old college try this time," he said, motioning me into the empty chair next to his desk. "What happened?"

"Oh, it was just one of those things. I worked hard, but it was a . . . well, personality conflict."

"Well," he said, beaming, "Mrs. Rosenburg, the woman who was handling your counseling, has been transferred to another office and I promised her if you came back in here I'd take care of you personally."

"Well, that's nice. Thank you."

"Listen," he said, consulting his expensive-looking

watch. "It's ten to one, how about lunch? I know a great place."

"Well, I don't think I can."

"Don't be ridiculous," his voice betrayed irritation. "I'm not going to do anything to make you uncomfortable. Do you like Mexican food?"

"Well, sure, but . . ."

"No 'buts' about it. I insist. It's a fantastic restaurant, the Villa Taxco. You'll love it." That was the beginning of my very unusual relationship with Jerry. Most of that first lunch we spent talking. He kept me on my toes, intellectually, and we talked endlessly. After several other dates, we were on better terms. One evening, we returned to my new, small apartment and he turned to me, peeved.

"Why haven't you told me, Canary?"

"What are you talking about?"

"Oh come on, you don't have to play games with me. I think I know what's been bothering you all along, but I've been waiting for you to come out with it yourself. You need to. You might as well get it off your chest." Although I knew I hadn't hinted at all, and that he was just thrashing about blindly, I told him. It came pretty easily, and he took it very well.

"Listen," he said, as I began the story, "I have a doctor, a friend, who's head of a Reproductive Endrocrinology Department. Can I give him a call and discuss your case with him? I know we've talked about this sort of thing before. What did you call it?"

"Transsexualism." Funny that a man who had a degree in psychology could have missed that word. "It means a changing of the sexes." About a week later I got an appointment with a man named Wells, with Jerry's help. I'd never seen so many hostile people under one roof in all my life!

"What do you want?" The reception nurse actually bellowed at me as I walked toward her.

"Could you please tell me where Dr. Wells' office is? I have an appointment," I said, ready to punch her, an instant response. She turned to help someone else.

"Excuse me," I said, trying to break in after about five minutes.

"Are you still here?" Her voice was louder and caustic.

"Yes, but I'm leaving." I walked until I could corner what looked like a young intern.

"Straight down toward the entrance," he said, pointing in the direction I had just come from, "and turn right. You'll see the department sign. You can't miss it." Thanking the man, I made my way back. The Reproductive Endocrinology Department was a different world. It was quiet. A lean, gay-looking blond nurse greeted me, with a trace of lisp in his voice.

"Hello. Can I help you?" he asked, tilting his head as he spoke.

"Yes, I'm here to see Dr. Wells. This is his office, isn't it?"

"Yes. This is Dr. Wells' office. Now, are you a patient of the doctor's?"

"Not exactly," I said, becoming uneasy. "I'm here for a consultation. I have an appointment for one o'clock."

"Your name?"

"Canary. Canary Conn."

"Oh, yes, here you are." He directed me to take a seat across the room to wait for the doctor. A middle-aged, dark-haired man came out after a while and called my name. When I rose in answer to his summons, he looked startled by my appearance.

"I'm Dr. Wells," he said, and, as we walked into his tiny office, he continued. "You're really beautiful." I smiled, but said nothing. "I know it must be difficult for you to talk about it," he said, shuffling some papers as he sat down, "but I'd like to know the extent of the surgery you've been through and any particulars of the situation, your health and such, which you might feel appropriate." It depressed me to think of rehashing the whole thing. If he had never performed a sex-change operation, what was he talking to me for? And if he had, why did he have to ask? I puzzled over why I was here.

"Miss Conn. Are you afraid? I mean, of talking about your problem?

"Oh, I'm sorry," I said, coming out of my daze.

Slowly, carefully, I told him my story, especially the last few months. After a few questions about my emotional state, he asked if I would submit to a physical examination. Before I realized what I could be letting myself in for, I was slipping into one of those backwards gowns and sitting on that flat hard table. This was the first time I would ever have been studied, and it was a strange feeling.

"I'm going to have a group of my students come in and observe the physical," Doctor Wells had said as he left the room. I didn't know quite how to object. The longer I waited, the more angry and upset I became about the prospect of wide-eyed coarse young interns studying me. I wiped away my tears as the door knob turned and a voice said something.

"This is the first stage, or at least what is termed such by the doctor south of the border, of the sex reassignment surgery," Dr. Wells began. "You'll notice . . ." He didn't even take the time to introduce me to the group of ten interns who were crowding in the small room to get a look at Dr. Wells' gestures. His hands were touching my legs, spreading them far apart, and I could feel the cold stirrups against the arches of my feet.

"Now, this is the labia-like structure, you'll notice what seems to be a graft of scrotal tissue, here . . . and here. . . ."

My face flamed red and hot. I could feel his hands poking at my genitals, none too gently. At first I was embarrassed—then angry. I wanted to make a scene. I wanted to sit up and leave the table, to call them animals for using me, for turning me into an exhibition. Let them get their education at someone else's expense, I wanted to say, but I didn't. There was something at stake here. Dr. Wells might do the surgery, no charge.

"Real butcher job," one intern said, brushing his red hair back from his face. They all turned to him and laughed; I felt the tears come to my eyes, but I couldn't let them see they had caused me pain. I covered my face with an arm, hoping, as I did as a child, things would get better when I took them away.

"Now this," Dr. Wells said, grabbing my penis,

"this will be used in the ultimate construction of the vaginal canal."

At the close of the examination, Dr. Wells had asked me to get dressed and meet him back in his office. There, we sat a minute while he told me he would do the second, final stage of the surgery free, providing he received an okay from the Psychiatric Department. I was thrilled. Clean sailing, from here on out, I thought, and mentally kissed Jerry. How could anyone deny me my right to a normal body?

Wells called the Psychology Department and set up an appointment for a little later in the afternoon. After the usual wait, I made my way down a narrow hall to room thirteen.

"Hello," a young man in his late twenties said. He was wearing horn-rimmed glasses and a bright print shirt. Rising from his chair, he extended a hand. "I'm Doctor Daniels, and you're? . . ."

"Canary." I hoped that he was the right man.

"Oh, yes. Do sit down, Canary. Dr. Wells called me about you a little while ago. Well, why don't we just start from the beginning." That was just what I dreaded. "First of all," he continued, taking off his glasses as he sat down, "how old are you?"

"Twenty-two."

"Are you married, or were you married at any time, Canary?" He folded his hands behind his head and leaned back a little.

"I'd rather not comment on that."

"Alright. I'm not here to make you uncomfortable. Believe me, I don't believe in the kind of people who badger patients to talk about things that obviously upset them. You know, Canary, it's my theory that when you feel I have earned your trust, you'll tell me uncomfortable things. Now, it's not likely that will happen in one hour, so there are things we'll have to skip."

"Thank you," I said, almost limp with relief. He was wrong, I was beginning to trust him.

"When did you first start feeling you had female tendencies?"

"I have memories of feeling something was wrong with me when I was two," I said.

"And dressing," he said, picking up a pencil to write on a small tablet on the desk. "When did you first start cross-dressing, Canary?"

"At about the same time," I told him, remembering the first time I borrowed a dress from Dee Dee.

"Did it give you any sexual stimulation at that time?"

"Of course not."

"How was your home life, Canary?" I knew what he was doing. Theories stated that homosexuals had a dominant mother image.

"My Dad was a very strong-willed individual," I said, "and my mother just about the same. I mean, from all I've read about marital relationships and normal active-passive roles on the part of normal marriage partners, my parents were pretty much that—normal, I mean."

The questioning continued along these basic lines. We touched on high points of my sexual identity crisis through high school and ended with my feelings directly after my first operation. I hadn't told him about Johanna and the baby, although I wasn't sure that was right. Despite an urge to be honest, my barrier against guilt and attack was vulnerable. By avoiding those days of confusion as a husband, as a father, they seemed to fade away, to become part of another world, the world of Danny. The hour came to a close.

"Well, I'm impressed, first with your intelligence, Canary." Doctor Daniels smiled at me. "I think it took a great deal of smarts to have realized at such an early age you had a gigantic problem to be solved. And then, of course, I'm impressed with your courage, for following through with your beliefs at all costs. It's my understanding that you've got your head screwed on pretty tight. You know, Canary, I wish you could see some of the people I've seen in this room in the last few months. People who have had to cope with one tenth the emotional shock you have can't even carry on an intelligent conversation." He paused.

"I'm going to recommend to Dr. Wells that he go right ahead and schedule you for surgery, for I really feel you're on the right track."

About a week later I finally heard from Dr. Wells' office.

"We've just received Dr. Daniels' report," the secretary said, "but the head of the Psychology Department, Dr. Wiley, has nullified it."

"What do you mean? Dr. Daniels authorized the surgery. What do you mean, 'nullified'?"

"I'm sorry. That's what has happened and you'll have to come in in person to set up a date to see Dr. Wiley to get the okay for surgery." I wanted to scream. Who was this Dr. Wiley? Where did he think he got the right to do this to me?

Two days later I sat in the crowded waiting room and studied the people around me. Five men in white coats entered the waiting room together and gazed around looking for someone. I had an appointment to see just one Dr. Wiley. But the woman at the reception desk called my name.

"You're to go with these doctors for your examination." I followed the men down a hall to a cold examining room. The men took seats, then began to watch me.

"Please sit down, Miss Conn, or is it *Mr*. Conn?" the oldest of the group said, smiling sarcastically.

"Are you Dr. Wiley?" I tried to stay calm.

"No," he said sharply.

"Well, what am I doing here with all of you?" I looked at each of them for a moment, trying to really see them.

"Dr. Wiley directed us to talk to you for him so . . ." He continued, but I wasn't listening. The hair on my head felt as though it were standing on end and I burned from his remark. If I'd been Danny, I'd have belted him one for Canary.

"Well, go ahead, say what you're supposed to say. You know why you're here, we don't." The man was smirking.

"Well, since you don't know what to do with me, I'll just have to see someone else. Someone, by the way, *human*."

The man's face slowly turned red. After a minute, I stood and left the room. There was laughter in the hallway, and it probably came from that room, but I wasn't going to check.

It took me two more visits to figure out what was going on, two more attempts to strike a professional vein in these people. It wasn't easy admitting to myself that so-called professional men would use a fellow human being in this manner. They had used me all along, beginning with Wells.

I was to be a study on transsexualism, that was it. No one had had any intention of doing the final surgery, although they had promised it. A new determination came out of my bitterness, and I decided to stop trying to deal with the world of the American medical man.

BACK TO THE BACCHANAL

Things began to change. Because I found myself increasingly put out with the kinds of demands men made of me I decided I should pursue other kinds of relationships. But what kind? I needed friends, companionship, people to talk to more than anything else. Going down the list of my contacts in Los Angeles, and the places I could go to get out for a while, I came up with an idea. There was the Bacchanal; gay people were opposed to the traditional roles I often found myself in and gay people were open to differences in others.

It looked the same, even though it'd been a year or so since I'd last visited the place.

"May I have your I.D.?" the man said as I walked in.

"Hey, Joe," I said, annoyed. "Don't you remember me? I used to come in here all the time with Jill. I'm Canary, remember?"

"Yeah, sure!" the man said, his face lightening a little. "Jill, sure. Say, how is she? I mean, I haven't seen her for some time now. Is she all right?"

"I don't know," I shrugged. "I haven't seen her since last summer." Reaching into my purse, I pulled out the dollar cover charge. It was nine times less than the charge for men there.

Bad beginning. Joe had touched two sensitive areas in my life. I didn't have a driver's license, the form of identification usually required for entrance by most gay bars; I didn't have one because I still didn't have a car, and I didn't relish the idea of standing in line at the Department of Motor Vehicles. And, of course, there was the matter of Jill.

Where was she? I had heard from her only a couple of times since my return from my parents'. At first, I'd heard she was seeing a girl from back East, but six months later, I ran into some mutual friends and they told me she had gone to New York to live with her parents.

The music was as loud as it had ever been. Making my way through the constant stream of new faces to an empty table at one side of the bandstand, I realized how hard it was to come here. So many of my inhibitions were going to be challenged.

"Hello," said a young-looking blond, a little taller than I was. She slid into an empty seat at the table next to mine. "My name's Max. What's yours?" At first I was annoyed, as if maybe the girl should have asked my permission to sit down or something, but then I remembered I was at the Bacchanal, where etiquette dictated that the strongest will and the boldest manners won. Play it cool, Canary, I told myself.

"My name's Canary," I said, extending a hand.

"Say, you're new in here, aren't you? I mean, I've never seen you here before. Is it your first time?" Her eyes were shining. Did I really know what I was letting myself in for? Females didn't really turn me on, but I wanted companionship, and in choosing the Bach, I hadn't considered the possibilities of a pass.

"No . . . I mean I've been here a few times before."

"Well, I would never have known," she said, tossing her long hair over one shoulder.

"Why's that?" I asked, trying to cool it down, something I remembered Jill doing whenever another lesbian had approached the table.

"Well, you're uptight—you know, not with it. You're apprehensive." Okay, I knew what she was driving at, but I didn't want to respond in a way that would prove her point.

"Do you want to dance, Max?" I took a long sip of the beer I'd just ordered and we walked to the dance floor. After a little bit of shock at the all-girl couples, I began to dance.

"Hey, Canary," my partner said, taking me by one arm, "you've got to loosen up a little, you know, 'butch' it up a little."

"Canary," she said, realizing I hadn't understood, "you're dancing too 'fem.' 'Butch,' well, that means you've got to be a little more masculine about your dancing. I didn't want to tell you, but all the sisters were eyeing you, baby, and if you don't want to be made by every dyke in here, honey, you'll do as I say." The band finished the song and announced they were going to take a break. On the dance floor it was one thing for this girl to put her arm around me, but as we sat down, I began to feel odd about the whole thing, as I had about Jill in our short-lived relationship.

"What do you do for a living?" I asked, deciding to make conversation with this girl, Max.

"I'm a secretary for a record producer," she said. "Say, you want another beer?" It took four beers for me to get back to the old game, just trying to act like a guy again. Max asked a bunch of her friends over, but they requested our presence at their table. As the two of us approached the tableful of strangers, one of them jumped up.

"Hey, you're Canary, aren't you?" She stuck out her hand. I didn't recognize her, but we shook hands and she smiled. "How's Jill?" she asked, bringing a chair for me from the next table. Max glared. Grinning, I fetched one for Max.

"Oh, Jill," I said, trying to be inconspicuous about my actions. "Well, I haven't seen her for a long, long time. Last time I heard, she had gone to New York."

"Oh, I've seen her since then," the girl said as Max and I got settled. "She was doing a movie, a bit-part player or something and I guess she'd doing all right." I turned to one girl and tried to start a conversation with her, but Max was right on top of my feelings.

"How you doing on your beer?" she said, putting her arm around me slowly to make sure that everyone knew I was her stake. It was a new feeling and I wasn't sure quite how to take it. A couple got up to dance, and I watched them, wondering about myself. What if I were attracted to this new girl? What if I had gone through the surgery and pain to find I still needed the kind of relationship my wife and I had had? Could it be that my happiness lay in just such a relationship, me still playing the game of acting like a guy? There was no doubt my return to this place indicated that a side of my personality that I had long forgotten would be aired. Was I wrong? Would I harm myself emotionally by going back to this role?

"Hey, hey," Max said, putting her hand against my chin and pulling my head toward her. "What are you so engrossed in thought about? Do you want to split? Maybe we can go somewhere and just rap."

What would Danny have done in a situation like this? A girl asking him to go out alone with her without knowing anything about him—what would he have thought? What would his concern have been? I tried to think from that side of it, but my mind went blank. All I could think of was the lonely apartment waiting for me, and the confusion I felt here.

"Okay, but I hope you have a car." Max got up, paid the check, retrieved my purse from the bartender, and came back, her voice taking a sudden low pitch.

"Let's go, Canary," she said, reaching for my hand.

"You know," she was saying in the car, "it really gets to a lot of girls. I've seen a lot of chicks in there, and I can always spot a new one."

"How's that?"

"Well, one thing most of the girls don't realize is that almost everybody is in there with either a friend or lover. Almost all the rest are new. No one seems to feel comfortable if they don't score on their first visit, and they don't want to go back there." It seemed lucky to me that I'd scored such a experienced, attractive girl. Many in the club had discouraged me with their short, short hair and an overly masculine appearance with mannerisms to match. A couple of them had even scared me.

Max seemed different, special, and I couldn't figure out why I came to that conclusion.

"You know," she continued, "gay life is an extremely lonely one. Most of the girls you see in the Bach are really screwed up, emotionally, and someday the lucky ones might meet another real person and become lovers, maybe live together."

"But what about their roles, I mean, if one girl pays for the drinks, does that mean she wants to play the guy, or is there another way to tell?"

"It's not that simple," she said, looking confused. "I mean, if a chick feels more dominant over the other chick, well nature just kind of takes its course, and physical roles in the bedroom . . . well, they have a lot to do with it."

What was she trying to tell me? Would she mean I would have to play a subordinate role in a lesbian relationship? I wasn't exactly sure of the degree of physical strength I had anymore, and I wondered about the possibility that I might have to take an inferior role to a female, physically. What would Danny have thought about that? He acted the part of the true male chauvinist pig and would have cringed at the prospect of a female physically superior to him. Could he rationalize himself out of it, as he had the time he found out one of the girls in his senior class was a karate expert?

"Where we headed?" I asked, as we passed Hollywood Boulevard and continued north.

"I thought we'd make it on over to a real freaky place called the Bla-Bla Café," she said, veering onto the Hollywood Freeway. "It's a fantastic place this time of night, because all the freaks—you know, hippies—start coming in. It's always good for an interesting time, and they have entertainment, too." A couple of days earlier I'd heard about the place, I realized.

"Isn't it some kind of showcase?"

"Yes, that's the one. Didn't you say you were a singer?"

"Yes," I said, wondering again what it would be like to perform as a female. "But I don't think that trip, I mean, performing in an after-hours club, is what I'm

looking for." Shrugging her shoulders, Max talked
about some of the acts she had seen there, and I flashed
suddenly on a place I had auditioned at, a place always
packed on Monday nights. That seemed to be showcase
night in most of the clubs around town, and I had gotten to know the people who owned that place. For a
while I was almost a regular and I invariably received
warm applause. My first time up had been pretty frightening, but no one seemed to be able to detect that I was
different. When I began to sing the entire club had
fallen silent—a silence I'll never forget. It was a beautiful night, especially since the club owner had come
backstage after my performance to offer me a job there.
I had declined for fear of eventual discovery, and that
was to be the pattern I would set for other auditions,
other clubs.

Leaving the freeway at Ventura Boulevard, we
sped a few blocks down to an older building covered
with abstract painting. As we entered, we were caught
in a huge cloud of smoke drifting through dim lights.
From what I could make out, I decided the coffee house
stretched back a fair distance in a sort of theater-like
layout.

"Can I help you ladies?" a young man asked, bow-
ing his head in a gentlemanly fashion.

"Table for two, please," Max said, putting an arm
around me as she smiled at the waiter. It embarrassed
me a little, as it had the first time in public with Jill,
and I found myself trying to act casual about the situation as we threaded through the crowd to an empty table.

Two months passed and I accomplished several
amazing things. I had become a regular performer at
the Bla-Bla Café. Every Tuesday night I was the featured performer, and although the club didn't do their
best business on that night, I had managed to keep them
pretty busy. And I was into some comedy, now, too,
something I'd never dreamed of doing. It happened the
first evening I was to appear.

"You're nervous, aren't you?" said a voice behind

me. It was Jimmy, a guy who I'd met at a party a few months before. He was now coming regularly to the club. Jimmy was about six feet five inches tall, close to four hundred pounds, and had a blond afro. His hair was almost as long as mine. On stage he would fling it back and forth in front of his bearded face while he played and sang.

"Yeah, Jimmy, I'm nervous all right. I can't even tune this damn guitar." That was my excuse, at least. Something else was bothering me, though. In the week since I'd accepted the owner's offer to put me on stage for a night, I'd worried about how to open my act, what to say, how to avoid comments that I was different, and how all of this would affect my life, my job—one I'd managed to keep for three months by then, another record. And on top of everything, there were never-ending doubts about my voice. Was it really female-sounding, or was it fake? After many recordings, many sessions listening to myself, I could still hear bits of Danny lingering in my singing style. What if someone else could hear it? I found myself losing my carefully built-up confidence. The lingering fear of humiliation on-stage was haunting me.

Someone flipped on the Juke Box sign, a signal that I had ten minutes before I was to start. I tried to concentrate on the efforts of my fat friend to tune my guitar, but the noise was overwhelming.

"Why don't we go in there," I said, pointing to the ladies' room. "Maybe the sound will be muffled in there." His eyes widened in surprise.

"Well, uh, it might be okay for you, but I don't know if I would fit!" Laughing, I knocked on the door to see if we would be intruding. Once inside, I wanted a go at the guitar myself.

"Here," I said, reaching for the guitar, "let me have a hand at it again, and maybe you can tell me which ones need tuning." Jimmy handed me my twelve-string.

"How's that? Is it high enough?" I sounded a string.

"Yes . . . that's it. That's fine."

Somewhere in the middle of our tuning process, Jimmy noticed that one of his red, white and blue-starred tennis shoes was untied. Bending, he tried to tie it, but it was impossible for him to reach the shoe over his huge stomach. I stopped tuning and started to laugh.

"Here, let me get that for you."

"No, no, you've got to get that thing tuned. You'll be on in a couple of minutes." While I worked, he brought his huge leg to waist level and put the untied shoe and his foot on the sink. One surprise! But the next surprise was funnier. The sink came out of the wall with a huge crash and streams of water sprayed over the tiny room. Somehow I got to the door and wedged it open. I was laughing so hard tears were streaming down my face. Jimmy had his hands over the pipes, trying to stop the flow of water. My fear of performing had disappeared; I was in the middle of a scene that must have been done by Laurel and Hardy once.

Grabbing a pile of newly laundered aprons, I tossed them to the flood victim. The water had traveled halfway down the hall towards the coffee house, and the owner was trudging through the water.

"What's going on here?" he asked, staring at Jimmy's wet beard. He burst into laughter. We pried open the back door, turned off the water to the sink, and mopped up the flood as quickly as we could.

"Okay, Canary," the owner said, "you'd better get up there and entertain them in case they don't know how to swim."

All the way through the audience to the stage I laughed, and as I turned around half the audience had joined me, not knowing why I laughed. I then started relating the events of the last ten minutes and they roared again. For a moment I'd completely forgotten I was a singer and I ignored the guitar around my shoulders. When I finished my tale, realizing the success of my first attempts at comedy, I began to play.

I must have done well with that, too, for each time I finished a song there was a round of applause. Before I knew it I'd finished my planned performance. Walking through the mass of tables and chairs, I met Jimmy and we smiled at each other.

"Just great, Canary," he said, rubbing the towel through his hair. "A real 'pro' job. I didn't realize you were so good."

It was great. Although my foray back into the Bacchanal had some awkward moments, it had helped me accomplish two things. I had started performing again, and I had made a decision—the lesbian world was all right, but I didn't want that kind of relationship.

MY FRIEND, THE SHERIFF

It didn't take long for the newness of performing to give way to the emptiness that I lived with constantly. There were just two things I wanted: a man, and more than that, my final operation.

Max called one evening, "Listen, Canary, why don't you come with me to my brother's birthday party?" I'd just arrived home and was feeding my tropical fish.

"Oh, I don't know, Max," I said. I was tired, but a little beaten down, too. "I think I'll just stay close to the nest. Maybe there's something good on television." What's the use, I was thinking.

"Now, don't be silly," she said, breaking in. "There'll be a lot of guys there and you might just meet one you like." Well, her brother was a foxy guy and he might have some foxy friends. But none of them would last more than a week with me, I knew, especially once I'd told them.

"Does your brother know, I mean, does he know about me?" I asked, wondering if she'd slipped.

"No, of course not!" Max answered angrily. "Don't you remember, I told you I would never tell anyone about it." Although I'd told her, I'd forgotten her promise. So many people slipped. The urge to tell someone could be almost overwhelming. And parties could be very frightening situations.

A couple of weeks before that night I'd gone to a party with a friend, Peggy, I'd met at the club. There were going to be some people from work there.

"I hope this is all you've described it to be," she

258

said, showing me a quick ironic smile as we entered the Ventura Freeway on-ramp. Her long brown hair was waving a little from the stream of air through the open window on the driver's side.

"Well, if that damned broken window doesn't freeze us to death before we get there," I said, "Denny promised me we'd have a lot of fun."

"He's the one from your office, isn't he?" I agreed. Denny and I had dated a couple of times. One frustrated, lonely evening I had told him about my situation. It had been a stupid thing to do, but I really needed to talk to someone. I didn't remember I had told him until I realized people at the party were staring at me. At first, I told myself it was paranoia, and I was tired or something.

"Is it true?" one guy asked suddenly, approaching me from one side.

"What do you mean?" I stalled, hoping he wasn't referring to me.

"Well, you know, is it true? That you're a man, I mean?" another man said, from my other side. Without answering, I turned on my heel and looked for Peggy.

"I don't understand, Canary. Did somebody say something to you?"

"I can't tell you right now," I said, spying Denny and some of his friends on the other side of the room, laughing and talking about me.

The next day at work I would jump every time someone came into the room, wondering how long it would take for the rumor to reach the supervisor via the grapevine. She would call me in and fire me, of course. Early in the afternoon I broke. Walking into the personnel office, I announced I was quitting.

"What's the problem, Canary?" the woman had said as she dialed the payroll department about my final check.

"I'd rather not talk about it," I had said. Shaking, I waited for my check to come down.

"Canary you worry too much," Max was telling me. "Don't worry. We'll have a groovy time. I'll pick you up about eight."

The time had gone by so quickly. I couldn't believe it had been almost a month since that party. Richard was due home any moment and I scrambled out of bed to prepare breakfast. The house was always so lonely without him.

"I love you, Richard," I mumbled aloud as I hurried around the kitchen preparing for his arrival. It felt good to be a wife of sorts. We hadn't gotten married, but it was just like I'd imagined. The whole situation seemed like a dreamworld. While I gulped down some orange juice, I reached over and flipped on the radio.

"Six forty-five on KHJ," the announcer said, and a record started up as I reached into the refrigerator to pull out a couple of steaks. It hadn't taken me long to learn what pleased my man. He was a meat eater; as long as breakfast began with steak, he loved it. I began to hum one of my newest compositions while someone read the news on the radio. "I'm a going to find me a brand new lover," I sang, rushing back into the bedroom to primp a little. Before I could finish, I heard the front door clicking.

"I'm coming," I yelled, realizing I hadn't undone the chain lock. "I'm coming."

"Hi, little bird," Richard said, walking through the door to put his arms around me. There was the scent of outside on him. "You got my breakfast ready?"

"Yes sir," I said, feeling his huge body squeezing me so tight I had to gasp for breath, and warming me as I needed it so badly. "Richard, I love you."

"I love you too," he said, putting his lips to mine, lifting me up in the air. When I stood back, I felt again the press of my good fortune. I was lucky to meet this man, a man who had everything I'd ever wanted. He was tall, almost six-four, dark-complected, reeking of masculinity, and very well-groomed, very handsome. He reminded me of the movie star Jack Webb, only a little younger, say early thirties, and he looked smart in his uniform. But of course, I always did like the uniforms they had in the sheriff's office.

"How'd things go?" I asked, hoping he would relate some of the events of last night to me. "Good night?" Richard was a deputy sheriff on night watch. That startled me at first for I hadn't told him right away about my situation. I decided to see how far I could go in a love relationship before I spoke up. It wasn't fair. I fell deeper and deeper in love, and found it harder to make the decision to speak to him.

At first he was shocked. Many times we'd gone to night clubs and restaurants filled with his co-workers. When I reminded him of their responses to me, he calmed down. Almost all of them seemed in favor of taking me home for themselves. Not one of them had suspected anything at all. In less than an hour after I'd told him, he made me the happiest girl in the world. "I love you," he had said, putting his huge hands over mine, "and it doesn't matter to me. I want you to come and live with me and maybe between the two of us we can save enough money to pay for your second operation."

The first few weeks we lived together settled into a routine rather quickly. Richard would leave the apartment at eleven each night all but two nights a week and return at eight in the morning. At first, I had enjoyed the newness of our relationship, for I could never remember being so happy. But then, with the advent of fall, Richard began to attend law school, and that cut our time together to a minimum. I became afraid. I had continued on in the job I had in Hollywood and the drive from Orange County, where our apartment was located and where Richard worked, was sometimes a two-hour drive in the morning traffic. That meant I had to leave just about the time he came home from work to make it to my job on time. This was an added pressure on our relationship.

Telling Richard hadn't been too difficult. Through a little practice, I'd developed a method, based on the type of person I was talking to. There were three basic kinds of people, I found. There were those who were apparently uneasy about their own masculinity. This kind of guy, on the first date, usually gave himself away with talk of homosexuals, lesbians, or occasionally, about transsexuals. These guys—I called them "the uptights"—I'd just treat as a casual one-time date. Then there were those who fell somewhere in the middle.

Sometimes I'd have to play them along for a while, but I evolved a way of telling them on the first date. It was easier on me that way. Middle-of-the-roaders were usually pretty indifferent about it. Some of them felt I had done the right thing; others just accepted me as "one of those things." I had very little trouble with this type of man.

The third type was a worldly, intellectual type of man who seemed to be the most understanding of all. I could spot them by their open-minded attitudes on politics, philosophy, religion, and the like. By simply starting a conversation on some controversial topic, I found I could talk to this kind of man right away. I had little apprehension about talking to an intellectual type.

I made mistakes of course. One time I went out with a doctor, someone I thought was a real intellectual sort. We were sitting at a dinner table in a French restaurant right off the Sunset Strip when I decided to break the news.

"You're what?" he screamed, jumping up from the table and tossing his napkin on his clean plate.

"I'm only kidding," I said, hoping the people around the restaurant would find something else to look at. My date walked out on me.

There were some people who surprised me, people who didn't fit into any of the categories. These rare few were close to me emotionally. It was this category that Richard fell into.

But we did have a couple of sore points. Richard's awareness of me created a whole new set of responsibilities and intensified my self-analysis. Now I was a girl under constant scrutiny, although it was usually unwitting. I felt as though I were thrown into a state of sexing everything I did: the way I held my cereal spoon, the way I knelt to pick up something, even my burps, sneezes, coughs, and hiccups. Richard, though very kind in many ways, became my nemesis, pointing out when he felt I was overexaggerating this move, that word, etc. I loved him, though he made me angry with this sometimes, and I kept reminding myself that while he could, if he wished, spend hours tearing me apart, the real truth was that, in a month of dating time together, he had not suspected the truth at all. This was my strongest argument when he became too critical. If I was so fakey, so weird, why hadn't he suspected something from the start? He would just shrug his shoulders and postpone his critique.

All that fall there seemed to be a deterioration in our relationship, a paranoia on the part of my pseudo-husband that would grow into a wall between us.

"Do you remember Joe Burke?" he asked one weekend as we lay beside each other on the bed trying to catch up on all our lost time.

"Joe? Yes, isn't he the guy in the highway patrol we went to that party with when we first started going together? Why?"

"Well, you know he asked about you when I saw him the other day, and how you were doing."

"Well say hello to him for me," I said, flattered I'd made an impression.

"Do you think he suspected something about you?" Richard asked, turning away, getting up from the bed. "I mean—you know what I mean." Well, I knew, but I didn't know how to take it. This was the first time he had confronted me with this kind of doubt about my looks. I felt upset, then hurt, then rapidly, frighteningly, suicidal.

"Richard," I said, on the verge of tears, "what is it? Do you want me to leave? I mean, are you ashamed of me?" I watched him as he walked back to the bed.

"Look," he said, reaching to pull me to him, "it's just that being away from you so much—I don't know—somehow it brings these doubts I have now. I didn't have them in the beginning. What would happen if the guys at work found out about you? I mean, how could I possibly explain? I love you, you know that. But I'm starting to feel kind of weird, Canary." My eyes were filling with tears as I buried my head in his chest. I wanted things to work out, just this one time. We had done almost everything I'd ever dreamed of in a love affair. I remember our first picnic.

"Let's go to Griffith Park today, come on, sleepy

head," Richard had wakened me one morning. It was the Fourth of July, and for once we'd managed to combine our days off. Waking up beside him was such a warm feeling. I can count each of the times we had slept all night together.

"Oh, wow, a picnic," I said, reaching around him, feeling the warmth of his body through my nightgown. "Isn't it a little too early to think of such things?"

Richard jumped out of bed, grabbed me and carried me into the kitchen, where he set me down with instructions to fix some sandwiches. He gave me that incredible warm feeling of being protected, which was something a little confusing to a lingering attitude carried over from my male days. Taking orders from anyone went against the grain.

But because Richard expected me to be his concept of a woman, and because he let me know that he loved me, I could handle a feeling of subordination pretty well. Later on that day we walked hand in hand through the acres of Griffith Park, a place for lovers, and I helplessly recalled the times I had once walked these grounds with my wife Johanna and our son. Then it was me who was the male, me who did the protecting. When Richard suggested we ride the merry-go-round, I almost froze. It was as though every part of my past were catching up with me, trying to reverse what had happened with Johanna. One time I had boosted Johanna up to one of those horses and had held my little boy Joey on one of the ponies while he rode, laughing and giggling.

"Come on, baby," Richard said, boosting me up onto the platform. A little dizziness started in my stomach and I smiled as he put me up on a pony.

When we found a spot for our lunch I was so happy that ordinary ham sandwiches tasted fantastic. It was me who fixed the lunch, not some other girl, and that gave me a real ego boost. I am really a woman, I remember saying to myself, and even though I've another operation to complete, my mental attitude has completely changed. I was a woman.

"Richard," I said, pulling my hand away from his hairy chest. "You didn't answer my question. Do you want me to leave?"

The question had come up again, as I had known it would. It was a relief that we weren't putting it off. I didn't want to live with the indecision.

"No," he answered, sighing and pulling my head close to him. "I'm too in love with you to even let your problem get in our way. I've never felt this way about any girl in my life. You're real, Canary, you're not like my wife."

No, I certainly wasn't like his wife, that was for sure. She had married him out of desperation when he returned home from the service. He was celebrating his discharge at a friend's party. She was barely eighteen, the product of an unhappy family life, and it didn't take her long to propose to Richard in hopes she could finally escape her home situation. After six years in the army as a Green Beret, fighting death on the front lines, Richard accepted readily. He soon realized his mistake, however. He woke up one day shortly thereafter to find his wife, his money, a lot of jewelry, and a new car missing. He never saw her again, and never retrieved any of the material possessions he had lost.

He had answered me once, but soon the problem came up again. One evening we were sitting on the couch watching television, holding hands. He got up from his seat and turned off the television, standing stiffly, with his hands behind his back.

"Something's been bothering me, honey, and I think we should talk about it." Watching him intently, I tried to compose myself despite the fluttering fear.

"Well," I said, motioning for him to come back to his seat.

"I think we should move you back into town," he said, his voice booming in my ears. He sat back down silently, his eyes narrowed as though he were expecting a great jolt of pain as he touched me.

"I understand," I said suddenly, quietly. The tenseness which had held my body rigid most of that day slipped away.

The first few days back in town were hard; I had to get used to being alone again. Richard had made a pledge to spend his two days off with me, and although he had assured me of his love, he felt until I had completed my surgery we ran too great a risk living together. My agreement was reluctant, for I felt I was losing what I most valued.

"Now, if you keep your job, I'll pay the rent on your apartment," he had said, "and between the two of us we should manage to save the money for your operation by December." It seemed a long way away, December, but in my depression tomorrow seemed a long way away. Getting in touch with Max helped because I didn't have to spend the five days he was working alone.

The months until December crawled and I could see changes in Richard's attitude as each week passed. It went from love to pity, and I could not rationalize the reality of that with any convenient excuse, not even his schoolwork. By that November, 1972, it finally came to a head. I was sitting up waiting for Richard, who had called me three times that day to say he was on his way and I suspected the worst. The phone rang.

"Hello."

"Hi, little bird," Richard's voice came, with a false cheerfulness. "I think I shouldn't come in tonight."

"What? I don't understand," I said. But I did.

"I think I'm being followed," he whispered.

"What are you talking about?"

"I think they found out about you at the department, and . . ." What a terrible excuse! I wasn't a criminal and I hadn't done anything to break any law. How could he say such a thing? "Well, listen, I think if I just stay away a couple of weeks, things will cool down, you know?" I knew. Although I realized he had just cut it off on the telephone I kissed him good-bye, as if unsuspecting, and hung up. It was over.

In spite of myself, I started analyzing. This had gone on a little longer, but it was over, it had run its course just like every other love affair I'd ever had. Carefully I went over everything that had happened in our relationship, trying to figure out what went wrong, but it always boiled down to just one thing. I am a transsexual and no matter what I hoped, no one could be expected to think of me as anything other than a transsexual, once they knew the story.

While I was with Richard I'd neglected my music a great deal, more and more as we went on. It was time to really get my life back together. I'd left the Bla-Bla because of his pressure, and because I'd grown tired of performing. But my attitude had changed, now, and I began to renew old friendships with musicians and singers. Through music, I somehow had always sustained my sanity, and when things got bad, really bad, I had taken my guitar in my hands to compose, to sing, or just to cry as I strummed a chord. I knew that after I sang a little, things wouldn't seem as bad.

Toward the end of December, I made one final trip to my savings account where, with Richard's help, my savings had doubled. I remember breaking into sobs, as I put the key into an old car I'd purchased a week earlier with part of my last check. I had done it. I had the money for my final operation.

CAN'T YOU HEAR ME?
I'M DYING!

After twenty-three years of waiting, hoping, suffering, I am here, I kept telling myself. As I climbed the stairs to the second floor of the hospital, I fought my fear of what was going to happen. It was the same hospital I'd had the first operation in.

"Thees way pleece, Mees," a middle-aged woman said, motioning me down the long corridor, when I told her my name. The smell of ether, antiseptics and blood filled my nose, and frightened me. I kept my eyes securely on her back, as I followed the nurse. To either side of me were bodies filled with pain, and I was sure if I got to look at them I would surely faint.

"Thees is your room, Mees," the woman said as we reached the end of the hallway. I followed her into an open door on my right, but almost challenged the armed guard at the door. The room seemed surprisingly like the one I'd had two years earlier. This one had a better view, though. There were two guest chairs, one in the corner by the window, and another to one side of the television, which hung from a special hook on the wall in front of the bed. Flinging the tiny Samsonite suitcase onto a chair, I busied myself with my coat and handbag while the nurse spoke low, rapid Spanish to the guard, who was peering into the room after us.

On my way to the hospital I had stopped in several of the markets of Tijuana to find some things to keep myself busy in the long hours I would have to spend in the hospital. These things got first priority as I unpacked. I had a chess set, various self-teaching books, a Spanish book among them, and tons (it seemed) of macramé and crochet material. When I had placed them on the table next to the bed, I grabbed the white gown lying across it and headed into the bathroom.

I thought I was ready for everything, but there were a few surprises. That afternoon, I was watching television when a tall Mexican man came into the room. I learned later he was a nurse trainee.

"You are Canary," he said, turning his body to display disdain.

"*Sí,*" I answered, "*yo soy, y tu?*" (Yes, I am, and you?)

"Alex," he said, walking into the bathroom. "You come in here pleece." Jumping from the bed, I followed him.

"Pull up your nightgown," he said. The plastic bag in his hands didn't look that dangerous, but the man frightened me.

"Please, what are you going to do?"

"*Huh? No comprendo.*"

Without an answer, he walked behind me and placed a hand on my bare back to push me into a bend position. I screamed when he jammed a four inch plastic tube up my rectum and squeezed the water-filled bag. This was my first enema.

That evening Dr. Lopez stopped by, full of assurances that the hospital would take very good care of me.

"Jus' you do as they say," he had said. "You remember, though, you are a little different to them." As he left he threw me a kiss, promising to return in the morning for a series of preoperative tests he insisted on.

I didn't like the waiting. After two years of scrimping, planning and saving, I wanted to get it over with. This was the longest any of his patients had waited between surgeries. The next couple of days would be exciting, anticipatory ones, ones with tests of every kind and three more enemas—a procedure that became increasingly painful. The food in this hospital hadn't changed. Apricot nectar, mush, tea, and cold toast seemed to be the standard fare. The three days before the operation passed much more quickly than I had expected. On the Sunday evening before surgery, the anesthesiologist came in to talk to me.

"Now, you going to be asleep when you go down to the operatin' rum. You don' take any *agua,* I min wator, from now on and don' eat nothin'! When you wake up tomorra mornin' you going to be in a lotta pain and you gonna be tersty, but you don't gonna drink no wator then, either. Okay?" As the man disappeared I wondered how I would remember anything when I'd awakened from surgery. The events of the past surgery had somehow faded, but I did remember that there had been a lot of pain and a lack of control over my thinking processes. It was important this time, too, to be asleep as they wheeled me down the hall. I didn't want that memory, and it didn't seem like too much to ask.

"Where am I?" I kept saying as the doors passed me on both sides. "Am I going to be operated on? I thought I was going to be asleep. What's happening? Don't you hear me?" No one seemed to notice me at all. "Where are we going?" I was still awake; the pills had failed again. On my back, I saw the lights of the operating room and the surgical team above me. They splashed a red dye-like liquid on my legs.

"Please, please, put me to sleep. I don't want to see this. Please, Dr. Lopez," I said, as I saw him.

"It's alright, Canary," he said, coming to me and taking my hand. "It's alright. The anesthesia just hasn't begun to work yet." He pointed to my arm and I watched as a man removed the rubber hose that had been wrapped around it.

"Please, Doctor," I said, as I felt myself slipping away.

It was over. I knew it was over. My mind wanted to enjoy the fact, to celebrate the occasion, but my body writhed with convulsions. I could hear people outside the door laughing at my screaming. I tried to stop the screams but they continued, despite my efforts. They had no right to laugh! I was dying, or I felt like it, and I had to listen to their taunts.

"Hey, *gringo,* shut up!" Someone hollered, but I continued to scream. Streams of tears poured down my face. I wanted to live! What was wrong? My voice started to give out, slowly, and reality came through in brief, vivid flashes. At first, it was like a nightmare, a cloudy dream, but the laughter and the taunts brought me back to the world of the hospital. My feet were cold, frozen-feeling. I raised my head to look at them, but it hurt me so much I fainted, and when I awoke Alex was staring down at me.

"*Callàte muchacho!*" he said over and over. At first I thought it was a dream, but gradually I awoke more and more, and became more and more aware of the pain ripping my insides apart. I was glad of it. And if I were dying, I would be glad of that too, because I wouldn't have to listen to them anymore.

"I'm not a *muchacho!*" I said to Alex angrily. "I'm a *muchacha,* now—a girl, don't you see? I'm a girl." There was silence.

This time I didn't wake so suddenly. I dreamed of being a woman, something I was unaware I had become in the last three years. I was Danny again, and Johanna and the baby were there, right there beside me. I wanted to talk to them, but I couldn't and I began to scream. My mother, my father, my sisters—they were all standing there, staring at me. I screamed again.

"*Màs agua, àndale,*" a voice said. More words followed, but I didn't understand them. "Canary, Canary, it's Dr. Lopez." The dream had ended, and I recognized his face.

"Here," he said, holding a cup of water to my mouth. "You got to drink as much water as you can."

"But the man said not to."

"Drink," he said, crisply this time.

Some hours later I learned that two days had elapsed since my operation. Lupe, another nurse, came in with a tray of liquids when the doctor left.

"It's Wednesday," she said. "You must drink thees." I couldn't eat or drink, I was in too much pain. As soon as I got a little comfortable, as soon as the pain diminished, it began to grow again. I remembered all the times I'd thought about reaching down, once the surgery had been finished, and touching my new self, but somehow the pain seemed to supersede everything else. The fact that I'd had momentous sex-change surgery didn't seem to matter much anymore. The only thing I wanted to do was sleep.

Mid-evening I woke again in a giant bolt of pain. Reaching, I found the nurse call button and pushed.

"*Qué quieres?*" a voice said. It was Alex. It must be mid-evening or so, I thought, checking the window for darkness, and trying at the same time to remember the Spanish I'd been cramming my head with.

"*Por favor, Alex, medicina.*" After a click, I closed my eyes and waited. The pain grew. The window darkened even more. I pushed the button once again.

"*Qué quieres?*" came the voice again. Again, I repeated my request for medicine. There was no response. And I had a problem. No one would come to me to help me if I needed it. A strange, wet feeling alerted me to a problem under the sheets. After a few minutes I lifted the sheet.

My leg, my gown and the bed were covered with blood. I put my head back and tried to breath calmly. I was totally immobile. Besides the catheter to collect my urine, I had a mold between my legs which was used to hold the newly constructed vagina open. Even if I had managed to dislodge those items I had to contend with the strap running from the bottom of one side of the bed over my feet to the other side. It was fastened under the bed. I knew I could never undo it.

"*Sí, Señorita,*" a middle-aged woman said as she entered my room. It had taken two hours for her to answer the button, but I was too happy to see her to complain.

"*Por favor,*" I said. "*Me duele.*" (I hurt). She called the doctor when she saw I was bleeding, and he took care of the situation with a single stitch. My pain increased and the doctor prepared a half dozen injections from a tray the nurse brought. I welcomed each prick of the needle. For a couple of days, it was much the same. When the pain came back I would call, and the nurses would ignore me until I was almost a nervous wreck. When I had finally given up, someone would wander in as if nothing had happened. I didn't have time to wonder about the details of my operation, only about the fact that I was a person in pain, and they were ignoring me. They might have disagreed with my operation, but how could they ignore the pain, ignore the person who hurt?

The fifth day after the operation, Dr. Lopez had discovered they were intentionally neglecting to change my sheets. The sheets were caked with blood from the first day after the operation, and filthy. I had been in too much pain to even notice, but a flare-up infection alerted him. When he asked if they had changed my linen that day, I shook my head, almost smiling.

"Were they supposed to? They haven't yet." He disappeared without a word.

Five nurses came back to change the sheets. As they did, Dr. Lopez stood there, muttering at them in phrases too quick for me to understand, but the tone of voice indicated his displeasure. When they had left and I lay in clean sheets, I decided to tell the doctor the rest of the story.

I hadn't been allowed to wash my face despite repeated requests. I was not able to receive telephone calls or to place them, and by this time my parents would have been frantic. Although the doctor had authorized a call to my parents three days ago, on a rare occasion that I saw a nurse, she nodded her head and disappeared. Food was another problem. I always received my food last, and my hot cereal was cold, my cold foods, like Jell-O, were soup. And my call button was never answered. Dr. Lopez assured me that things were going to be different and that he would instruct a nurse to be assigned to the floor so that an eye could be kept on me. For a while I began to feel confidence.

As the hours passed, and I was alone, the confidence faded. When I had not seen a nurse for more than eight hours, I began to be afraid, and stretching carefully, I pressed the call button over and over again. I guess they were trying to get even with this young blond American girl. The doctor had said they were jealous of me.

For a while I thought of disconnecting the catheter, still connected to my bladder, to get up somehow. But even had I managed to disconnect the plastic tube, I would have to contend with the packing mold which, according to Dr. Lopez, had to be left in for a minimum of eight days or the entire operation would be a failure. That thought kept me confined to the bed. I didn't want to go through the pain again. For the evening hours, I lay in the bed quietly, watching the sky outside darken and deepen into black. I guess it was about one in the morning when I began to feel a chill. The nurses were to have returned with a blanket but only a thin sheet covered me, and the rooms had no individual heating units. Reaching for the call button, I tried again.

Then I thought of Richard. I wondered how he would feel about me, now that I had finished the procedure. I missed him. Shaking with fear, with loneliness and with pain, I started to cry, then to scream.

"Somebody, please. Please, come here." I cried and reached for the button, keeping it in my hand. A peculiar wet feeling was gathering around my legs. At first I was too frightened to peer under the sheets, but as the chill increased, I reached up for the chain over my head. With the light on, I lifted the sheets. Then I panicked.

The sheet under me was a pool of blood, and more was flowing from between my legs. I pressed the button again and again and began to scream for help. Thinking about detaching myself from the bed, I propped myself on one arm, but then fainted and fell back. When I woke up, some ten or fifteen minutes later, the blood had made its way down one side of the bed to the floor. I was weaker, now, and the pain didn't matter. I was bleeding to death.

This time I tried to signal an S.O.S. in Morse code, a dot, dot, dot—dash, dash, dash—dot, dot, dot, over and over again, frantically. Sobbing, I began to pray aloud, then I screamed again and again until my voice faded into hoarseness. Grabbing a book from the table, I tried to throw it through the window, but it fell from my fingers into the pool of blood. The chills had changed to small convulsions as I tried to calm myself.

"Now you are not going to die, Canary, just settle down. You are going to be all right, Canary, someone will be here soon. . . ." I kept talking to myself, trying to fight back the thought that this was God's punishment for trying to be a female, for killing Danny, and I began to think about all the small humiliations of the past three years.

"Why should I go on living?" I began to say aloud. "Why should I live in a world that doesn't want me? I don't care anymore!" A new burst of pain silenced me.

My breathing was shallower than before. My head was swirling. Johanna, the baby, my parents, Richard, the rest of them. All of them would be free of their "unmentionable." Bending my head I looked once more at the side of the bed, half-covered with my life's liquid. It looked pretty somehow, red on white. I couldn't help thinking now how ironic it was that I had worked and saved all this time to pay for my own death. I would be my own executioner.

"My scissors," I said aloud, realizing I had a sure-fire way out. I didn't have to wait to die. Reaching down carefully I found the small drawer of the bedside table and pulled. It wouldn't budge, or maybe it was just that I had become too weak to open it. After a minute's rest, I felt I had gathered some strength. The scissors were in there, I knew they were. I had put them there the night before the operation when I had finished cutting some macramé strings. This time when I tried, the drawer slid open easily. Streams of tears filled my eyes and overflowed as I realized that it was almost over now. The pain was almost gone.

I grabbed the scissors and brought them toward me. As the point came to rest on my breast, I tried to voice the Lord's Prayer. Somehow I couldn't remember the words, and because of the bleeding and the increasing pain I felt myself going into shock. I had to move. I had to end it all, now.

"God help me," I said, my voice cracking through the tears as I shakily raised the scissors over my heart for what would be my final decision. "God help me."

"You gonna be fine now," a voice was saying. "It's

okay now, everythin' is okay." At first I was sure I had died, but as I opened an eye, I recognized Dr. Lopez.

"Where am I?" How could I still be alive?

"I decided to drop in to see you after a party, Canary, and it was a good thing, too, because you had begun to bleed badly. Do you remember that at all?" I shook my head.

"I had my suspeecions that the people here were not treating you well at all, but I did not suspect that after I told them . . ."

Later I found out that he had arrived about an hour after I had blacked out. When he asked me about the scissors I just smiled at him, telling him I had forgotten to put them back in the drawer. I didn't want him to know how close I had come. The hospital administrator came briefly into my room and the two men left together, speaking in low Spanish. Alex, and the others responsible for leaving me alone for so long were transferred to another floor. Although there were new faces on the shifts, the attitudes were the same. These people hated someone, something they didn't know. While my room was being attended to, the doctor saw to it personally that I was able to call my parents, who had almost decided to call the American consulate to search for me.

The next day, when the doctor came to call on me, we discussed again the problems I had incurred and he explained why he had not transferred me to another hospital.

"It's, well, a problem," he had said. "Een Mexico there are few who understand the problems of transsexuals or the phenomena of transsexualism. Thees, unfortunately, it ees the only hospital that will permit such operations. Before now, there hasn't been thees problems." This man sitting before me had a lot of courage, I decided. It wasn't as though he had to perform transsexual surgery to survive, for he was one of the oldest and most respected surgeons in all of Mexico. He was a pioneer in fields such as cancer prevention and cures and dared to announce his findings about such things. He had the largest practice in Tijuana, which is among the top three largest cities in Mexico, and he certainly didn't have to perform sex change surgeries, but he recognized a need for them. His medical knowledge and concern were several paces in front of his colleagues in the States.

"I'm going to see how you are healin' up," he said, suddenly. "Eef you are far enough along, I think I'm goin' to take out the catheter and mold." At first I couldn't believe him. That meant freedom, after a week in bed—and a chance to observe the results of my operation. I asked him if I could use a mirror to see his work. He agreed, smiling, and he watched my response to his unbelievable surgical technique.

"You like it?" he said.

"Oh, yes!" I had actually made it. I was a girl. My penis had been amputated and its tissue inverted to be utilized for the formation of a vagina as a continuation of the first surgical process. The mold had been placed inside the vagina to hold the new tissue open long enough to permit healing. Up to this point, the doctor had only dressed the wound, cleansing it with a special non-burning antiseptic, and checking the hundred and twenty-five stitches as well as turning the vaginal mold to insure symmetry.

"Yes," the doctor said, after he and a nurse had successfully removed the mold. "I think you are ready to do some walking."

"Does that mean you remove the catheter?"

"Yes, that's right."

The nurse brought an instrument full of water and injected the water into one side of the catheter hose. My bladder contracted, and the doctor slid the hose out of my urethra. It hurt for a moment, but my happiness outweighed the discomfort, and I sobbed with tears of gratitude. He spread my legs and gave me my first douche. Putting a long plastic tube into my new vagina and using the kind of bag used in enemas, he cleansed the vagina with a fluid. The feeling was so different, so unusual—somthing inside of me, rather than outside. Raising a metallic rod, which reminded me of one of the many dildos I'd once packaged, he showed me what he would be using, after he covered it with KY Jelly, to dilate my vagina.

"Thees is going to hurt," he said, "but it is the first time, and each time you do it the pain will decrease."

Lying back, I anticipated a terrible pain, but it never came. Although I could feel the rod inside me, as he rotated it gently, it didn't really hurt. It was the most amazing feeling.

"I can't describe it, Doctor, I've never felt that kind of feeling before." He laughed then, saying I should remember the feeling for it was that of being a woman. After a few minutes, I was left alone with instructions to move most carefully to the bathroom if the urge to urinate came. The first time, I moved slowly and tried to think about what it would feel like. I had always sat down to urinate, but I realized suddenly I didn't know *where* the urine would come out of me, now. When the urge came, I felt like I had no control. As quickly as I could, I made it to the bathroom, and sat down to cry in confusion.

For about an hour I sat there, sure it had all been a failure. I kept thinking I would never be able to go to the bathroom again, and if I did, I would not know how to control or direct it. Despite myself, after a while a small burst of urine came from me, and I was delighted.

"It's working," I said aloud, my tears turning to joy. "I'm going—I'm going!"

The next day I spent more time on my feet. I refused to return to bed, although the nursing staff resented my new independence. And I received a surprising call from Dr. Lopez.

"Canary, I'm quite concerned about your staying alone in the hospital while I go to Stanford for the symposium." I remembered his mention of it.

"Now, it's entirely up to you, but I thought if you are feelin' better, I'd take you with me." I felt I couldn't refuse him, no matter how I felt, and I was sure that service in the hospital was not going to improve.

"Yes, well, I thought you would, so I took the liberty of calling the physician in charge at Stanford and he said you could lecture, if you feel like it."

"Are you ready, Miss Conn?"

"Yes, I guess so," I said, standing up from the

wheelchair. Before I realized it, I was on stage and standing in front of a huge audience—doctors, nurses, reporters and other people—all of whom knew about me. If it weren't for a great doctor with a funny accent, I wouldn't have been there at all. For the first time in my life, I began to think about my worth as a person— not a male, not a female, but a human being—and this formed the theme of my opening lines.

'Ladies and gentlemen, my name is Canary Conn. I am a human being." I stopped for the applause—then continued with my experiences with the medical communities of the United States. I laid it on the line, for myself and for others who lived in alien bodies and needed help to get out of them. As honestly as I could, I told these people about the problems and concerns of a young child who feels that something is wrong, that there has been some horrible mistake. Transsexuals are people who feel thay have the wrong genitals, and they are expected to play social roles that do not suit their feelings.

Because so little is actually known about sexuality and what the roles of biology and environment actually are, it can be hard for the parents of a child to avoid guilt feelings for a sense of "different-ness" their child may have. Some transsexuals come from a family with an absent father, or one who feels withdrawn from his family, and a mother who therefore dominates the situation, although she may feel depressed about her role. Although there are many different factors involved, there are also biological bases for transsexualism.

Because the fetus begins as a sort of tissue which is basically feminine, there are many possible ways that the necessary male hormones which differentiate the fetus might not be present at the time they are needed, or that unneeded male hormones are added to a fetus which is female by chromosomal makeup.

I explained the practical problems that could be met by a person who desires sex change; therapy with hormones is required for some time, and psychological counseling is a prerequisite to surgery. The psychiatric community needs to examine its attitudes, so that a transsexual may receive supportive therapy from them, rather than discouragement, or suggestions to adapt or to "be normal."

This was my first chance to speak openly and freely to members of the American medical profession gathered in large numbers, and I wanted to say as much as I could in a way that would benefit others in my situation. When I had finished speaking, I opened the floor for questions.

"What makes you think you're a girl?" one man said, rising and identifying himself as a doctor in psychology. For a moment I thought of the dozens of similar questions I had been faced with in the last few years.

"Emotionally," I began, "I've always known."

"Well, can you elaborate?" the man broke in, his face reflecting a mild hostility.

"In order to illustrate," I said, "let me ask you a question. If you, as a male, had become involved in an accident as an infant and your genitals were severed, your parents might have consulted with Dr. Lopez, or any one of the other doctors here, and decided to perform a sex change operation on you early in your life. They would then treat you as a normal female and rear you as one. How do you think you would feel? Would you feel like a boy or a girl?"

"Well—uh—that is—well, I'd feel like a boy, of course. I mean, I'd have to." The audience laughed, and the man sat down suddenly.

"It stands to reason," I said, "that you would, indeed, feel as though something were wrong, at the very least. Your emotions, your physical makeup, even your sex drive toward what would be the opposite sex would all be important factors in leading you to believe you were somehow in the wrong situation. At least, you and everyone else here has to agree that the possibility does exist that these doubt feelings would manifest themselves sooner or later. It's my theory that just such an accident happened to girls like myself—that we were somehow mutated in our prenatal development by drugs, diseases, etc."

"What do you feel a doctor should do when confronted by a transsexual needing help?" asked a woman who identified herself as a reporter from the *San Francisco Chronicle*.

"I believe a doctor should try to act like a human being, first of all," I said, remembering incidents from the university hospital. "Unfortunately male physicians begin to believe they are gods, all-knowing. When confronted by such a situation, a transsexual who turns to them for help, many of these men become hostile, and many more, inhumane."

"What do you believe should be done to insure that transsexuals receive the kind of treatment they deserve?" someone asked.

"We need education, all of us. It's most important to eliminate the kind of mental abuse that can be given out by doctors toward insecure, frightened transsexual patients. A doctor should be informed that the person on the other side of his desk is a potential suicide case. He would have to be warned that playing God with someone's life, someone who has been guilt-ridden most of his or her life, and who has decided that the only solution is a surgical correction, is a dangerous undertaking. A transsexual is not a toy to be discarded once you've studied it and found what you think is the working part. The solution to the problem can be found through education with action, providing the love, surgical help, and understanding that we need."

"Would someone you had sex with know you were a change?"

"I haven't had time yet to find this out, but I have been assured that it would take a very careful examination to determine the differences between a transsexual and a person born with female genitals. Female to male transsexuals have a more difficult time since it is very hard to construct a workable penis."

"Are all the operations done in two stages, as yours was?"

"No, there's an increasing trend to do it all in one stage—something I really feel, after being half and half for such a long time while securing the money for the completion of the change, is much better psychologically."

"Is there some kind of chromosomal difference between a female transsexual—one born with male genitals—and a person naturally born a female?"

"From what I've been given to understand, most female transsexuals are XY rather than the normal female XX chromosome reading. That is, *genetically* they are normal males. But if a chemical or biological disorder should come into play, then the genetic coding is no longer really valid in that person's case."

"Do you feel that all transsexuals are the products of chemical or biological disorders?"

"Transsexuals are the result of many factors, I believe. There are both some chemical and some environmental stimuli which could affect a person's feelings about their sexuality. I understand that many transsexuals have chemical disorders such as unusual amounts of hormones of the 'wrong' kind; there are many times in a fetus's development that sexuality could be affected. I don't really have the answer to this one. But as far as my doctor and I have determined in my case, my mother ingested an unusual form of antibiotic early in pregnancy that could have somehow caused my fetus to mutate. Although the doctor immediately took my mother off the antibiotic, there was time at a critical point in my development for changes to occur."

"Do you think people who undergo sex change surgery have special needs?" another reporter asked.

"Yes. This kind of trauma requires special help. In many cases, there are problems with a career as the opposite sex. There are mountains of records to be changed—birth certificates, social security records, driver's licenses, banking accounts, etc.—and problems with red-faced or disbelieving clerks. A transsexual needs psychological counseling, mainly because of the special adjustments which have to be made and the need for support while they are happening."

"Are you happy?" one woman asked, watching me seriously as I thought about my reply.

"Yes, I am. There are a number of problems in my life, and there are many adjustments I am still going to have to make. But for once in my life I feel the problem of my basic identity has been solved, and I can now get to the other problems of living. Yes. I have never been happier in my life."

THE GREATEST VOYAGE

Those first few months after the second operation were full of unwinding. After having spent so much time and energy on solving the problem of obtaining the money for that operation, I had to somehow find new goals. In this quest for my future, I finally made a decision I'd been avoiding for as long as I could remember, a decision to be *myself*.

Richard and I had gotten back together after the operation. It wasn't exactly an ideal relationship, because he was still plagued with fears of someone finding out about me. Although I deluded myself, thinking that if we were to break up again I could laugh it off, I still loved him and dreaded the prospect of never seeing him again.

Music had become even more important to me. Songwriting and singing filled several hours of each day, and I was writing many new songs. Richard and disability insurance were my means of support until I could recover from my surgery, and for the first time in many months, I had time to think and to create. Song after song came out of me. It was heaven until the bottom suddenly dropped out, just two weeks after I'd received an okay from Dr. Lopez to start having sex.

I was busy preparing my tiny apartment for my pseudo-husband, who had called from a nearby Chicken Delight where he was getting some dinner for us. I hadn't told him yet that it was alright to have sex now, for I still hurt and I was afraid to offend my lover with a scream of agony or to frighten him if I were to faint. I wanted my first time to be perfect.

I was a virgin, there was no denying that, and I was guarding my vagina as if it were made of gold. But I had decided that tonight was the night. I knew it. Whether it was the old movie I had watched earlier in the day, the young couple I'd seen walking hand in hand at the grocery store, or the fact that I was just plain horny, I knew that tonight was the night, and I was ready.

After two solid hours in the bathroom, bathing, powdering, and perfuming myself in the right places, I took the time to douche, something which was still a new game to me. When I dressed, I put on a pair of special panties, canary yellow, with "I love you" written across the front in bold pink. Yes, I had to admit, I'd really gone all out.

Sitting on the couch in my sexiest cocktail dress, I began to reflect on the first few days home after the trip to Stanford. I hadn't quite grasped what had happened to me until one evening when I was dilating (inserting a stainless steel, penis-shaped rod into my vagina to prevent it from closing), something which I still have to do on occasion, my finger slipped into the newly created hole. I remember freezing as if I had discovered something wrong. Until then I had never entered the vaginal cavity with anything other than the metal rod, but now I did so. As I examined the inside walls with my finger and marveled at what had been constructed, I closed my eyes and imagined myself a male again, touching me. I remembered the feeling of touching a female, and I was the same. I was actually a girl.

Since the operation I had different feelings towards myself. Now I walked with my hips cast forward a little, and there was a strange new feeling when I sat down to go to the bathroom. Somehow, it was as though I were starting all over again, like a small girl just after she had begun to discover her body. It was all new but natural, more natural than I'd ever remembered. For the first time I could ever remember, I felt whole.

"I'm coming," I said, hearing the front door knock. "Hold on, I'm coming." As I opened the door, I got a feeling something was wrong, something terrible was about to happen, Richard hurriedly made his way inside the house after a quick peck on my forehead.

"What's wrong?" I asked; that wasn't his usual greeting.

"I . . ." he stammered, "I have to talk to you."

"Well, what is it?" I asked, closing the door and taking a seat beside him on the couch. "What's wrong? You look so down."

"Never mind me," he said sharply. "It's *you* that's going to have to make the decision. I think you know what I'm talking about." When I had talked to him on the phone a few minutes earlier he hadn't given any sign of being upset. Staring at him, I tried to think back to our many telephone conversations during the day, but I couldn't remember anything that could have upset him so.

"What are you talking about? What do you mean, '*me* who has to make a decision'."

"I want you to marry me," he said, putting his hand in mine. "I want you forever, but you're going to have to, well, you're going to have to give up your career—singing, songwriting, the whole bit. I won't have it any other way."

Although I had sensed his distaste for my music from the beginning of our relationship and I sympathized with his position, I knew if I continued to pursue my career, there were certain realities I'd have to contend with. I'd never thought that he would issue me an ultimatum like this. He was saying it was my career—ten years of songwriting, singing, learning to sing as a female, and most important, giving of myself creatively—or him. That one factor, my ability to continue creating, had been the single most important link with some better world through all of the problems I had had.

"You can't be serious, Richard," I said, feeling a lump in my throat.

"I've never been more serious," he said, rising to pull the curtains closed. "Whatever you decide, it'll be all the way. If you decide to take me up on my offer and become my wife, you'll have to throw your guitar, your tapes, your lead sheets, *everything,* away—tonight."

The thought of throwing away more than two hundred songs, songs that had been my life's work, nauseated me. I began to cry as I rose to put the boxes of chicken on the table.

"Richard, if I decided to go on in music, would we still be at least friends?"

"No," he said, his voice booming with authority. "If you decide to go it alone, you'll never see me again. Never."

Almost two months had passed since that evening and I was still a virgin. A friend had called me to give me some good news. He had been casting for a movie.

"And you're in it if you want to be," he had said, "but you'll have to pack and be down to the studio by five o'clock, no later, today. Okay?"

"Okay!" I said, feeling excitement at the prospect of being in a movie. "I'll be there, for sure." For the first time in two months I was beginning to feel good about my decision to break with Richard. He had kept his word; I never saw him again. At first, as I expected, I felt guilty, for I was still in love with him and continue to be. But as time passed and the last remaining burden of worry left me, I realized I was a woman now, a truly liberated one at that, and I was in the mood for life. It took me less than an hour to pack my clothing, and I was at the studio in plenty of time to catch the bus for the cast and crew, headed for Barstow—our shooting location.

"You ever acted before?" a man asked from across the aisle. I thought for a moment about just how to answer the question.

"Why yes," I said, "I've been acting ever since I was a child."

The movie took six days to shoot. I had signed up as an extra and wound up being a bit part player with shots in all the major scenes. Acting was not the only new experience. I was keen to try out the results of my operation and chose for the endeavor a film producer, who promised love and money, swept me off my feet

and on to his motel water bed, where I was deflowered
in royal Hollywood fashion.

It took me a little while to realize that I would
have to learn how to use and enjoy my new equipment.
My first time wasn't that romantic or satisfying, but like
any first time, it served to clear the air a little. As time
went on I would have more experience with sex, and I
found a basis for comparison. There really is little difference between orgasm as I experienced it while male,
and now, while female. The feeling as a male was a little more intense, and, as I remember, oftentimes painful. Now my orgasm is more subtle and seems to come
in small waves.

After my dalliance with the producer, one of my
so-called friends on the set, in whom I had confided,
told the man about me. The producer was so incensed
that he spread the word around the set, and within a
day I was an object of attention and the recipient of
many curious stares. Luckily, it was the last day of
shooting, as I was becoming rather tired of the movie
business.

We had been staying at a Howard Johnson's motel
and it was customary that this particular establishment
have a going-away dinner for movie casts. All the hier-
archy, from stars to prop men were gathered around the
room from the head table on down to corner back tables. There was one person who seemed to be the object
of concern—me.

But I'd changed somehow since the operation.
Now I was more bold, more confident in what I was.
Challenges were welcomed rather than avoided, and I'd
developed a better concept of my own identity. It didn't
matter to me any longer if anyone knew the circumstances of my recent life, of my changes. I was *me*, not
me the male, Danny, nor me the female, Canary, but
me the person. As the waitress served what would be
our last dinner in Barstow, I thought about the irony of
this situation. All these people staring at me had worked
right alongside me for the duration of the movie. Many
of the men had propositioned me at one time or another, and no one had suspected anything odd about
me. The joke was on them. As I finished my dinner, I

took a casual glance around the room before I rose to make my way over to the cashier's cage.

"May I help you, ma'am?" the woman asked, smiling at me.

"Yes," I said, "could you give me one of the biggest cigars you have in the case down there?" I watched as the woman bent to choose a huge brown cylinder, wrapped in cellophane.

"That'll be fifty cents," the lady said, watching me tear the cigar wrapper from it and stick the brown cigar in my mouth.

"Do you have a match?" I asked, feeling the cigar distort my speech.

"Uh, yes," the woman said, her eyes widening to silver dollar size. "Here." I turned so I faced my audience and lit the cigar. Taking it out of my mouth just long enough to lick both sides of it, the way Danny had, when he had smoked one of these horrid things, I strode through the tables. It was all I could do to contain my laughter as I puffed my way through the shocked cast, with their awed faces, out the back door and to the bus.

"They wanted a show," I said aloud, "so I gave them one." And I was laughing.

Life started taking on new meaning in the next weeks. Songs were pouring out of me, songs for myself, and I was productive in many other ways as well. Somehow I stumbled into writing my own column for the *Hollywood Citizen News*. Stumbled was really the word, too, for I had met a fantastic person who treated me, in many ways, as Cornbluit had, back in high school. Leo Guild wasn't content with second-rate work, and he encouraged me to improve this or that, but at the same time, reassured me that I was indeed going to accomplish much, and soon.

As a reporter, I felt a tremendous sense of freedom, and I was in awe of Leo, who has been in the newspaper business over 30 years and has worked alongside Walter Winchell, Louella Parsons, Sidney Skolsky and others.

"You're only as good as the last story you've written," he'd say to me. "And the kinds of stories you get depend on how much *chutzpah* you have." Guts, that was the quality at test, and I was amazed to find just how much *chutzpah* I did have.

I'd been writing the column, a weekly one, only a month when I got a chance to test my supply. My prestige as a new reporter was far from that of Earl Wilson or Rona Barrett, and I really had to hustle to obtain press passes to concerts, movie premieres, press conferences and other events of that nature. I was beginning to wonder if my new job was really worth the effort.

A friend, Sally, called me one night and told me about a huge rally at the Century Plaza, which was going to be attended by Senator Henry Jackson. She suggested we get on over there. At first I was a little hesitant at the thought, fearful of being turned away at the door, something which had happened before. But I had planned nothing else, and eventually I gave in.

We decided to take Sally's car since it was a later model, and they seemed to have less trouble when trying to convince a valet to let you have press parking. As we entered the Plaza parking area, a police officer stopped us.

"Can I help you ladies?" the man asked, bending down to look at both of us.

"Yes, officer, could you direct us to the press parking lot?" I showed him one of my press passes. Before long, we had parked the car and were heading down the main lobby of the huge hotel toward the elevator.

"I'm sure my source said the Senator's board room, and I'm pretty sure she said he'd be there to meet friends and newsmen at 7:30." Her source had been correct. At exactly 7:30, the Senator from Washington appeared outside the board room. I froze. I'd never seen a Senator before, and the prospect of just shaking hands with him awed me.

"Come on," Sally urged. "This is your big chance. Look, you're the only reporter here." To my surprise, she was right. Other than five or six people who didn't seem to be connected with the press at all, we were the only ones in the room. I had a peculiar feeling we had found a very secret meeting judging from the crowds of people, who were, at that same moment, filing into the huge convention room *downstairs* to hear the man speak. How had I managed this?

I fumbled for the KIIS button I'd received earlier in the week for becoming one of the radio station's roving reporters. As the Senator turned to greet us, I pinned it on my baby blue sweater. He stuck out his hand, and I went into shock. I really felt I'd arrived. Seeing that I was stuck somehow, Sally performed the introductions.

"It's nice to know you," the Senator said, smiling, "I hope all the other reporters downstairs are as pretty as you." With a wave of good-bye, he disappeared into the board room and the door closed behind him.

"Sally," I said, "did you see that? I actually shook hands with him! Me—Canary!" Turning, we made our way down the hall to the elevator, and I checked out my burgeoning sense of self-confidence.

I had intentionally kept my past a secret in my new journalistic career, as though this were one last test to prove no one need ever know or suspect anything odd about me. Just the fact that the Senator had commented on how pretty I was, had something to say for the great distances I'd traveled.

Descending to the convention area, we were suddenly surrounded by hundreds of people filing into the room. There were policemen and women in great numbers, and even a few police dogs who sniffed for dynamite under plants.

"Are you press?" a man asked, coming from out of nowhere.

"Yes," Sally and I said simultaneously.

"Well, the press conference begins in fifteen minutes right down at the end of this corridor." We thanked the man and headed in the direction he'd indicated. It seemed odd that so many people had shown up and I'd not heard anything about the rally over the wire services the week before. As we approached the room marked "press conference," I saw a woman who wore a button reading "Save Israel Emergency Rally," and things began to fall into place. The second Middle East war had just begun the week before.

A man in the room told us the conference had

been delayed until after the rally, and that it would be held backstage then.

Sally's feet were hurting so we decided to head for home. Then we somehow stumbled on a room marked "private party dining area" and noticed it was prepared for a salute dinner for Senator Jackson. Winking at Sally, I told her I was about to give my *chutzpah* a run.

"Press," a man of about fifty said, smiling at the huge pin on my sweater. "Why of course, won't you go on into the dining room and have a seat? We'll be serving in a few minutes." When we had picked a table and started a conversation with some of the dignitaries, I spied the Senator and his aides ascending the steps to the dais to take their seats at the long table. While he spoke, liquor was served quietly. Then we had a fantastic dinner of smoked salmon flown in for the Senator from Washington that day. We made our way quietly out of the dining area when cigars were being lit and coffee served.

Later that evening I thought about the events of those few hours, and realized that I'd never given myself credit for courage, *chutzpah,* and it was something I'd had all along.

About a month later I began featuring stars in my column. I interviewed many people, but the most interesting, for me, was Fabian, once a singing idol of America, something, although he never suspected, I identified strongly with. We spent about an hour in a closed interview talking about such things as autograph seekers, teeny boppers, and more.

Today, I am content doing the things I do, because I never gave in to unending discouragements from people who tried to dissuade me from pursuing my goal of finding an identity in keeping with what I knew to be my true self.

"In your case," a pastor of the church I once attended had said, "suicide would be justified, and I'm sure it would make things easier for all those concerned."

"What do you need your second operation for?" a doctor had asked me when I had approached him in desperation. At that time I was half female, half male, and I had no one else to turn to for help. "You're just obsessed with having yourself cut on."

"Why don't you just give it all up?"

"I mean, you're just hoping for too much. You'll never make it."

"There's no *chance* you'll ever sing again."

"I don't care what you say, you'll always be a male to me."

"No recording company would ever dare sign you. Why, you're a transsexual!"

But who really cares? I have had the courage to make choices about solving my problems, and I have followed through with them in the face of every kind of adversity—sure of the validity of my feelings. Whenever I go to The Troubador to cover a singer for my column, or drive past the Capitol Records building, or walk in the neighborhood where I once lived with Johanna and the baby, I thank myself, for in reality *I* was the only one I ever knew who had the guts to stick by me all the way.

In my lives, I've crossed the unknown, that mystical world in abstract creation, the void between masculine and feminine—a place I call hell—and I've managed to maintain myself. I created, I create, and I shall create. I believe I've truly traveled the greatest voyage and lived to tell about it.

ABOUT THE AUTHOR

Today CANARY CONN is a vivacious, attractive young woman. She is a writer, singer, and radio personality. Her voice has a fascinating resonance and her songs a purring rhythmic quality and solid commercial sound. She writes her own newspaper column and is pursuing her career as a composer, performer and recording artist. The nation's media have discovered Canary, and she is receiving notice in newspapers and magazines. She is now lecturing on the transsexual phenomenon.

We Deliver!
And So Do These Bestsellers.

☐ CAVETT by Cavett and Porterfield   (2044—$1.95)

☐ HELTER SKELTER by Vincent Bugliosi   (2222—$1.95)

☐ WHEN I SAY NO, I FEEL GUILTY by Manuel Smith   (2268—$1.95)

☐ GODS FROM OUTER SPACE by Erich Von Daniken   (2466—$1.50)

☐ LINDA GOODMAN'S SUN SIGNS   (2777—$1.95)

☐ DORIS DAY: HER OWN STORY by A. E. Hotchner   (2888—$1.95)

☐ THE MOTHER EARTH NEWS ALMANAC
     by John Shuttleworth   (2927—$2.25)

☐ CHARIOTS OF THE GODS? by Erich Von Daniken   (5753—$1.25)

☐ LIFE AFTER LIFE by Raymond Moody, M.D.   (10080—$1.95)

☐ FUTURE SHOCK by Alvin Toffler   (10150—$2.25)

☐ GUINNESS BOOK OF WORLD RECORDS by the McWhirters   (10166—$2.25)

☐ WHAT DO YOU SAY AFTER YOU SAY HELLO?
     by Dr. Eric Berne   (10251—$2.25)

☐ BURY MY HEART AT WOUNDED KNEE by Dee Brown   (10277—$2.50)

☐ EVERYTHING YOU ALWAYS WANTED TO KNOW
     ABOUT SEX by Dr. David Reuben   (10436—$2.25)

☐ SOME MEN ARE MORE PERFECT THAN OTHERS
     by Merle Shain   (10565—$1.75)

☐ ALL CREATURES GREAT AND SMALL by James Herriot   (10759—$2.25)

☐ DR. ATKIN'S DIET REVOLUTION by Dr. Robert Atkins   (11001—$2.25)

☐ THE PETER PRINCIPLE by Peter & Hull   (11122—$1.95)

☐ THE LATE GREAT PLANET EARTH by Hal Lindsey   (11291—$1.95)

Buy them at your local bookstore or use this handy coupon for ordering:

Bantam Books, Inc., Dept. NFB, 414 East Golf Road, Des Plaines, Ill. 60016

Please send me the books I have checked above. I am enclosing $_____
(please add 50¢ to cover postage and handling). Send check or money order
—no cash or C.O.D.'s please.

Mr/Mrs/Miss_____

Address_____

City_____State/Zip_____

NFB—7/77

Please allow four weeks for delivery. This offer expires 7/78.

Bantam Book Catalog

Here's your up-to-the-minute listing of every book currently available from Bantam.

This easy-to-use catalog is divided into categories and contains over 1400 titles by your favorite authors.

So don't delay—take advantage of this special opportunity to increase your reading pleasure.

Just send us your name and address and 25¢ (to help defray postage and handling costs).